LIGHT UP WITH ENGLISH

An English Literature Workbook For CSEC® English B

POETRY

CLAVIA WILLIAMS-MCBEAN

Light Up With English: An English Literature Workbook for CSEC® English B - Poetry

Author: Clavia Williams-McBean

Contact: claviawilliams@yahoo.com or acesjamaica@gmail.com

First published 2019

Also in this series:

Light Up With English: An English Language workbook for Grade Seven students

Light Up With English: An English Literature workbook for Grade Eight students

Light Up With English: An English Language workbook for Grade Eight students

Light Up With English: An English Literature workbook for Grade Nine students

Light Up With English: An English Language workbook for Grade Nine students

Light Up With English: An English Literature workbook for CSEC® English B – Prose

Light Up With English: An English Literature workbook for CSEC® English B - Poetry

Light Up With English: An English Literature workbook for CSEC® English B – Drama

Light Up With English: An English Literature workbook for CSEC® English B – Paper 01

Other Works:

Argumentative Writing: A Preparation Guide for Caribbean Secondary Education Certificate (CSEC) English A Examinations

Persuasive Writing: A Preparation Guide for Caribbean Secondary Education Certificate (CSEC) English A Examinations

Short Story Writing: A Preparation Guide for Caribbean Secondary Education Certificate (CSEC) English A Examinations

School-Based Assessment in English: A guide and workbook for students

School-Based Assessment in Mathematics: A guide and workbook for students

Other resource:

English ABC: the interactive Facebook page where you can ask questions, get information on topics relative to English A, English B and Communication Studies while you have fun interacting and competing with friends online.

TABLE OF CONTENTS

INTRODUCTION

Light up with English: An English Literature workbook for CSEC® English B – Poetry is the first workbook of its kind to be added to the Caribbean educational landscape. It was designed based on the learning objectives of the CSEC® English B syllabus to make classroom instruction more effective and maximize learning outcomes. It is my aim that while learning the content for the CSEC® syllabus, students will make connections to their unique life experiences. Also, they should increase their knowledge and appreciation of the cultures presented in the different poems.

The workbook incorporates activities which cater to the varied intelligences in the classroom. It also incorporates the use of Information Communication Technology (ICT), formative assessment and collaborative learning to make learning more interactive and fun. It is believed that the nature of the activities will allow students to become excited about learning both English Language and Literature. It is my hope that this Workbook will ignite, in students, the desire to do well in English, and the flame will continue to burn outside the classroom and far beyond their high school years.

Literature is more than a subject on a timetable. It is a mirror of life with all its accomplishments, disappointments and complexities. Studying literature can help you to identify, understand and solve some of these complex issues in your own life. The study of literature also supports language learning as well as the individual's personal and professional development. It is my hope that **Light up with English** will be an essential part of enhancing the teaching and learning of English at your school.

To Teachers: Thank you for making this workbook a part of your instructional resources for the teaching of English. This book is meant to be complementary to classroom teaching and is not designed as a tool for teaching itself. Teachers are free to incorporate the various activities as they see fit in their classrooms. It is believed that with many instances for guided practice, **Light up with English** will enable formative assessment and active learning and will help teachers as they evaluate the effectiveness of the teaching and learning process. At the end of each poem, there is a slot for students to complete the 3-2-1 activity which works as follows:

Three – After completing the activities on a poem, instruct each student to write **three** things he/she learned from the activities.

Two – Next, instruct the student to write **two** things he/she found interesting or about which he/she would like to learn more.

One – Then, have the student write **one** question he/she still has about the material.

This activity will help to keep the students focused on their learning. It may also help you to quickly assess your students' learning, interests and misunderstandings. **Cooperative learning is also encouraged as students can answer a question posed by their peers.** Finally, the most important step in the 3-2-1 activity is reviewing the students' responses. This information should be used to guide future instruction.

Rubrics and checklists are also provided to enable formative assessment. Encourage your students to assess their own work (self-assessment) and that of their peer(s) (peer-assessment) **before** you assess their work. It is important to allow for self- and peer-assessment **before** your assessment to develop independent and critical assessment skills within your students.

Finally, use the stickers to motivate your students to continue to work efficiently and accurately. Sign and date across each sticker as the students earn them or award the actual stickers (sold separately) to the students. You may use the stickers for activities not in this Workbook as well.

To Students: This is YOUR book. All the activities are here to make learning English fun and to give you many opportunities to practise as you learn. The activities will call on you to be creative and use the knowledge and skills you acquired in other subjects. Some will require you to work as a team. Do not be afraid to try or make mistakes. Learning English is a process. This process becomes easier through constant practice and by working along with your teachers and your peers. Be sure to follow your teacher and use the 3-2-1 activity to assess your learning at the end of each topic. Think about what you have learned and any questions you may have. It is very important that you are actively involved in your learning if you want to do well. Challenge yourselves by completing the different activities to earn the most stickers. Finally, HAVE FUN!

Good luck and LIGHT UP your life WITH ENGLISH!

CSEC English B

Have you ever wondered why the Caribbean Examination Council has only one syllabus for both English A and English B? Why not have two syllabi since they are two separate subjects? Why have one school-based assessment (SBA) for both subjects? The fact is English Literature complements English Language and the study of English as a language is not complete without an understanding of literatures written in English. As such, although you have an examination for English A and one for English B, the English A examination requires you to demonstrate your understanding of literary works (poems and prose extracts) on Paper 1, and on Paper 2, you are expected to express yourself in a literary form – short story. At the same time, the English B examination requires you to understand English language as used by authors, poets and playwrights and express your opinions, judgements and understanding of literary works using correct grammatical structures and expressions of the English Language. English Language and English Literature are integrated, and this integrated approach is reflected in the single syllabus for both examinations. The syllabus also states:

> This *integrated syllabus* provides a map to help students to develop the ability to read and enjoy literary texts; to explore social and moral issues using the skills acquired while learning to 'read' texts; to evaluate the way their personal ownership of language promotes and optimises their own growth; and creates opportunity to practise using the acquired language to express themselves effectively. *In short, the syllabus crafts an essential interweaving of literature and language study* as the platform for raising UNESCO's "Pillars of Learning": to know, to do, to live together, to be, and to transform self and society. (p.1)

The syllabus also encourages teachers to integrate both language and literature to help students to improve their competence in the language and literature of English.

This integrated approach is taken in this English B workbook series. The skills in focus in English A are used while exploring the poems, drama and prose texts prescribed by CXC for the 2018 – 2023 English B examinations. I hope you sharpen your language skills while developing your understanding of English poetry, prose and drama.

What is Literature?

Literature is defined as "a body of artistic writings … that are characterized by beauty of expression and form and by universality of intellectual and emotional appeal". It is differentiated from other types of writing by its artistic form. We will investigate the artistic form of each genre of literature later. I like to tell my students that literature is a mirror of life with its good and evil sides. It is for this reason, you may find characters in stories who remind you of people you actually know or persons responding to situations in ways you understand or can relate to because you have had similar experiences. Indeed, poets, playwrights and authors often write about what they have seen or experienced in real life situations or desire to see in their real or imaginary lives. Literature is life as it was, as it is, as it will be and as it is imagined.

Genres of Literature

Directions: The CSEC English B examination focuses on prose, poetry and drama. Match each of the following features with the genre of literature it is **most likely** to be associated by placing each in the assigned box. If the word or phrase is a feature of all three genres place it in the middle.

Features: *characters, props, stage directions, theme, rhyme, language of ordinary people, lighting, setting, performance, costume, literary devices, metre, lines, stanza, paragraphs, acts and scenes, plot, chapter, limited words, fixed forms, type of narration, spectacle, rhythm*

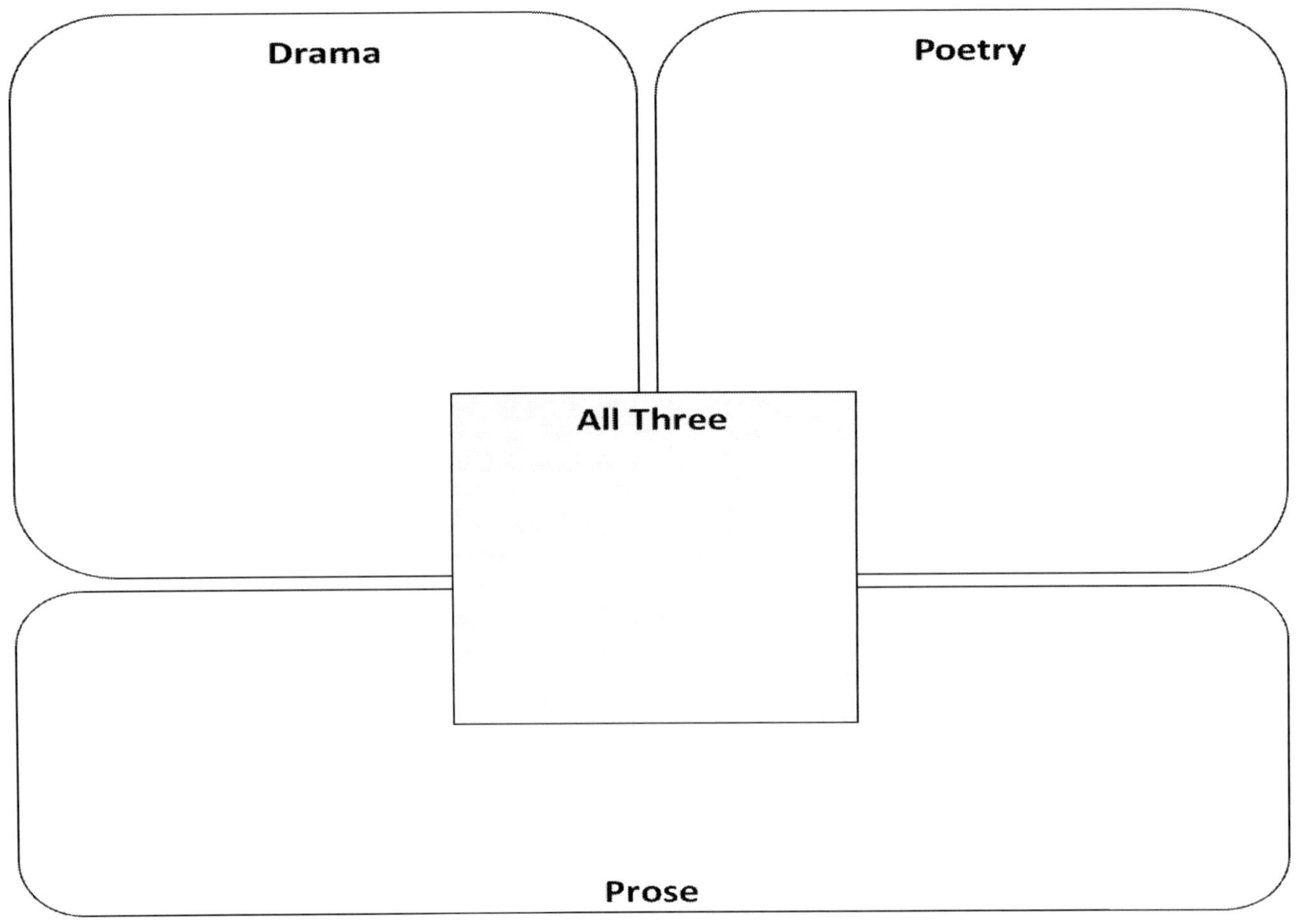

Activity 2: Genres of My Literature Texts

Directions: Classify your literature texts according to the genres of literature.

Prose: ____

____

____

____

Poetry: ____

____

____

Drama: ____

____

____

____

Which genre do you think you will enjoy most? Why? ______________________

____

____

____

____

Which genre do you think you will be comfortable teaching your classmates about? Why? __________

____

____

____

____

Which genre do you think you will need the most time to understand well? Why? ______________

____

____

____

____

Poetry

Objectives

After completing the activities in this section, you should be able to accurately:

- ☐ define poetry;
- ☐ list at least 10 elements of poetry;
- ☐ define each element of poetry;
- ☐ identify the elements of poetry in an assigned poem.

Poetry is another artistic form of literature. It shares many elements in common with the other genres: prose and drama. However, it is differentiated from the other genres primarily through its conciseness, greater use of figurative language to create meaning, images and experiences. We will take a closer look at the elements of poetry later. We first need to understand CXC's focus in relation to poetry. The English syllabus indicates that when studying poetry for the CSEC examination, primary focus should be placed on:

a. fixed forms, metre, rhythm and rhyme;
b. the economy of language;
c. the organic relationship between sound and sense; and,
d. the figurative language employed to give the poem levels of meaning. (pp. 34 – 35).

Therefore, as we go through the poems on the list for this year, we will focus on these elements of poetry.

Elements of Poetry

The elements of poetry include rhyme, rhythm, metre, words, imagery, literary devices, form, persona, theme, lines, stanza, and historical background. Is it not ironic that the shortest genre of literature has the most elements? It should tell you that no matter how short a poem is, you should not take it lightly. It is quite possibly packed with hidden meanings. We will focus on these elements as we study the prescribed poems.

Activity 1: Hidden Messages

Directions. Poems sometimes contain hidden messages. Therefore, you must practise to find out what is behind the words and symbols that are written on the pages. The definition of each element of poetry is presented as a secret message below. The secret message is written in symbols. Use the code key below to find what each symbol means. Write the letter above the symbol and you can read the secret message. After you have figured out the message, write the name of the element that is being defined on the line below the hidden message.

Example

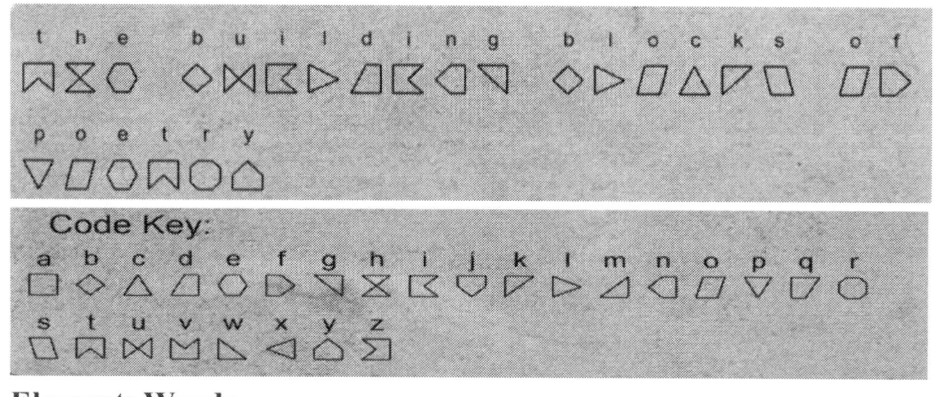

Element: <u>Words</u>

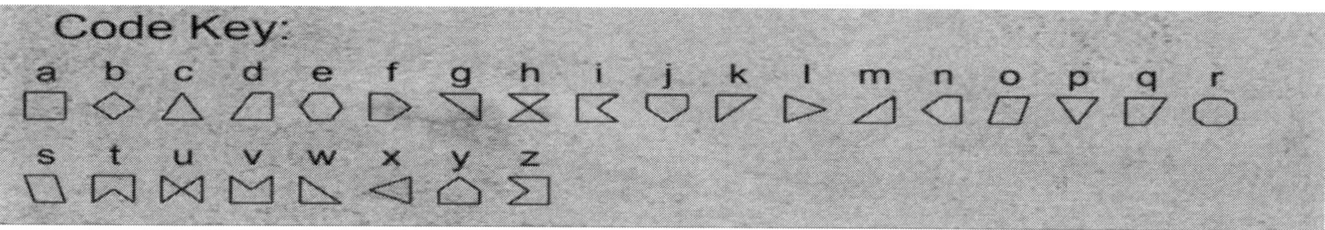

1.

Element: ______________________

2.

Element: ______________________

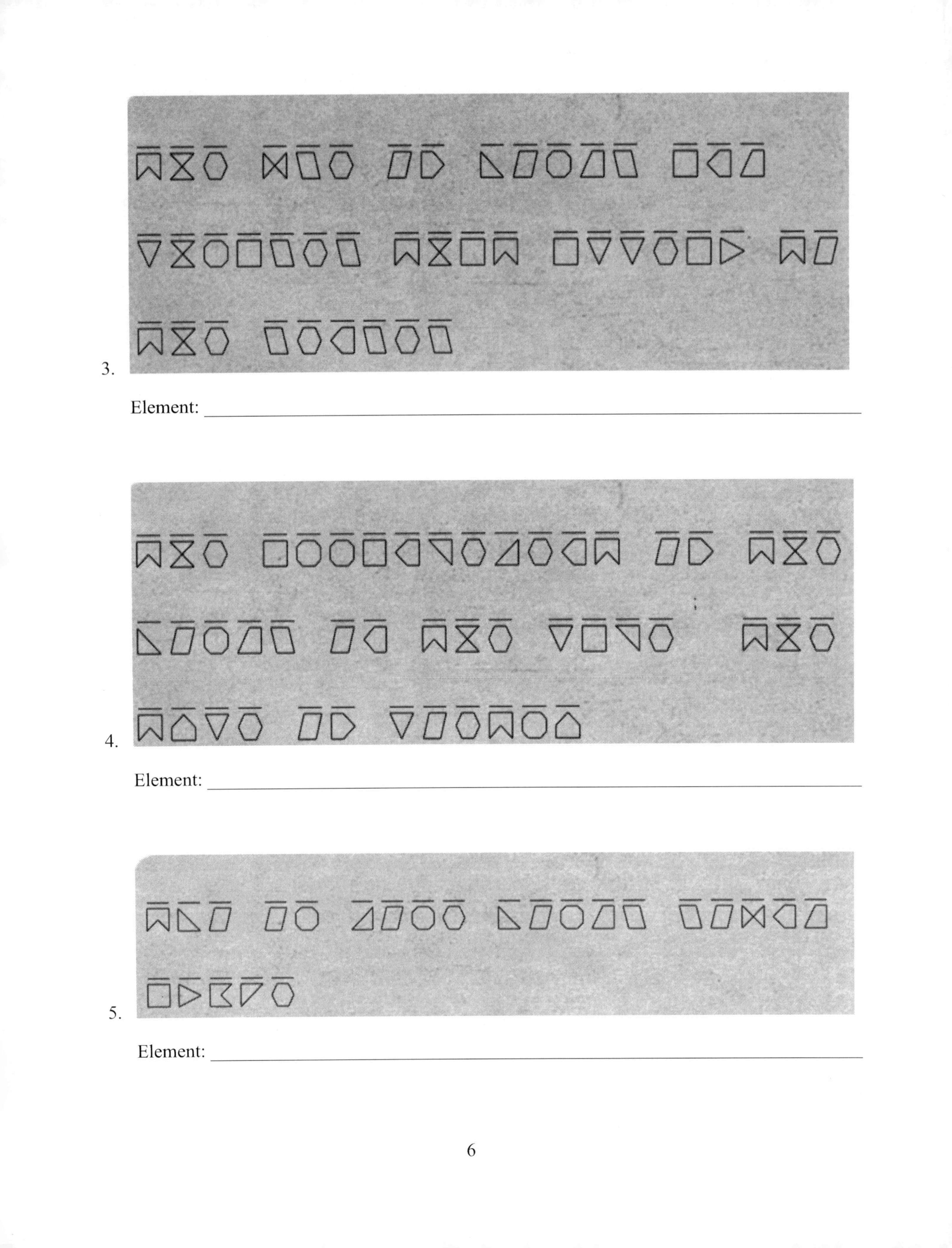

3.

Element: ____

4.

Element: ____

5.

Element: ____

6.

Element: ______________________________

7.

Element: ______________________________

8.

Element: ______________________________

9.

Element: ______________________________

10.

Element: ______________________________

11.

Element: ______________________________

Activity 2: Identifying the Elements of Poetry

Directions. Your teacher will assign you a poem from the prescribed list. Before the teacher begins instruction on each poem, the assigned students will be expected to:

1. recite the poem from memory (without looking in the text);
2. provide a personal analysis of the poem.

Your analysis should include:

1. the identification of the elements of poetry defined in Activity 1;
2. a paragraph on how the poem benefited you personally and as a student of English.

Since it is highly likely that more than one student will be assigned a poem, the students may recite and analyze the assigned poem as a group.

Earn a 

for making the best presentation on your assigned poem and a AWESOME JOB!! for completing all the steps on time.

Follow the steps below to help you prepare for your recitation and analysis.

Step 1: Make your predictions. The first thing you read in a poem is the title. The title is like the topic of the poem. It gives you a general idea of what the poem is about. However, you will not know specifically what the poem is about or what the poet's position or view on the general topic is until you read the entire poem. When you read the title, connect it to your personal experiences and knowledge. What do you know about the general topic in the title? Based on what you know, and before you read the poem, generate as many ideas about what you could possibly find in the poem. Look at the title, "Little Boy Crying" for example. What are the possible reasons for a little boy to cry? How would you respond to a little boy who is crying? Your experiences and prior knowledge are very valuable in poetry and literature as a whole. Use them as a starting point to understand what the poem is about. Do not be disappointed if what you expect to find is not in the poem. Remember people have different experiences and the poet is sharing one of his or hers. What you should do is note in what way your expectations are different from what you found in the poem.

Activity: What I Know

Directions. Write the title of your assigned poem below. Then, make THREE predictions on what you expect the poem to be about. Your predictions should be related to the title of the poem.

Title: ____

____

Predictions

1. ____

   ____

2. ____

   ____

3. ____

   ____

Step 2: Read for Understanding – At this stage, you are reading the poem to get a basic understanding of it. To do this, read the poem silently and underline the unfamiliar words in the poem. Define each word before reading the poem again. Write the meanings of each unfamiliar word in your assigned poem below.

____

____

Now that you know the meanings of these words, read the poem again silently to understand what the poem is about.

Step 2: Read Aloud – Poems are meant to be heard and performed, so read the poem aloud a few times and listen to the sound of your voice as you read. Try out different tones (happy, sad, sarcastic etc.), pace (fast or slow) and pitch (high or low tone) to communicate the appropriate emotions and meanings.

Step 3: Summarize the Poem – Briefly state what the poem is about in your own words. A good way to do this is to write a sentence which states what happens in each stanza (if your poem is divided into stanzas). Then combine the sentences into ONE paragraph. Most of the poems on the prescribed list are divided into stanzas. If your poem is not divided into stanzas, look for sections with the same rhyming words and summarize those individually before putting them together in a paragraph. The aim is to have one short paragraph which states what happened in your poem exactly as presented in the text. Write a summary of your assigned poem below. Write your separate individual sentences **before** you combine them into a paragraph.

Step 4: Preparing for your Performance – Imagine that your poem is a monologue in a play. Consider the gestures, facial expressions, movement and posture that would compliment your recitation. Write out the words of the poem below. Include stage directions[1] to yourself.

[1] Instructions in the text of a poem indicating the movement, gestures, position, or tone of an actor, or the sound effects to be used while a line is being recited.

Now that you have a clearer idea of how you want to perform your poem, rehearse in front of your family members, peers or teacher. Ask for suggestions on how you may improve your recitation.

My Recommendations

Make recommendations to yourself about how you may improve your performance. Ask your peers, family members and/or your teacher for their recommendations on how you may improve as well.

Self	Peer/Family Members
Teacher	

Peer reviewed by: ______________________________ Date: ______________________

Teacher reviewed by: ___________________________ Date: ______________________

Based on the feedback from yourself, your peers and teacher, make the necessary changes. If you have no improvements to make, move on to the next step.

Step 4: Identifying the Elements of Poetry – We have listed eleven elements of poetry in this workbook. You will need to go through your assigned poem and identify each of these elements. Where do you begin? A good place to start is with the historical background of the poem.

Historical Background

Understanding a poem's cultural context can often help our understanding of some aspect of the poem itself. The social, political, and economic environment surrounding a writer can, and usually do, affect how and what the writers write about. What do you know about the poet or the time and place in which your assigned poem was written? Fill in the required information in each of the following boxes based on the life and works of the poet of your assigned poem.

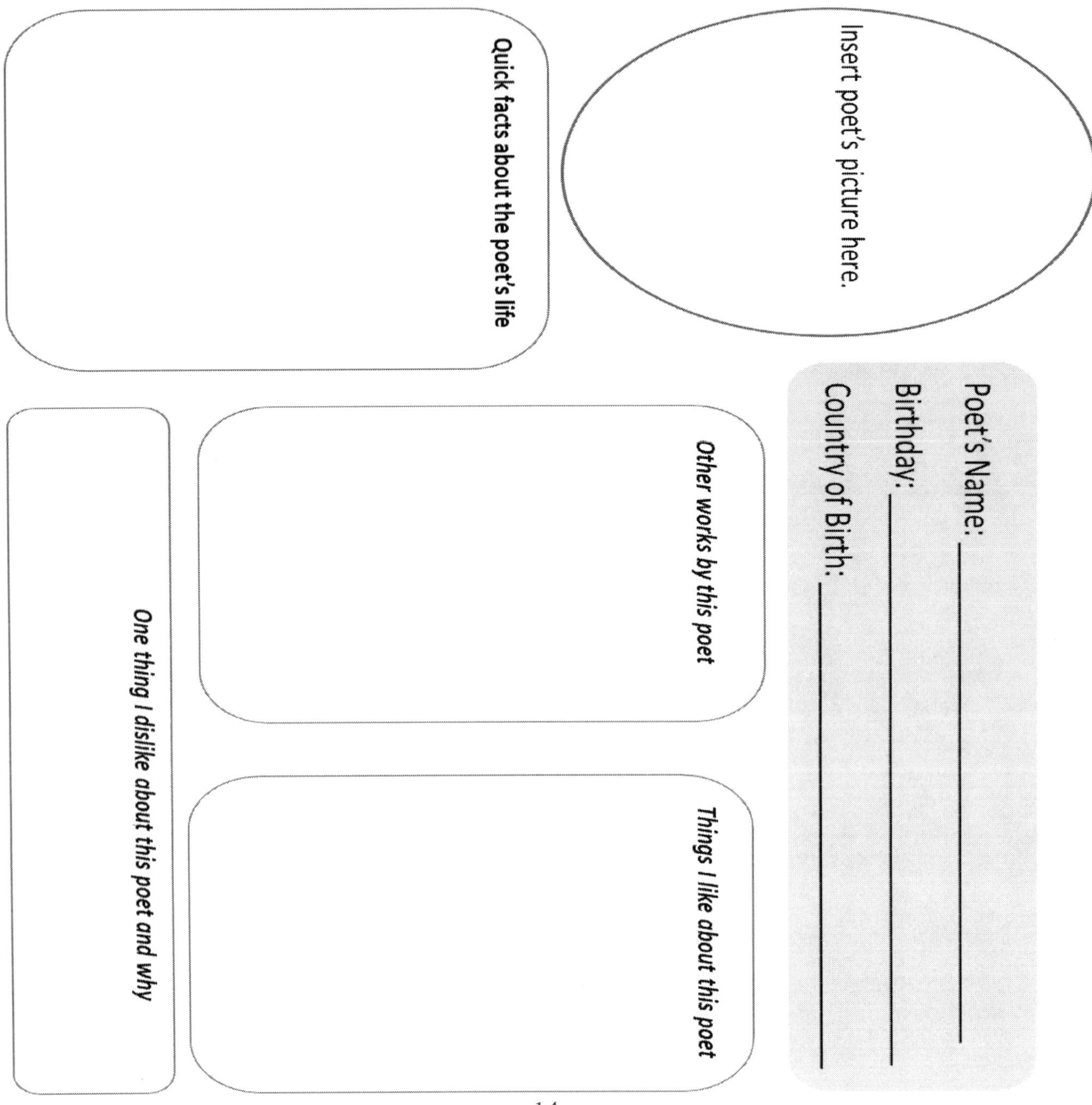

Fill in the required information in each of the following boxes based on the historical context of your assigned poem.

Title: ______________________________

Year the Poem was Written: ______________________________

Country/City in which the Poem was written: ______________

____

Is the poem a part of a series/anthology/cycle?

If yes, what is the name of the series/anthology/cycle?

What is the series/anthology/cycle about?

Important events during that period in the City:

Country:

World:

You now have background information on the poet and the poem that may enhance your understanding of the poem.

Can you identify any similarities between the background information on the poem and the poet and what is presented in the poem?

The research says …	**In the poem …**

You should then look at the elements of poetry that are similar to those in drama and prose: the literary elements.

The Literary Elements

These include characters, setting, plot, theme and stylistics. Though some of the stylistics features are similar to those used in drama and poetry, there are some stylistic features of poetry that are different. This is similar to how the technical elements of drama (lighting, costumes, set, props, etc.) are unique to drama. Many of the unique stylistics features of poetry are not found in the other genres at all or are not as emphasized in the other genres. Let us identify the literary elements in your assigned poem.

Characters

There are characters in poems as well. The characters include the persona as well as any other person, place or thing that plays a role in the poem. The persona is like the narrator in a story. It is simply the voice in the poem. The voice in which we hear the poem is not necessarily the poet's. It could be a child, an object, a supernatural being or another person. However, it could be the poet as well. That is why it is important to do research on the poet while analyzing a poem. It will help you to identify if the poet is the persona in the poem. Understanding who is speaking helps you to understand and assess the credibility of the opinions and emotions presented in the poem. To identify the persona, ask yourself: Who is talking in the poem? Whose voice are you hearing as you read, perform, listen to the poem? There may be more than one voice in the poem so pay attention to the number of voices you hear in the poem. To identify the other characters, look to see if the persona is speaking to someone or something in the poem? Look also to see if the persona mentions any other characters.

Who are the characters in your assigned poem? Justify your answer.

Characters	Your Identification	Evidence
Persona(s)		
Other Characters* Addressed Mentioned		
Type of Narration: 1st Person 2nd Person 3rd Person		

**** Other characters include the characters who are mentioned or to whom the persona is speaking.***

Tone

After you have identified to whom the voice(s) in the poem belong, you need to identify in what tone of voice is the persona speaking. You have probably heard the expression, "It's not only what you say. It's also **how** you say it". How you say what you say can completely change the meaning of what is said. That is why tone is important. It gives you a better understanding of the people, places, events and themes in the poem. ***Tone refers to how the words in the poem are delivered. It more commonly refers to the poet's or persona's attitude to the subject of the poem.*** Tone is indicated by word choice, punctuation marks, facial expressions, gestures, body language and so on. Look at the following example. Which of the following classmates do you think is really sorry for being engaged in a classroom quarrel? Why?

Simon: (*barely audible and staring at his feet*) I'm sorry.

Chase: (*eyes rolling and looking in the ceiling*) I'm sorry.

Savanna: (*arms on her waist and staring defiantly at her classmates*) I'm sorry.

James: (*solemnly*) I'm sorry.

In the example, all the students said the same words, but how they said the words differed. Based on how they said the words, different things were communicated.

Use ONE adjective to describe Savanna's attitude. ______________________________

Justify your selection. ______________________________

____

____

In poetry, the poet relies heavily on word choice, punctuation and literary devices to indicate his or her attitude towards the subject of the poem. This is similar to how you communicate your tone when you write text messages or email.

Write a text to a friend simply asking where he or she is.

____

You have been waiting on your friend's arrival for over an hour. Write a text in which you angrily or in frustration inquire where he/she is. Do NOT use the word angry or frustrated.

____

____

How did you communicate the different tone? ______________________________

____

____

Activity 1: Toning Your Vocabulary

Directions. To accurately describe tone in poetry, you need a large vocabulary of words. Do a Google search for "List of Words to Describe Tone". Print and paste one of the lists provided below.

Define the unfamiliar words in your list below.

Activity 2: Categorizing Tones

Directions. Tone can be divided into three main categories: positive, negative and neutral. Now that you know the meanings of the words that can be used to describe tone, categorize them as positive, negative and neutral in the table below. List the words in alphabetical order in each column.

Positive	Neutral	Negative

Activity 3: Tones in My Poem

In the same way you may begin a text conversation in anger and later become soft and apologetic or vice versa, tone can change in a poem. Therefore, when you are identifying tone in your poem, be sure to look for:

1. words, phrase and punctuation marks that help to show the poet or persona's feeling
2. any change in the tone in the poem.

Directions. In the first box, write words, phrases and/or punctuation marks that you think indicate the tone in your poem. Then, find a suitable word from your tone list to describe the group of words, phrases you have identified.

The poem says ... **Therefore, I think ...**

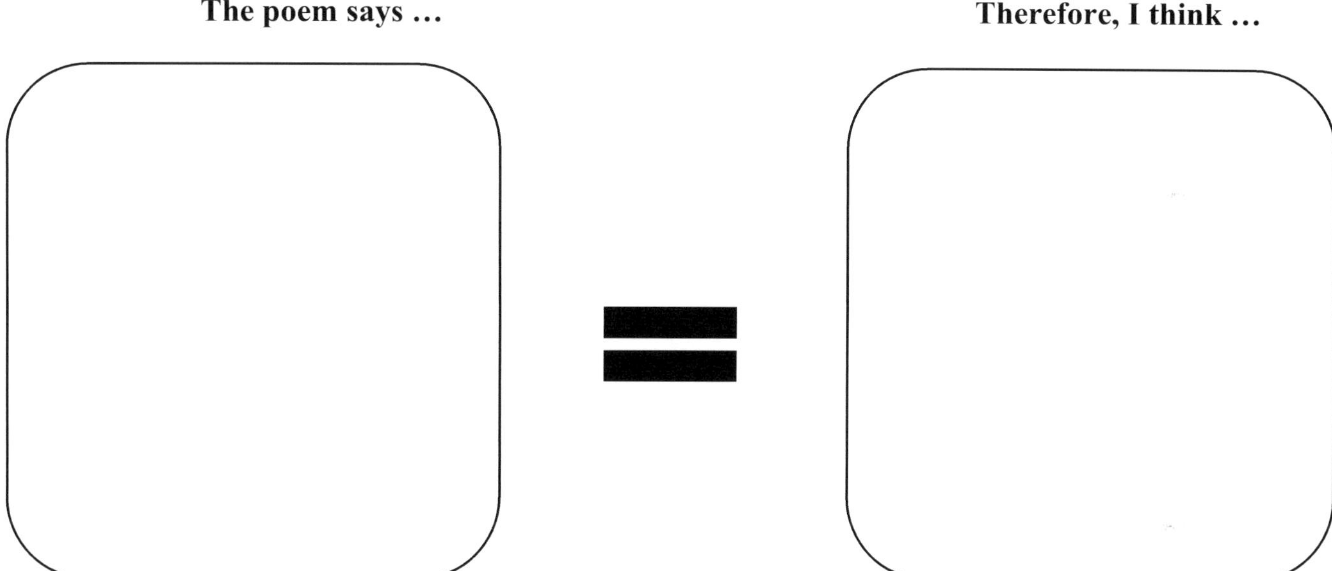

If the tone changed, complete the diagrams below to support the change in tone.

The poem says ... **Therefore, I think ...**

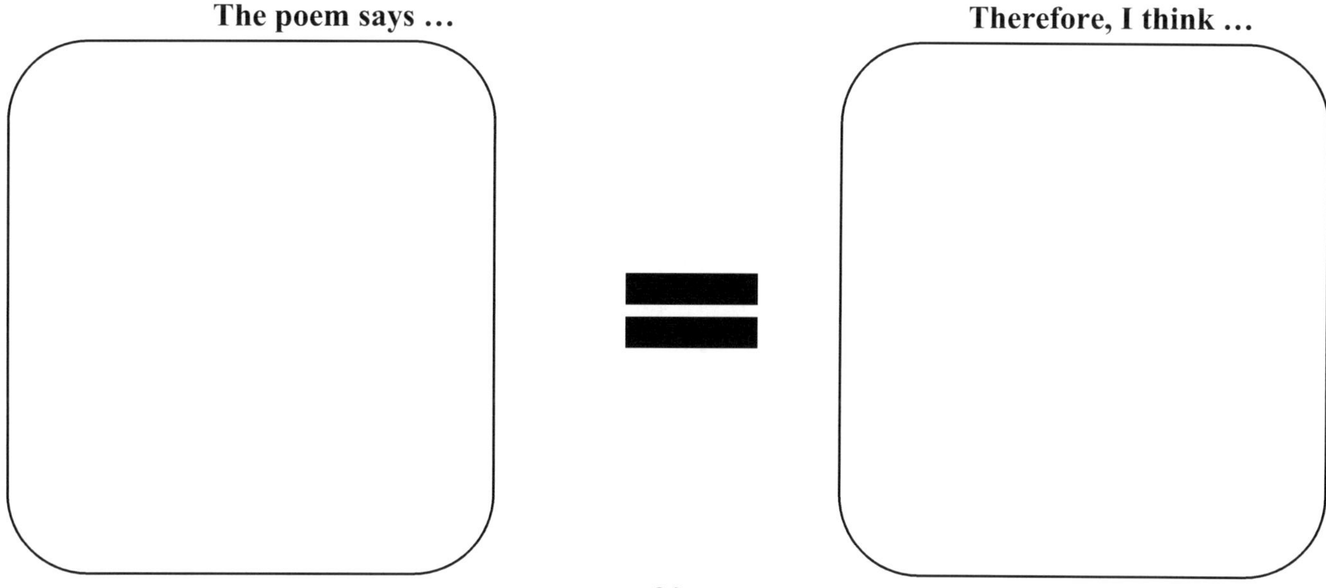

1. In which line did the tone change? ______________________________

2. Why did the tone change? ______________________________

____

____

____

Setting

Like in prose and drama, ***the setting is the time and place in which the opinions and emotions in the poem are being expressed***. In identifying the time, you should look for details that tell you the time of day or the historical period. The place includes the immediate location as well as the historical, social and economic context in which the poem is written. Do not be surprised if there is no information in the poem that allows you to describe the physical location and time. Poets do not have to establish a setting. Again, that is why it is important to do research on the historical background of the poem and poet. It helps you to understand the external setting of the poem.

1. Describe the setting of the poem.

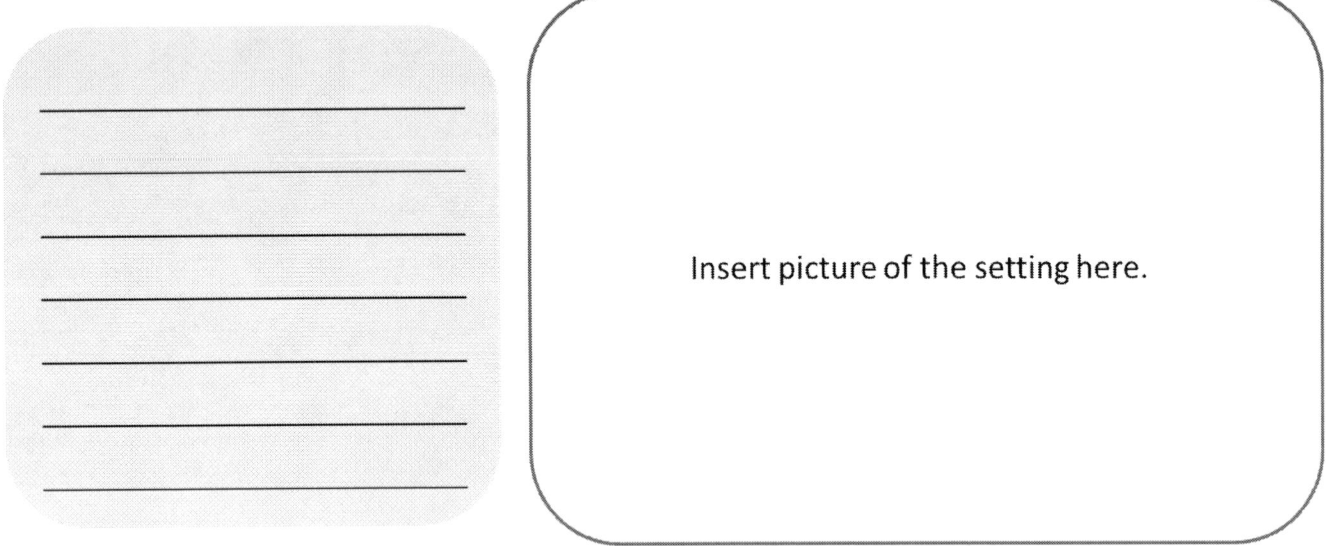

Mood

Setting also refers to the mood in the poem. **Mood is the overall emotion or feeling that is created IN THE READER after reading the poem.** The words used by the persona to present the setting, theme and incidents in the poem can cause the reader (you) to feel different emotions and be left with an overall feeling. To identify the mood, think about how you feel or how you are expected to feel after reading the poem. In poetry and life in general, how you feel is more specific than "good" or "bad". Therefore, you will need to have a wide vocabulary of words to describe mood as well.

Activity 1: My Mood List

Directions. Do a Google search for "List of Words to Describe Mood in Poetry". Print and paste one of the lists provided below.

Paste your list here.

Define the unfamiliar words in your list below.

Activity 2: Categorizing Tones

Directions. Moods can be divided into three main categories as well: positive, negative and neutral. Now that you know the meanings of the words that can be used to describe mood, categorize them as positive, negative and neutral in the table below. List the words in alphabetical order in each column.

Positive	Neutral	Negative

Activity 3A: Mood Emojis

Directions. Emojis are used to express emotions. Identify the emotion expressed by each emoji below. First, write what you use it to mean while texting. Then, use a word from your mood list to describe the emoji.

You should notice from this activity that there are different levels of intensity to the same emotion. Therefore, ensure the words you choose match the intensity of the emotion as well.

Activity 3B

Directions. Draw an emoji that indicates how you feel right now. Without naming the emoji, show it to your classmates and see who can correctly identify your feeling. See if you can accurately identify how your classmates are feeling based on their emojis as well.

Activity 4: Moods in My Poem

Like tone, your mood can change as you read different sections of the poem. Therefore, when you are identifying mood in your poem, be sure to look for:

1. words, phrases and punctuation marks that help to make you feel a specific emotion;
2. any change in the mood in the poem.

Directions. In the first box, write words, phrases and/or punctuation marks that you think indicate the mood that is created in your poem. Then, find a suitable word from your mood list to describe the group of words and/or phrases you have identified.

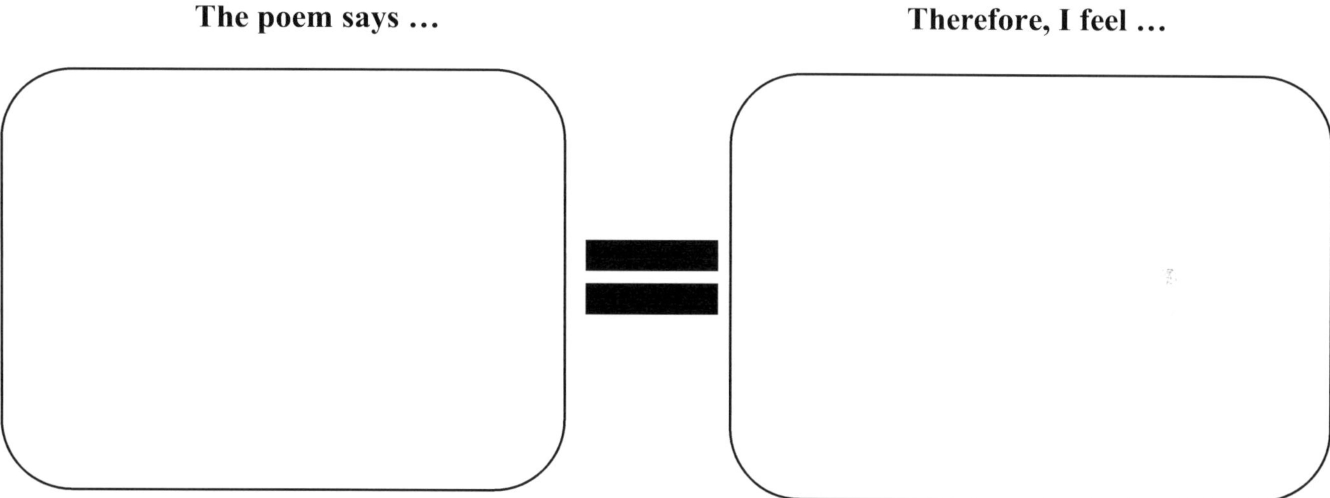

If the mood changed, complete the diagrams below to support the change in mood.

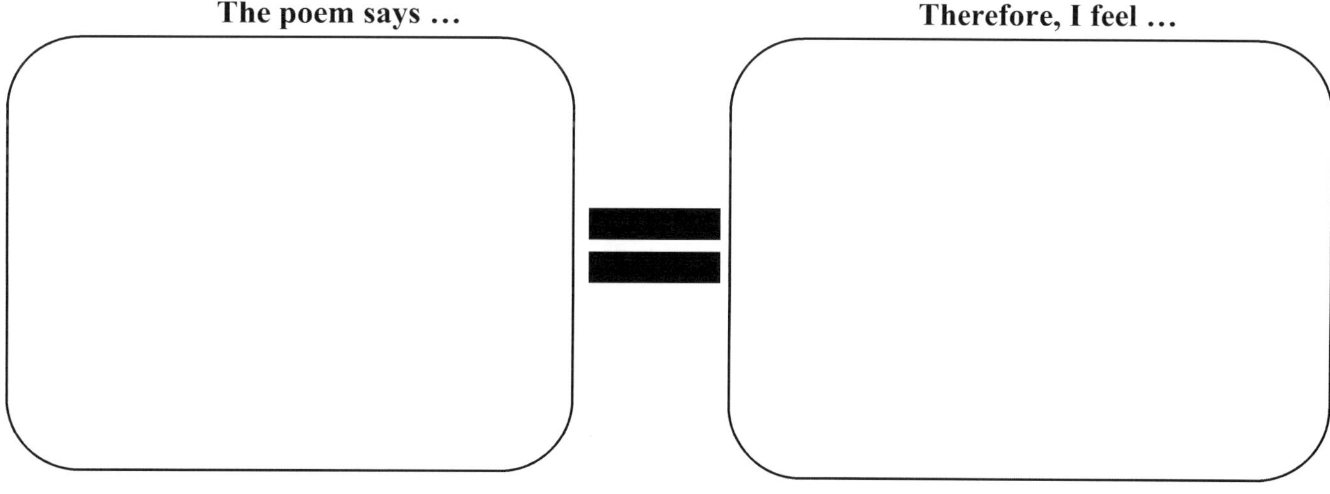

1. In which line did the mood change? ____________________________
2. Why did the mood change? ____________________________

____

____

Theme

A theme is a main idea or main lesson that the poet wants to bring across to the readers. It is usually a single sentence and not a word or phrase. For example, religion is not a theme because there is no message in that one word. Instead, think of religion as the category and then write a sentence that summarises the message, lesson, moral or truth the poet is communicating. (e.g., *Religion can divide people as much as it can bring them together.*) All the events in the poem should contribute to its development. You identify the message in the same way you would in prose or drama:

1. look for evidence of major ideas/issues being addressed in the poem;
2. search for evidence that suggests the writer's opinion, attitude or feeling towards that major idea/issue.

Major issues may include education, love, racism, religion, gender, childhood experiences, nature and so on. Then, ask yourself, based on the words, thoughts, actions and/or emotions expressed in the poem, what is the specific message related to the major idea or issue the poet wants to express. There may be one or more themes in a poem. Fill in the diagram below with relevant information from your assigned poem.

NB. The theme is usually a generalization that is directly stated or suggested and unifies the poem.

1st Major Idea

Evidence from the Poem
Words:
Emotions:
Actions:

Poet's Message

2nd Major Idea

Evidence from the Poem

Words:

Emotions:

Actions:

Poet's Message

Plot

The plot is the sequence of events in a poem. Think of it as what happened from beginning to end. Since a poem is usually much shorter than a story or a play, the summary of the events in the poem should be much shorter. You have already written a summary of the poem in Step 3. Is there anything you would like to change from that first summary? Make your changes below. Remember to write ONE PARAGRAPH. If you have no changes, move on to identifying the stylistic features of your assigned poem.

Stylistics

Stylistics refers to the poet's style – the way he or she writes. The stylistic features we will look at include form and literary devices. The other elements of poetry can be used to describe form or literary devices

Form

The form of the poem is the arrangement of the words on the page. It also refers to the type of poem. In discussing the arrangement of the words on the page, we will pay particular attention to lines, stanza, rhyme, rhythm and metre as elements of poetry. Being able to identify these elements will help you to describe the form of the poem and identify the type of poem.

Lines and Stanza

The first thing you should notice is the number of lines in the poem. ***A line is a single row of words in a poem.*** It is not necessarily a sentence. It could be a phrase or even a single word.

a. How many lines are in your assigned poem? ____

Then, you should check whether the lines are separated in sections (groups of lines) or if they are all together. ***The sections or groups in which lines are separated are called stanzas.***

b. How many stanzas are in your poem? ____

Next, identify the types of stanzas.

c. What type of stanzas are present in your assigned poem? (You may select more than one type below.)

☐ Monostich – stanza with ONE line

☐ Couplet – stanza with TWO lines.

☐ Tercet – stanza with THREE lines.

☐ Quatrain – stanza with FOUR lines.

☐ Cinquain – stanza with FIVE lines

☐ Sestet – stanza with SIX lines

☐ Septet – stanza with SEVEN lines

☐ Octave – stanza with EIGHT lines

☐ Spenserian – stanza with NINE lines

Put your answers to a, b and c into a sentence. Fill in the sentence below with the information from your assigned poem.

The poem consists of __________ lines which are divided into ________________________________.
Number of lines — *Number and type of stanza*

OR

The poem consists of ____________ lines that are not separated into stanzas.
Number of lines

Now you must identify the relationship among the ideas presented in the different lines and stanzas. Does the idea presented in the first line or first stanza change in the lines and stanzas that follow? If there is a change, how did it change? Ways in which you may describe the relationship among the ideas presented in lines and stanzas include:

1. **Repeated** – present the same idea in the same words
2. **Similar** – present the same in different words
3. **Extended** – provide additional details or examples in support of the main idea
4. **Contradicted** – present an idea that is the opposite of the main idea.

Go through your poem line by line and write repeat, similar, extend or contradict as the case may be.

Example:

My parents kept me from children who were rough	***Main idea***
Who threw words like stones and who wore torn clothes.	***Extension*** *of the description of the kinds of children from whom his parents kept him*
Their thighs showed through rags. They ran in the street	***Extension***
And climbed cliffs and stripped by the country streams.	***Extension***

In the example above, the first line tells us that the persona's parents prevented him from playing with 'rough' children and each line provided further description or additional details about the types of children who were considered 'rough'. Therefore, lines 2 to 4 extend the main idea.

After you have completed the line-by-line identification, use the relationship between the lines to help you to identify the main idea in the first stanza and then the relationship among the stanzas. When you were writing the summary of your poem in Step 3, you first had to identify the main idea in each stanza. What is the relationship among those main ideas? Complete the diagram on **page 38** with information from your assigned poem. In the squares, write the main idea in each stanza of your poem. Then, colour the arrows to indicate the relationship between the stanzas.

1. **Repeated** – GREEN
2. **Similar** – YELLOW
3. **Extended** – BLUE
4. **Contradicted** – RED

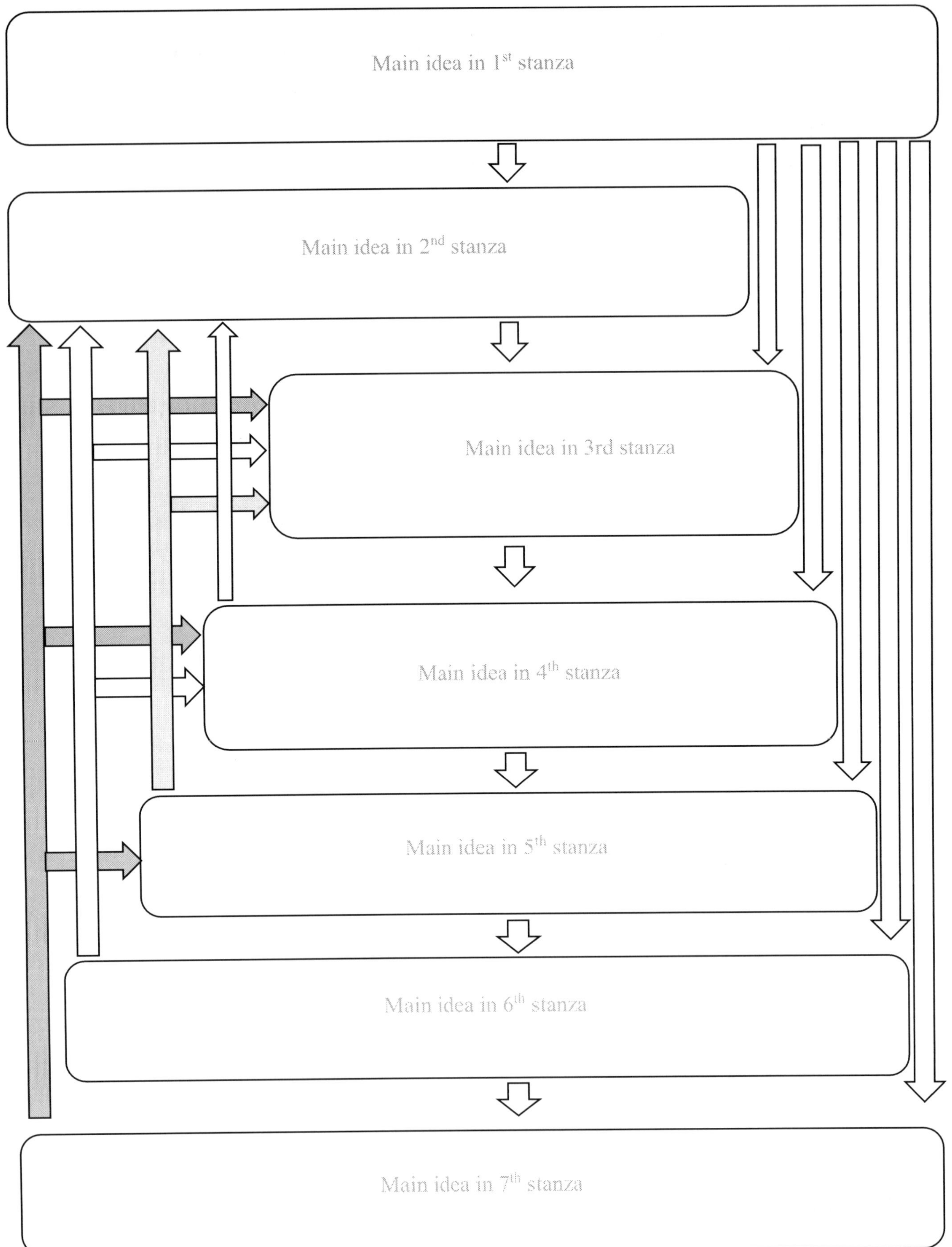

As you can see from the graphic organizer, the relationship among the stanzas is not linear.

Rhyme

Next, you need to look to see if there are rhyming words in your poem and identify any patterns among the rhyming words. ***Rhyming words are words that sound alike*** (e.g., you – too; dutiful – beautiful).

a. Are there rhyming words in your poem? ______________________________

b. What type of rhymes are they? (You my select more than one type below.)

☐ End rhymes – the rhyming words are at the end of the lines.

☐ Internal rhymes – the rhyming words are within the lines or one word in the middle and the other at the end of the line.

☐ Identical rhymes – the rhyming words are the same.
E.g. There's something about **you**
that make me want to embrace **you**.

☐ Slant rhymes – the rhyming words do not completely rhyme (half-rhymes).
(E.g. street – stream)

☐ Eye rhymes – the rhyming words only look like they should rhyme. They rhyme when you look at them but not when you pronounce them. (E.g., though – rough).

Rhyme Scheme

You now need to identify the rhyme scheme. What do you know about houses in a housing scheme? They usually look alike. All the houses usually have the same pattern or design, especially at the front of the houses. ***Rhyme scheme refers to the pattern of the end rhymes in a poem.*** If the rhyming words have a pattern, then there is a rhyme scheme. To identify the rhyme scheme of a poem, you label each rhyming word alphabetically. End rhymes that sound alike should be given the same letter throughout the poem.

Example: Literature is a mirror **A**
That gives you glimpses of your soul **B**
Flashes of youth as you grow old, **B**
Love, life, passion and terror **A**

The rhyme scheme for the stanza above is ABBA.

Throughout the poem any word that rhymes with **'*mirror*'** will be labelled ***'A'*** and any word that rhymes with **'soul'** will be labelled '***B***'. As new end words appear, they should be given the next letter in the alphabet. Go through your assigned poem and identify the rhyme scheme. ***Some poems do not have end rhymes or rhyme scheme.***

____

____

You also need to identify the type of the rhyme scheme. There are different types of rhyme schemes. Some of the most frequently used rhyme schemes include:

- ☐ Rhyming couplets – A two-line stanza with end rhyme (E.g., AA, BB or CC)
- ☐ Rhyming Triplet – three lines rhyme (AAA, BBB, CCC)
- ☐ Monorhyme – Every line in the poem rhymes.
- ☐ Alternate Rhyme Scheme – Every other line rhyme. (E.g., ABAB, CDCD, EFEF)
- ☐ Enclosed Rhyme Scheme – The first and fourth lines rhyme and the second and third lines rhyme. (E.g., ABBA, CDDC, EFFE)

Look at the stanza used as the example for identifying rhyme scheme above. What type of rhyme scheme is present there? ____

Identify the type of rhyme scheme present in each stanza of your assigned poem. If the poem has no stanzas, describe the rhyme scheme in the poem as a whole. Remember, it is possible that the poem does not contain rhymes or a rhyme scheme.

____

____

____

____

____

____

____

Rhythm and Metre

The rhythm of a poem is the beat of the poem. The beat is established through the pattern of stressed and unstressed syllables in the poem – metre. A stressed syllable is one on which great emphasis is placed while an unstressed syllable is less emphasized. An easy way for you to identify stressed and unstressed syllable is to say the words out loud and listen to determine whether the syllable contains long vowel or 'y' sounds or the short vowel or 'y' sounds. Syllables with long vowel or 'y' sounds are stressed and those with short vowel or 'y' sounds are unstressed. For example, **eat** would be a stressed syllable because you must make the long eeeee sound when you pronounce it. However, **egg** would be unstressed because you make the short 'e' sound (eh) when you pronounce it. Listen also to determine if one syllable is louder and higher than another. Louder and higher syllables are stressed as well. On the other hand, short, soft, low syllables are unstressed.

Hint: Your dictionary usually tells you which syllable is stressed, and which is unstressed when you pronounce a word.

When you are analyzing a poem, a stressed syllable is indicated by ictus (/) and an unstressed syllable is indicated by a breve (˘). A pair of stressed and unstressed syllable is called a foot which is indicated by a (|).

Examples: remix = remix remorse = remorse

/ ˘ ˘ /

Both words have two syllables. However, in the first word "remix" the stress is on the first syllable 're' as it has the long eeee sound. In the second example, "remorse", the stress is on the second syllable 'morse' because it has the long oooo sound.

Identifying the metre can be difficult, but it is oftentimes necessary in poetry. So, keep practising. Keep saying the words aloud to determine where you place the emphasis. When all else fails, use your dictionary.

Activity 1: How Many Feet Make a Line

Directions. Write a line from your assigned poem and identify the stressed and unstressed syllables and the feet in your line.

____

____

How many feet are in your line? ____

After your teacher has given you the go ahead, identify the types of syllables and feet in the other lines in your poem. You do not need to rewrite the poem to make your identifications.

Types of Rhythm

Identifying the feet in your poem will help you to identify the type of rhythm the poet used in the poem. This is the reason metre is connected to rhythm. The types of rhythm are only identifiable after you have identified the metre in each line of the poem. There are FIVE main types of rhythm in poetry:

1. Iamb – a foot containing one unstressed and one stressed syllable (e.g., re**morse**)
2. Trochee – a foot containing one stressed and one unstressed syllable (e.g., **re**mix)

3. Spondee – a foot containing two stressed syllables (**Why mourn**?)
4. Dactyl – contains THREE syllables. The first syllable is stressed and the second and third syllables are unstressed (e.g., **beau**-ti-ful)
5. Anapest – contains THREE syllables. The first syllable is unstressed and the second and third syllables are stressed (e.g., I'd **fore-go**)

The number of feet in a line is also important. It can help you to identify the beat and the type of poem. ***If there are five feet in a line of poetry, it is called a pentameter***. If each foot is an iamb, then the line is an iambic pentameter. Iambic pentameter is one of the most commonly used rhythms in poetry. Its primary function is to give a natural flow to the words used in the poem, especially if the poem is a serious one.

Using the definition of iambic pentameter, define each of the following beats.

a. Trochaic pentameter: ____________________

____

____

b. Dactylic pentameter: ____________________

____

____

c. Anapestic pentameter: ____________________

____

____

Write TWO examples of a pentameter from your assigned poem below. Then, write the type of pentameter that is evident in each example. Please note that your poem may not have a pentameter. Ensure you identify the stressed and unstressed syllables and each foot in each example to make identification of the type of pentameter easier.

____

____

____

____

____

Types of Poetry

We have spent some time looking at form as the different ways the words on the page may be arranged by the poet. We will now spend some time looking at form as type of poetry. The arrangement of the words will help you to identify the type of poetry. The types of poetry we will focus on are sonnets, ballads and free verse.

Activity 1: Comparing Types of Poetry

Directions. Complete the following table by inserting a matching description in the spaces provided. The descriptions you insert may be similar to or different from the one that is already inserted for you. The first one is done for you. For some categories, there is one aspect for which no description is provided. You are required to provide **all three** descriptions.

Earn a  ***by completing the table correctly.***

	Sonnet	Ballad	Free Verse
Lines and Stanzas	*No refrain*	*Usually has a refrain*	*No refrain*
		Usually has quatrains	
Number of Lines			
Rhyme & Rhythm		*ABCB or ABAB rhyme scheme*	
	Written in iambic pentameter	*Written in iambic triameter and iambic tetrameter*	

	Sonnet	Ballad	Free Verse
Structure	*Fixed form*		
			Uses a variety of literary devices
		Usually narrative (tells a story)	
Types (of sonnets, ballads, free verse)			
Example of ONE poet and ONE of his/her poems			

Based on the features of each type of poetry listed in your table, what type of poetry is your assigned poem. Justify your identification by demonstrating how the different features of your selected type of poetry are present in your assigned poem.

____

____

____

____

____

____

____

Literary Devices

Literary devices are present in all genres of literature. However, poet's make arguably greater use of literary devices. Literary devices allow the poets to convey deeper and additional meanings. In that way, the poems remain relatively short but say much more than the number of words on the page. You are familiar with many literary devices, particularly similes and metaphors. Throughout this workbook, you will get familiar with the different types and examine the effect of their use and the effectiveness with which the poets' use them. But let us define a few that are frequently used at this point.

Alliteration: ______________________________

____

____

Analogy: ______________________________

____

____

Allusion: ______________________________

____

____

Assonance: ______________________________

____

____

Comparison: ______________________________

____

____

Consonance: ______________________________

____

____

Contrast: ______________________________

____

____

Euphemism: ______________________________

____

____

Hyperbole: ______________________________

____

____

Imagery: ______________________________

____

____

Irony: ______________________________

____

____

Metaphor: ______________________________

____

____

Onomatopoeia: ______________________________

____

____

Oxymoron: ______________________________

____

____

Paradox: ______________________________

____

____

Personification: ______________________________

____

____

Proverb: ______________________________

____

____

Pun: ______________________________

____

____

Repetition: ____

____

____

Sarcasm: ____

____

____

Satire: ____

____

____

Simile: ____

____

____

Symbol: ____

____

____

Can you think of any other literary device to add to the list? List and define them below.

____

____

____

____

____

____

____

____

____

____

____

____

____

____

Activity 2A: Identifying Literary Devices

Directions. Examples of the different literary devices are presented below. Read each example and write the name or names of the literary device on the line.

1. My sister is on a see food diet. ______________________________
2. I was saddened by the long sorrowful howling of the wind. ______________________________
3. The clattering, pitter-pattering of the rain ______________________________
4. She is a Judas. ______________________________
5. Your father has gone to a better place. ______________________________

Activity 2B: Literary Devices in My Favourite Song

Directions. Paste the lyrics of your favourite song below and identify the literary devices in the song.

Activity 2C: Pair Work

Directions. Choose any FIVE of the literary devices in your list and create an example of the literary device. Then, share your examples with your friend to see if he or she can correctly identify the device you have created.

Earn a  SUPER WRITING ***for creating examples of at least TWO unpopular (less frequently used) devices.***

Activity 2C: Literary Devices in Your Assigned Poem

Directions. Identify the literary devices in your assigned poem below.

Effect and Effectiveness of Literary Devices

After you have identified literary devices, you will be expected to 'examine' them. To examine a literary device, you need to scrutinize it carefully and comment on its effect or effectiveness. To assess the effect and effectiveness, you need to know the different ways in which literary devices contribute to poems.

Literary devices contribute to poems in many ways:

a. **Engagement** – sometimes poets use these devices to pull in the audience. Literary devices can create images that appeal to our senses and emotions and thereby connect us to the person or the object of the poem. For example, describing a place as cold does not convey the same experience as "as cold as ice". The latter is a more vivid image that causes the reader to better feel how cold the place is. It helps you to imagine more precisely what is being described. Imagery pulls the audience in as well. When you are clearly able to see, hear, taste, feel and smell what is going on in the poem, your interest and emotions are more likely to be evoked.

b. **Tone and Mood** – Literary devices can convey the poet's tone – attitude towards the subject. For example, oxymoron can convey the persona or the poet's mixed emotions, hyperbole can convey the intensity of the emotion or attitude and depending on what the subject is compared to, similes and metaphors and other devices used for comparison can show whether the poet or persona has a positive, negative or neutral attitude towards the object of the poem. Literary devices can create or change the mood in the poem as well. Imagery contributes to the sensory experience of the poem by appealing to our five senses. Again, when you can see, smell, taste, feel and hear all that is happening, your emotions are more likely to be stirred. Also, rhymes usually create a more enjoyable, light, happy mood, and the absence of rhymes is usually connected to a more serious atmosphere. Please note that poems with serious topics can also use rhymes and vice versa.

c. **Theme development** – Literary devices contribute to the development of the themes in the poems as well. To identify the theme in a poem (or story or play) ask yourself:

   1. What is this poem about? Write one sentence.
   2. Who/What is the protagonist in the poem and who/what is the antagonist?
   3. How does the poet feel towards the protagonist and the antagonist? *(Literary devices can help you to identify the poet's feeling or attitude (tone) towards the protagonist and antagonist in the poem.)*
   4. What is the main conflict between the protagonist and the antagonist? Write in one sentence.

5. What is the poet's attitude towards the conflict? *(Literary devices can help you to identify the poet's feeling or attitude (tone) towards the conflict in the poem.)*
6. How is the conflict resolved? In favour of the protagonist? Antagonist? Neither? How the conflict is resolved can also indicate the poet's attitude towards the characters in the poem as well as the issue or main idea in the poem.
7. Based on what you know about the subject of the poem, the poet's attitude towards the characters and the conflict and how the conflict is resolved, what is the poet's main message, moral, lesson or truth?

d. **Tension** – they can create, increase or lessen tension or conflict in the poem.

Effect: This is the outcome of the use of the literary device on ***you***. How does each make you feel or what does it help you to understand?

Effectiveness: This is really your assessment of how well the poet has used a literary device. In your estimation, how well has ***the poet*** used the device? Though this question is asking for your opinion, your opinion is not whatever you want to think. It must be grounded in knowledge of poetry, the purposes of the different literary devices, and the specifics of the situation in which the device was used. In answering this question, you:

- ✓ make an evaluation of how well or appropriately the playwright has used the technique(s)
- ✓ justify your evaluation by explaining how fitting or appropriate the poet's use of the device is based on the conflict, character, situation, theme, the audience and so on.

Activity 1: Classifying Literary Devices

Directions. The ability to classify devices by their purpose will help you to examine their effect and effectiveness. You can comment on if the writer has achieved his/her desired purpose by using the device. Classify the devices according to purpose by listing them in their corresponding box. The first one is done for you.

Sound Devices	**Devices of Comparison**
Onomatopoeia	**Metaphor**
__________	__________
__________	__________
__________	__________
__________	__________
__________	__________

Devices of Emphasis

Repetition

Devices with Contradictions

Irony

Reference Devices

Allusion

Devices with Double Meanings

Symbols

Activity 2. Effect and Effectiveness

Directions. Choose any ONE of the devices identified in your assigned poem and comment on its effect and effectiveness.

CONGRATULATIONS!!! You have just completed your analysis of your poem.

Checking My Progress

At the end of each poem, you will be required to check how much you have learnt. You have just finished the introductory activities on poetry. Before we move to the activities on the first poem, review what you have learnt or are still uncertain about. Complete the 3-2-1 activity below. It works as follows:

Three – Write **three** things you learned from the lessons on elements of poetry.

Two – Write **two** things you found interesting or about which you would like to learn more.

One – Write **one** question you still have about the material.

Share your question with your classmates and listen to their responses. Did they clarify things? If not, maybe it is time you did some independent research.

Finally, record ONE question from one of your classmates and provide an answer to that classmate.

Checking What I Know!!!

3. ____

____

____

2. ____

____

1. ____

Helping My Peers!!!

Peer's question: ____

____

My answer: ____

____

____

"Once Upon A Time" by Gabriel Okara

Objectives

After completing the activities on "Once Upon A Time", you should be able to accurately:

- ☐ make predictions based on the title of the poem;
- ☐ identify the elements of poetry in the poem;
- ☐ critically assess your peers' recitation and analysis of the poem;
- ☐ examine the effect and effectiveness of literary devices used in the poem;
- ☐ evaluate social conventions used in your society.

Getting Started

Activity 1: Before you begin …

Before you begin to read any piece of writing, it is usually a good idea to think of what you already know about the topic. Write down what you know about the title of the poem by completing the table below. The table should be completed as follows:

It says … - Write the title of the poem.

I know … - Write what you know about the title. In this case, when is the phrase 'once upon a time" usually used?

And so … - Make a prediction about what you think the poem will be about based on the stated title and what you know about the title.

It says …	
I know …	
And so …	

Activity 2: You've Got Manners

In society, individuals are praised for being polite or having good manners. Good manners are usually demonstrated if you conform to certain social conventions. Social conventions are accepted rules that govern everyday behaviour. They have become so common place that we oftentimes do them without even thinking about it. E.g., saying "please" when you ask for something.

Directions. For each item below, state the acceptable social convention or if the convention is listed, state when it is appropriate to do or say it.

	Social Convention	**When to do or say it**
1.	Thank you.	
2.		Say this after someone sneezes.
3.		Appropriate greeting after 6 p.m.
4.	Goodbye.	
5	Nice to meet you.	
	Good morning.	
6.		Say this after someone says, "Thank you".
7.		If you accidentally hit someone, you say this.
8.	Come back anytime.	
9.		When an elderly person or pregnant woman enters a public office or bus in which you are seated, you do this.
10.	Shake hands	

Have you ever said any of these phrases without meaning it? Share an experience.

Why did you say it if you did not mean it?

Have you ever believed someone's expression of any of these social conventions was sincere and realized later that it was not? Share an experience. How did you feel? If you have not had the experience, how do you think you will feel?

Activity 3: The Featured Presentation

Use the checklist below to assess your peers' recitation of "Once Upon A Time".

Checklist for the Poetry Recitation

Directions. The checklist below consists of a list of statements highlighting important things to consider when reciting a poem and three emojis. If your answer to the statement is yes, put a tick beside the statement and under the happy face. If your answer to the statement is no, put a tick beside the statement and under the sad face. If you are unsure, put a tick beside the statement and under the unsure face.

Checklist for Poetry Recitation			
1. Performance is no longer than three minutes.			
2. The words of the poem are said exactly as presented in the text.			
3. The performer adapts the role of the persona in movement, posture and general demeanour.			
4. Performer conveys the appropriate emotion.			
5. Performer makes appropriate use of facial expression, gestures, tone etc. to convey the meaning of the poem.			
6. Performer makes appropriate use of stage.			
7. Performance is audible and confident.			
8. Performance is entertaining.			

Directions. Based on your ticks in the checklist, rate your classmates' recitation of "Once Upon A Time" by shading the stars below. Five stars mean you believe the recitation was excellent. Then justify your rating.

Your Rating	**Your Justification**
☆☆☆☆☆	

What is the most common rating received by the presenter from your classmates? ____________________

What is your teacher's rating? ____

If you have the same rating as your teacher, you earn a  .

Choose TWO areas from the checklist where you ticked 'no' or 'unsure' and make ONE recommendation to the presenters on how they could have improved in those areas.

Selected area 1: ____

Recommendation: ____

____

____

Selected area 2: ____

Recommendation 1: ____

____

____

Elements of Poetry in "Once Upon A Time"

Your classmates will present their analysis of "Once Upon A Time". In this analysis, they will identify, explain and discuss the historical background, literary elements, form and literary devices used in the poem. You will be expected to critically assess the analysis being presented. This will be done in a step-by-step process.

Step 1: Listen for Information – While you listen to the analysis, complete the different activities with information presented in the analysis.

Step 2: Consult Your Peers – Share with a peer to see if he/she heard anything you might have missed or if you heard anything, he/she missed.

Step 3: Rate the Analysis – Look at the number of answered and unanswered activities you have and rate the overall analysis.

Historical Background

Directions. In this section, the presenters are expected to provide relevant information for all the areas in the picture below. However, you are only expected to write the ***poet's name, birthday, country of birth, quick facts and other works by the poet*** from the presenters' analysis. Complete the other sections based on your own feelings about the poet.

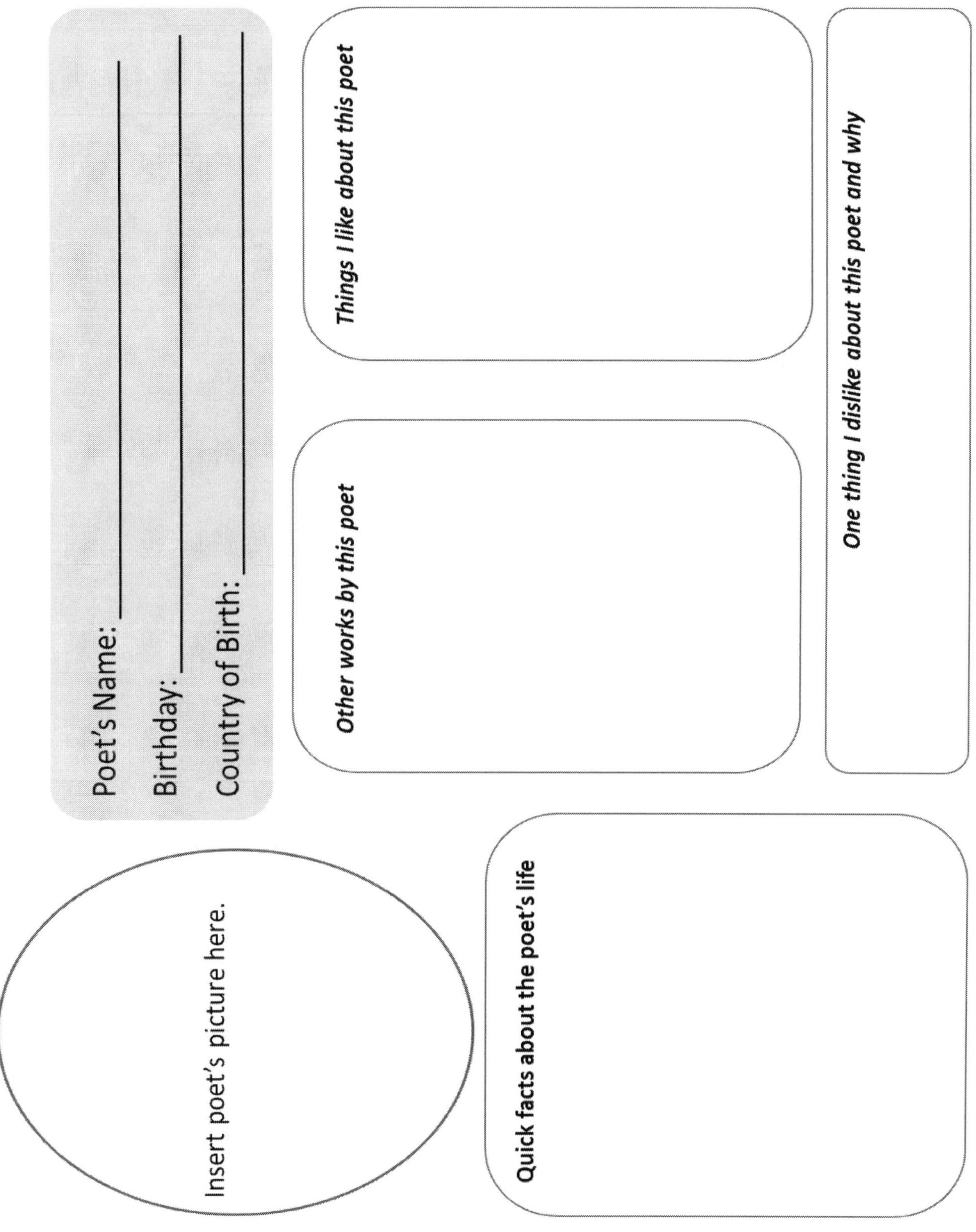

Literary Elements In "Once Upon A Time"

Directions. Write the literary elements identified by the presenter(s). After the presentation, you will be allowed time to identify these elements for yourself and compare your answers to the presenters' answers. Look at your notes on each element if you are unsure. Complete the table as follows:

1. Write the presenters' identifications.
2. Tick whether you agree or disagree with each identification.
3. Whether you agree or disagree, write one piece of evidence from the poem to support your decision.

Characters		
Persona:	**Agree**	**Disagree**
Evidence:		
Tone:	**Agree**	**Disagree**
Evidence:		
Other characters:	**Agree**	**Disagree**
Evidence:		
Type of Narration:	**Agree**	**Disagree**
Evidence:		

Setting		
Time and Place:	**Agree**	**Disagree**
Evidence:		
Mood:	**Agree**	**Disagree**
Evidence:		

Theme		
1st Theme Category: **Message *(one sentence):***	**Agree**	**Disagree**
Evidence		
2nd Theme Category: **Message *(one sentence):***	**Agree**	**Disagree**
Evidence		

Plot in "Once Upon A Time"

Directions. Summarize each stanza in a single sentence. Then, combine the sentences into a paragraph. Use suitable transition words and phrases to make the paragraph more coherent. Remember to use your own words.

Stanza 1:

Stanza 2:

Stanza 3:

Stanza 4:

Stanza 5:

Stanza 6:

Stanza 7:

Stylistics in "Once Upon A Time"

We will look at the form of the poem and the literary devices used in the poem.

Form of "Once Upon A Time"

Directions. Fill in the blanks with information from "Once Upon A Time".

"Once Upon A Time" is a ____________________ (*Type of poem*). The poem consists of ___________ (*Number of lines*) lines which are divided into ________________ (*Number of stanzas*) stanzas. The first four stanzas are _____________ (*Type of stanza*) while the fifth, sixth and seventh stanza are ________________ (*Type of stanza*), ________________ (*Type of stanza*), _______________ (*Type of stanza*), respectively. The poem has __________________ (*Type of rhyme scheme*) and mostly _____________________________ (*Type of rhythm*).

Answer the following questions.

1. Why do you think the type of stanza changes after the fourth stanza?

____

____

____

____

____

____

____

2. What does the rhyme scheme or the absence of a rhyme scheme contribute to the poem?

____

____

____

____

____

____

____

____

Literary Devices in "Once Upon A Time"

For each poem, you should be able to:

- ✓ list the main devices used;
- ✓ explain each device used;
- ✓ comment on the effect and effectiveness of each device used.

The main devices used in "Once Upon A Time" are contrasts, similes and metaphors. These devices are devices of comparison. In explaining devices of comparison and especially similes and metaphors, I usually used the formula: **A = B, B = C. Therefore, A = C.**

Where

A – the first thing being compared

B – the second thing being compared

C – What you know about B

Example: The boy is a lion. - **metaphor**

The boy (A) is being compared to a lion (B).

A lion (B) is fierce, powerful, revered (C).

Therefore, the boy (A) is fierce, powerful and revered (C).

NB. The context and the tone in which the comparison is made should be used to determine what aspect of B is being compared.

Identify a simile or metaphor from "Once Upon A Time" and explain it by using the formula.

___

___

___

___

___

___

___

___

Practise to explain similes and metaphors by using the other similes and metaphors in "Once Upon A Time".

Activity: Effect and Effectiveness

Directions. Choose ONE simile and ONE metaphor identified in "Once Upon A Time" and comment on their effect and effectiveness. If you need to remind yourself of what is required when you are asked to examine or comment on the use of a literary device, read the notes presented of **pages 52 – 53** of this Workbook.

Device	Evidence
Effect:	
Effectiveness:	

Device	Evidence
Effect:	
Effectiveness:	

Activity 2A: Contrast

Directions. Contrasts are used in literature to show how two or more things or persons are different. They may be seen as the opposite of similes and metaphors. Identify the differences shown in "Once Upon A Time" in the different areas in the table below. The table should be completed as follows:

It says ... - Write the line, phrase or sentence exactly as written in the poem.

On my own ... - Write what you think the contrast mean.

Then	**Now**
People	
It says ...	**It says ...**
On my own ...	
It says ...	**It says ...**
On my own ...	
It says ...	**It says ...**
On my own ...	

<table>
<tr><th>Then</th><th>Now</th></tr>
<tr><td colspan="2">The Persona</td></tr>
<tr><td>It says …</td><td>It says …</td></tr>
<tr><td colspan="2">On my own …</td></tr>
<tr><td>It says …</td><td>It says …</td></tr>
<tr><td colspan="2">On my own …</td></tr>
<tr><td colspan="2">Childhood vs Adulthood</td></tr>
<tr><td>It says …</td><td>It says …</td></tr>
<tr><td colspan="2">On my own …</td></tr>
</table>

Use ONE word to describe how the persona feels about the changes he has made? Use the tone table to help you. ____

Find evidence from the poem to support your chosen word. ______________________

____

____

Activity 2B: Examining Contrasts

Directions. Examine any TWO contrasts identified in "Once Upon A Time". If you need to remind yourself of what is required when you are asked to examine or comment on the use of a literary device, read the notes presented of **pages 52 – 53** of this Workbook.

Device	**Evidence**
Effect:	
Effectiveness:	

Device	**Evidence**
Effect:	
Effectiveness:	

Assessing Your Peers' Presentation

Directions. Compare the information your peers provided with your own analysis and rate your classmates' analysis of "Once Upon A Time" by shading the stars below. Five stars mean you believe the analysis was excellent. Then, justify your rating.

Your Rating	Your Justification
☆☆☆☆☆	

What is the most common rating received by the presenter from your classmates? ________________

What is your teacher's rating? ____

If you have the same rating as your teacher, you earn a ______.

Choose ONE element of poetry that you think the presenters need to make improvement in analyzing and make TWO recommendations to the presenters on how they can improve in analyzing that element.

Selected area: ____

____

Recommendation 1: ____

____

____

____

Recommendation 2: ____

____

____

____

Now that you have finished analyzing "Once Upon A Time", look back at the predictions you made before you analyzed the poem and answer the following questions.

1. To what extent were your predictions right?

   Not at all ☐ A small extent ☐ Somewhat ☐ To a large extent ☐ Spot on ☐

2. Explain your selection for question 1.

   ____

   ____

   ____

   ____

   ____

Activity 2: Dear Younger Self

Directions. In "Once Upon A Time" the persona shares childhood experiences and expresses a desire for things to be like they were when he was a child. If you could speak to your younger self, what would you say? Create a piece (letter, story, song, dramatization, video etc.) in which you speak to a younger version of yourself. In this piece you should include:

- ✓ One thing you used to do when you were younger that you are unable to do now.
- ✓ One thing you used to do when you were younger that you are happy you no longer have to do.
- ✓ One advice you would give to your younger self to help him/her better transition into adolescence or adulthood
- ✓ One simile
- ✓ One metaphor

Earn a 

for creating the best piece.

Use the **Dear Younger Self Checklist** to ensure you have the piece. After you are finished putting a tick beside each statement, make recommendations to yourself about how you may improve your piece. Ask your peers and teacher for their recommendations as well.

Checklist for Dear Younger Self

Directions. The checklist below consists of a list of statements highlighting important things to consider when preparing for your piece and three emojis. If your answer to the statement is yes, put a tick beside the statement and under the happy face. If your answer to the statement is no, put a tick beside the statement and under the sad face. If you are unsure, put a tick beside the statement and under the unsure face.

Checklist for Dear Younger Self	Happy	Unsure	Sad
1. Piece includes a missed experience.			
2. Piece includes an experience you no longer must engage in.			
3. Piece includes an advice on how to manage adolescence or adulthood.			
4. Piece includes at least one simile.			
5. Simile is effectively used.			
6. Piece includes at least one metaphor.			
7. Metaphor is effectively used.			
8. Performance is entertaining.			

My Recommendations

Make recommendations to yourself about how you may improve your performance. Ask your peers, family members and/or your teacher for their recommendations on how you may improve as well.

Self	Peer/Family Members
Teacher	

Peer reviewed by: ______________________ Date: ______________

Teacher reviewed by: ______________________ Date: ______________

Based on the feedback from yourself, your peers and teacher, make the necessary changes.

Checking My Progress

At the end of each poem, you will be required to check how much you have learnt. Before we move to the activities on the next poem, review what you have learnt or are still uncertain about in "Once Upon A Time". Do so by first checking the objectives you have accomplished so far.

Directions. Go back to the objectives at the beginning of the activities on "Once Upon A Time". If you think you have accomplished an objective, without looking back at your notes, put a tick in the box ☐ before the objective. If you are unsure you have accomplished the objective, put a question mark (?) and if you are sure you have not accomplished the objective, leave it unchecked (blank). Ensure you pay more attention to your unchecked boxes and the boxes with your question marks as you study. Also, ensure that you can perform the number indicated in each objective (e.g., list **three** genres). You have accomplished the objective when you can list the indicated number (three).

Now complete the 3-2-1 activity below. It works as follows:

Three – Write **three** things you learned from the lessons on "Once Upon A Time".

Two – Write **two** things you found interesting or about which you would like to learn more.

One – Write **one** question you still have about the material.

Share your question with your classmates and listen to their responses. Did they clarify things? If not, maybe it is time you did some independent research.

Finally, record ONE question from one of your classmates and provide an answer to that classmate.

Checking What I Know!!!

3. ____

____

____

2. ____

____

1. ____

Helping My Peers!!!

Peer's question: ____________________________________

____

My answer: ______________________________________

____

____

"Little Boy Crying" by Mervyn Morris

Objectives
After completing the activities on "Little Boy Crying", you should be able to accurately:

- ☐ make predictions based on the title of the poem;
- ☐ identify the elements of poetry in the poem;
- ☐ critically assess your peers' presentation and analysis of the poem;
- ☐ discuss different types of conflict in literature;
- ☐ examine the effect and effectiveness of literary devices used in the poem.

Getting Started

Activity 1: Before you begin …

Before you begin to read any piece of writing, it is usually a good idea to think of what you already know about the topic. Write down what you know about the title of the poem by completing the table below. The table should be completed as follows:

It says … - Write the title of the poem.

I know … - Write what you know about the title. In this case, why would the little boy be crying? How do people usually respond to children's crying?

And so … - Make a prediction about what you think the poem will be about based on the stated title and what you know about the title.

It says …	
I know …	
And so …	

Activity 2: The Faces of Discipline

Directions. Answer the following questions.

My Side

1. Have you ever been disciplined by your parent or guardian? How did you feel? List THREE emotions. ______________________________

2. How do you view **your parent** immediately after he/she has disciplined you? List THREE emotions. ______________________________

3. If you could get anything you wished for, what is ONE thing you would wish for your parent/guardian after he/she has disciplined you? ______________________________

   ____
   ____
   ____
   ____
   ____
   ____

Ask Your Parent/Guardian

1. Why do they discipline you? Give TWO reasons.

   ____
   ____

2. How do they feel when they see you crying because they have disciplined you? List THREE emotions.

   ____

3. If they could get anything they wished for, what is ONE thing they would wish for you after they have disciplined you?

   ____
   ____
   ____
   ____

Activity 3: The Featured Presentation

Use the checklist below to assess your peers' recitation of "Little Boy Crying".

Checklist for the Poetry Recitation

Directions. The checklist below consists of a list of statements highlighting important things to consider when reciting a poem and three emojis. If your answer to the statement is yes, put a tick beside the statement and under the happy face. If your answer to the statement is no, put a tick beside the statement and under the sad face. If you are unsure, put a tick beside the statement and under the unsure face.

Checklist for Poetry Recitation			
1. Performance is no longer than three minutes.			
2. The words of the poem are said exactly as presented in the poem.			
3. The performer adapts the role of the persona in movement, posture and general demeanour.			
4. Performer conveys the appropriate emotion.			
5. Performer makes appropriate use of facial expression, gestures, tone etc. to convey the meaning of the poem.			
6. Performer makes appropriate use of stage.			
7. Performance is audible and confident.			
8. Performance is entertaining.			

Directions. Based on your ticks in the checklist, rate your classmates' recitation of "Little Boy Crying" by shading the stars below. Five stars mean you believe the recitation was excellent. Then justify your rating.

Your Rating	Your Justification
☆☆☆☆☆	

What is the most common rating received by the presenter from your classmates? ____________________

What is your teacher's rating? ____

If you have the same rating as your teacher, you earn a  .

Choose TWO areas from the checklist where you ticked 'no' or 'unsure' and make ONE recommendation to the presenters on how they could have improved in those areas.

Selected area 1: ____

Recommendation: ____

____

____

Selected area 2: ____

Recommendation 1: ____

____

____

Elements of Poetry in "Little Boy Crying"

Your classmates will present their analysis of "Little Boy Crying" In this analysis, they will identify, explain and discuss the historical background, literary elements, form and literary devices used in the poem. You will be expected to critically assess the analysis being presented. This will be done in a step-by-step process.

Step 1: Listen for Information – While you listen to the analysis, complete the different activities with information presented in the analysis.

Step 2: Consult Your Peers – Share with a peer to see if he/she heard anything you might have missed or if you heard anything, he/she missed.

Step 3: Rate the Analysis – Look at the number of answered and unanswered activities you have and rate the overall analysis.

Historical Background

Directions. In this section, the presenters are expected to provide relevant information for all the areas in the picture below. However, you are only expected to write the ***poet's name, birthday, country of birth, quick facts and other works by the poet*** from the presenters' analysis. Complete the other sections based on your own feelings about the poet.

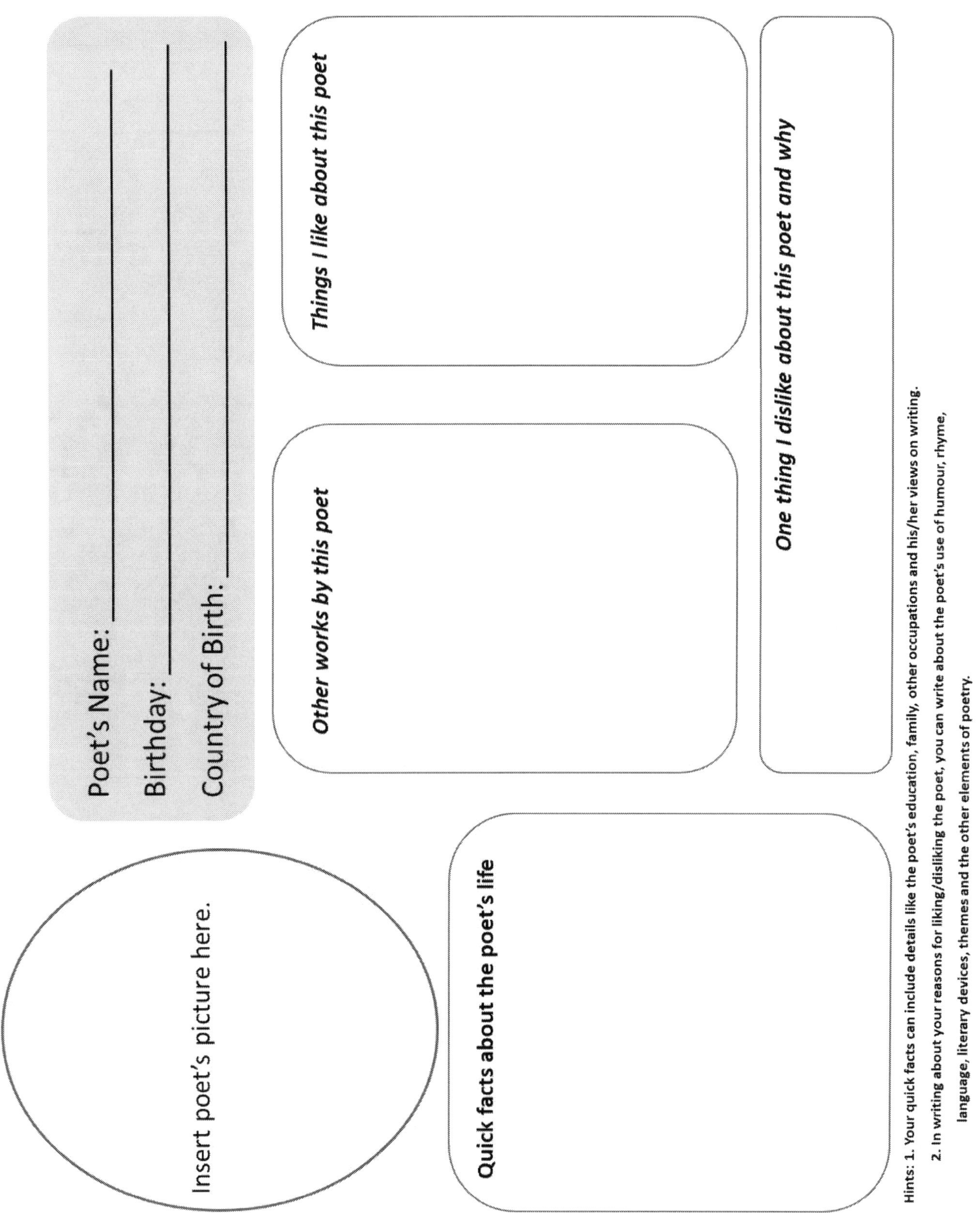

Literary Elements in "Little Boy Crying"

Directions. Write the literary elements identified by the presenter(s). After the presentation, you will be allowed time to identify these elements for yourself and compare your answers to the presenters' answers. Revise your notes on each element if you are unsure. Complete the table as follows:

1. Write the presenters' identifications.
2. Tick whether you agree or disagree with each identification.
3. Whether you agree or disagree, write one piece of evidence from the poem to support your decision.

Characters		
Persona:	**Agree**	**Disagree**
Evidence:		
Tone:	**Agree**	**Disagree**
Evidence:		
Other characters:	**Agree**	**Disagree**
Evidence:		
Type of Narration:	**Agree**	**Disagree**
Evidence:		

Setting		
Time and Place:	**Agree**	**Disagree**
Evidence:		
Mood:	**Agree**	**Disagree**
Evidence:		

Theme		
1st Theme Category: **Message *(one sentence):***	**Agree**	**Disagree**
Evidence		
2nd Theme Category: **Message *(one sentence):***	**Agree**	**Disagree**
Evidence		

Plot in "Little Boy Crying"

Directions. Summarize each stanza in a single sentence. Then, combine the sentences into a paragraph. Use suitable transition words and phrases to make the paragraph more coherent. Remember to use your own words.

Stanza 1:

Stanza 2:

Stanza 3:

Stanza 4:

Conflict

A conflict is an opposition between two or more persons or things. In literature, conflict usually makes a story more interesting. Conflict exists in poems, especially narrative poems, as well. The opposition may be:

a. between one character and another character (**man vs man**);
b. between character and the values and practices of society (**man vs society**);
c. between a character and forces of nature, for example, a hurricane (**man vs nature**);
d. or between a character and him/herself (man vs self). This type of conflict is an internal conflict in which the character is in 'two minds'. He or she may hold a particular belief as sacred but be in a position where he/she is forced to go against that belief for a greater good.

Answer the following questions.

1. Identify the types of conflict in "Little Boy Crying". Provide a specific example of EACH type of conflict you have identified.

____

____

____

____

____

____

____

2. Compare the types of conflict present in "Once Upon A Time" and "Little Boy Crying".

____

____

____

____

____

____

____

____

____

Stylistics in "Little Boy Crying"

We will look at the form of the poem and the literary devices used in the poem.

Form of "Little Boy Crying"

Directions. Fill in the blanks with information from "Little Boy Crying".

"Little Boy Crying" is a ____________________ (*Type of poem*). The poem consists of ____________ (*Number of lines*) lines which are divided into ________________ (*Number of stanzas*) stanzas. The first stanza is a ________________ (*Type of stanza*) while the second and third stanzas are ________________ (*Type of stanza*). The fourth stanza is a ________________________ (*Type of stanza*). The poem has ______________________ (*Type of rhyme scheme*) and mostly _____________________________ (*Type of rhythm*).

Answer the following questions.

1. Look at the words of the poem as they appear in the World of Poetry. Which stanza stands out and why?

____

____

____

2. What is the importance of the form of the last stanza?

____

____

____

3. How does getting the perspective of both the child and the father contributed to your experience of the poem?

____

____

____

____

____

Literary Devices in "Little Boy Crying"

Activity 1: Identifying the Devices

Directions. Write the names of FOUR literary devices used in the poem. Then, write an example of each of the listed devices from the poem. Ensure you write the line number(s) for each example given.

Literary Devices	Examples
1. ______________:	______________________________
	______________________________
2. ______________:	______________________________
	______________________________
3. ______________:	______________________________
	______________________________
4. ______________:	______________________________
	______________________________

If you have identified a simile or metaphor, explain it by using the formula.

Identify and explain a contrast made in the poem.

Activity 2: Effect and Effectiveness

Directions. Choose TWO devices identified in "Little Boy Crying" and comment on their effect and effectiveness. If you need to remind yourself of what is required when you are asked to examine or comment on the use of a literary device, read the notes presented of **pages 52 – 53** of this Workbook.

Device	**Evidence**
Effect:	
Effectiveness:	

Device	**Evidence**
Effect:	
Effectiveness:	

Assessing Your Peers' Presentation

Directions. Compare the information your peers provided with your own analysis and rate your classmates' analysis of "Little Boy Crying" by shading the stars below. Five stars mean you believe the analysis was excellent. Then, justify your rating.

Your Rating	Your Justification
☆☆☆☆☆	

What is the most common rating received by the presenter from your classmates? ________________

What is your teacher's rating? ____

If you have the same rating as your teacher, you earn a .

Choose ONE element of poetry that you think the presenters need to make improvement in analyzing and make TWO recommendations to the presenters on how they can improve in analyzing that element.

Selected area: ____

____

Recommendation 1: ____

____

____

____

Recommendation 2: ____

____

____

____

Now that you have finished analyzing "Little Boy Crying", look back at the predictions you made before you analyzed the poem and answer the following questions.

1. To what extent were your predictions right?

   Not at all ☐ A small extent ☐ Somewhat ☐ To a large extent ☐ Spot on ☐

2. Explain your selection for question 1.

   ____

   ____

   ____

   ____

   ____

Activity 2: Before and After

Directions. In "Little Boy Crying" the persona shares a view of the child before and after being slapped. Create a piece (picture, poses or dramatization) in which you illustrate the before and after views of the child.

OR

Create a piece (picture, poses or dramatization) in which you illustrate the conflicting feelings of the father.

Earn a 

for creating the best piece.

Checking My Progress

You have just finished the activities on "Little Boy Crying". Before we move to the activities on the next poem, review what you have learnt or are still uncertain about. Do so by first checking the objectives you have accomplished so far.

Directions. Go back to the objectives at the beginning of the activities on "Little Boy Crying". If you think you have accomplished an objective, without looking back at your notes, put a tick in the box ☐ before the objective. If you are unsure you have accomplished the objective, put a question mark (?) and if you are sure you have not accomplished the objective, leave it unchecked (blank). Ensure you pay more attention to your unchecked boxes and the boxes with your question marks as you study. Also, ensure that you can perform the number indicated in each objective (e.g., list **three** genres). You have accomplished the objective when you can list the indicated number (three).

Now complete the 3-2-1 activity below. It works as follows:

Three – Write **three** things you learned from the activities on "Little Boy Crying".

Two – Write **two** things you found interesting or about which you would like to learn more.

One – Write **one** question you still have about the material.

Share your question with your classmates and listen to their responses. Did they clarify things? If not, maybe it is time you did some independent research.

Finally, record ONE question from one of your classmates and provide an answer to that classmate.

Checking What I Know!!!

3. ____

____

____

2. ____

____

1. ____

Helping My Peers!!!

Peer's question: ____

____

My answer: ____

____

____

Writing Literary Essays

In the Poetry section on Paper 02 of your English B examination, you will be required to write an essay using information from TWO poems. One of the questions will name the two poems you should use, and the other will allow you to choose any two poems on the prescribed list. Since we have gone through two poems, it is time for you to practise writing these essays. Go through the steps below to help you to write a superior essay.

"Once Upon A Time" and "Little Boy Crying" present childhood experiences.

Write an essay in which you outline the childhood experience in EACH poem. In this essay, you must also discuss the impact of the experience on the persona in EACH poem and examine ONE device that is used to present the childhood experience as a whole in EACH poem.

Step 1: Before you begin to write, you need to understand exactly what is required of you. The first step is to underline the key phrases that will help to focus your attention on what you are supposed to write. I call these the **issues of focus** in the question. You are usually required to focus on three things in your CXC English B essays. I have underlined the first two for you. **Underline the third.**

In the exam, if you do not have enough information on all three sections of the question, move to the other question and repeat this step. The question on which you have the most to write should be the question you select. Thinking about what you know about the specific issues of focus in the question will help to prevent you from beginning to write an essay, maybe because you like the topic, and then finding out half way through that you do not have enough to write. Without this step, you may have to waste time and frustrate yourself by starting over.

Step 2. After you have identified the issues of focus you need to circle the terms that indicate how you should present information on each issue. For this question, you are required to "outline", "discuss" and "examine". Look in your CXC English syllabus and record the meaning of these terms as used by CXC.

Outline: ______________________________

____

____

Discuss: ______________________________

____

____

Examine: ______________________________

____

____

Understanding what CXC means by the terms it uses will help you to write what is required. If you do not focus on the verbs used, you may write an essay that does not truly reflect your ability because you ignored what was required.

Step 3. You should plan for your essay before you begin to write. Planning also helps you to choose the question you know the most about. By planning you get an opportunity to write down your thoughts before you get carried away in writing the actual essay and forget the points you wanted to raise. Planning will also help you to see, before you begin to write the essay, whether you have enough information to write a complete essay for your selected question. Again, if after you have written your plan you do not have enough content to respond to all the issues of focus in the question, you should select another question.

Activity 1 – Planning your Essay

At this stage, generate as many ideas as possible. Plan for writing the essay by inputting the required information in the diagram.

The plan should include:

1. Childhood experience in EACH poem (Write a brief title for the experience e.g., mother taking her son to school)
2. Impact of the experience of the persona in EACH poem. (Name the persona and list two ways he is impacted by the experience.)
3. Device used in EACH poem to present childhood experience. (Write the name and provide an example of a device.) In the essay, link the use of the device to the theme or issue identified in the question.

My Literary Essay Plan

Childhood Experiences

"Once Upon A Time"	**"Little Boy Crying"**
______________________	______________________
______________________	______________________
______________________	______________________

Persona Impact

"Once Upon A Time"

____

____

____

____

"Little Boy Crying"

____

____

____

____

Devices Used

"Once Upon A Time"

____

____

____

____

"Little Boy Crying"

____

____

____

____

Step 4. It is now time to write your essay. The first thing you must figure out is how to organize all the information you want to use to answer the question. To organize your essay well, think of it as making a sandwich. Think of the top bread as you write your introduction, the lettuce, tomato, cheese, meat and so on as you write each paragraph in the body of your essay and the bottom bread as your conclusion. Look at the picture below to see how.

The placement of the introduction and the conclusion is constant. The introduction is always the first paragraph you write, and the conclusion is always the last paragraph. The body of the essay can get a bit confusing because you may write about all the issues all at once. Therefore, this is where you need to pay greater attention to organization. If your essay is not well-organized, you may lose marks because the marker will be unable to follow your line of argument.

To help you to figure out what to write about and when to write about it in the body of the essay, it is useful to write about each issue as it is presented in the question. You could write about the first issue in the first poem and then the first issue in the second poem. Then, move on to the second issue in BOTH poems, one after the other, before you move on to the third issue in BOTH poems. Look at the outline below to write this essay.

Paragraph 1 – Your introduction (Top Bread) – Ensure you define any key terms (not the verbs), name the two poems you will be writing about and the three issues of focus in the question.

Paragraph 2 – 1st body paragraph (Ketchup) – Outline the childhood experience in "Once Upon A Time". Include specific details from the poem. **(1st issue in the 1st poem)**

Paragraph 3 – 2nd body paragraph (Mayonnaise) – Outline the childhood experience in "Little Boy Crying". Include specific details from the poem. **(1st issue in the 2nd poem)**

Paragraph 4 – 3rd body paragraph (Tomato) – Discuss the impact of the experience on a PERSONA in "Once Upon A Time". Include specific evidence from the poem. **(2nd issue in the 1st poem)**

Paragraph 5 – 4th body paragraph (Lettuce) – Discuss the impact of the experience on a PERSONA in "Little Boy Crying". Include specific evidence from the poem. **(2nd issue in the 2nd poem)**

Paragraph 6 – 5th body paragraph (Cheese) – Examine ONE device used in "Once Upon A Time" to present childhood experience. **(3rd issue in the 1st poem)**

Paragraph 7 – 6th body paragraph (Meat) – Examine ONE device used in "Little Boy Crying" to present childhood experience. **(3rd issue in the 2nd poem)**

Paragraph 8 – Conclusion (Bottom Bread) – Summarize the points you have raised in your essay. Do not raise new points in the conclusion.

Another useful tip to help you to organize the body paragraphs is to PEE in the body paragraphs. Of course, you are not going to literally urinate on the paper. PEE is an acronym I use to help to organize body paragraphs. It simply means:

P – Point **E – Evidence** **E - Explanation**

P – **Point** – State your **point.**

E – **Evidence** – Provide **evidence** from the story to support your point.

E – **Explanation** – **Explain** the link between the point you have made and the evidence you have provided. Without explicitly showing how the point and the evidence are connected, you leave it up to the marker to make the connection and he/she may not see the connection. However, if you clearly show the connection, you will remove the possibility of any misunderstanding.

Look at how this acronym is applied in one of the body paragraphs from the essay question above.

In "Little Boy Crying", the poet effectively uses the allusion to a fairy-tale to present the childhood experience in the poem. In the poem, the boy sees his father as an 'ogre' and a 'giant' and imagines chopping down the tree his father has climbed down. This is an allusion to the fairy-tale of Jack and the Beanstalk. The allusion is effective as children are more likely to read or have these tales read to them, so it is fitting that a child would conjure these images. The giant as an antagonist in the fairy-tale is also a fitting description for the father who is perceived by the child as an antagonist in the poem. Consequently, the allusion to fairy-tale was effectively used to present the child's perspective of the experience.

Circle the point, evidence and explanation in the paragraph above.

If you PEE in your body paragraphs, you will include the necessary content and organize the content well.

You should also ensure you use suitable transitional words and phrases between sentences and paragraphs to make each paragraph and the entire essay more unified. Here is a list of transitional words and phrases and their uses. Use them appropriately to improve your essays.

Uses	**Transitional Words and Phrases**
To show order of ideas	First (second, third, etc.), firstly (secondly, thirdly), next, finally, most important, less important
To provide examples	For example, an example is, to illustrate, as an illustration, evidence of this can be seen, on another occasion
To add information	In addition, additionally, also, too, furthermore, as well, moreover, and, equally important
To show contrast	In contrast, conversely, on the other hand, while, but, however, still, yet
To show similarities	Similarly, likewise, in a like manner, in the same way
To show that one idea resulted from another	As a result, therefore, so, thus, consequently, as a consequence
To show conclusion	In conclusion, in sum, to sum up, finally, hence

Activity 2 – Transitional Words and Phrases

Directions. Identify the transitional words and phrases used in the sample paragraph and explain why they were used.

____

____

____

____

____

____

____

____

____

____

Activity 3 – Writing Literary Essays

Directions. Use the outline presented on pages 91 – 93 to write your complete literary essay. Use the checklist below to ensure you write it well.

	😁	😵	😔
The Introduction			
1. Key terms (not the verbs) are defined.			
2. The two poems are named.			
3. The three issues of focus in the question are stated.			
The Body			
4. The childhood experience is **outlined** in each poem.			
5. The impact of the tension on the persona is **discussed** in each poem.			
6. A device used in each poem to present childhood experience is **examined**.			
7. The writer PEE in each body paragraph.			
The Conclusion			
8. The conclusion summarizes all the points raised in the essay.			
9. No new point is raised in the conclusion.			
Overall			
10. Adequate, suitable transitional words and phrases are used within and between the paragraphs.			
11. Essay is factual and written in the correct tone.			
12. Essay is free from grammatical errors.			

Activity 4: What's the Verdict?

Directions. Identify the different parts of the essay and of each paragraph in your completed essay. Then, use the rubric for poetry essays in the CXC English syllabus to assess your essay writing skills. Then, ask your classmate to use the same rubric to assess your essay while you do the same for him/her.

My Recommendations

Make recommendations to yourself about how you may improve your essay. Ask your peers and your teacher for their recommendations on how you may improve as well.

<table>
<tr><th>Self</th><th>Peer</th></tr>
<tr><td>

</td><td>

</td></tr>
<tr><th colspan="2">Teacher</th></tr>
<tr><td colspan="2">

</td></tr>
</table>

Peer reviewed by: ______________________________ Date: ______________

Teacher reviewed by: ____________________________ Date: ______________

Based on the feedback from yourself, your peers and teacher, make the necessary changes. If you have no correction to make, move on the next poem.

Earn a 

for writing the best essay.

"My Parents" by Stephen Spender

Objectives

After completing the activities on "My Parents", you should be able to accurately:

- ☐ make predictions based on the title of the poem;
- ☐ identify the elements of poetry in the poem;
- ☐ critically assess your peers' presentation and analysis of the poem;
- ☐ examine the effect and effectiveness of literary devices used in the poem;
- ☐ discuss the roles of parents in your society.

Getting Started

Activity 1: Before you begin …

Before you begin to read any piece of writing, it is usually a good idea to think of what you already know about the topic. Write down what you know about the title of the poem by completing the table below. The table should be completed as follows:

It says … - Write the title of the poem.

I know … - Write what you know about the title. In this case, what does the use of the pronoun 'my' tell you about who the persona is? What do you expect to find out about the parents?

And so … - Make a prediction about what you think the poem will be about based on the stated title and what you know about the title.

It says …	
I know …	
And so …	

Activity 2: My Parents

Directions. Inset a picture of your parent(s) or guardian(s) below. Then, in each of the shapes attached to the box in the center, insert the required information.

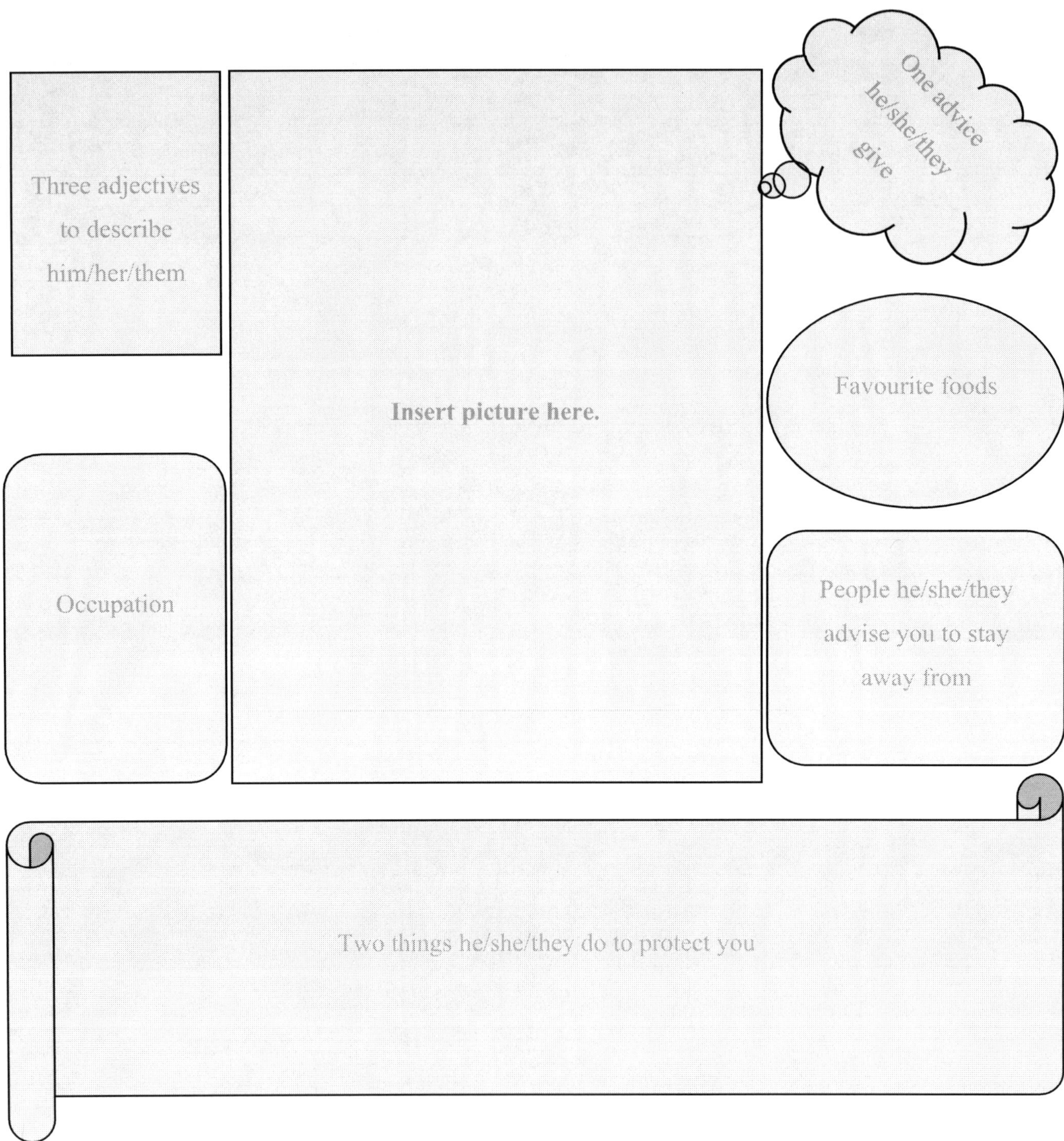

Activity 3: The Featured Presentation

Use the checklist below to assess your peers' recitation of "My Parents".

Checklist for the Poetry Recitation

Directions. The checklist below consists of a list of statements highlighting important things to consider when reciting a poem and three emojis. If your answer to the statement is yes, put a tick beside the statement and under the happy face. If your answer to the statement is no, put a tick beside the statement and under the sad face. If you are unsure, put a tick beside the statement and under the unsure face.

Checklist for Poetry Recitation			
1. Performance is no longer than three minutes.			
2. The words of the poem are said exactly as presented in the text.			
3. The performer adapts the role of the persona in movement, posture and general demeanour.			
4. Performer conveys the appropriate emotion.			
5. Performer makes appropriate use of facial expression, gestures, tone etc. to convey the meaning of the poem.			
6. Performer makes appropriate use of stage.			
7. Performance is audible and confident.			
8. Performance is entertaining.			

Directions. Based on your ticks in the checklist, rate your classmates' recitation of "My Parents" by shading the stars below. Five stars mean you believe the recitation was excellent. Then, justify your rating.

Your Rating	Your Justification
☆☆☆☆☆	

What is the most common rating received by the presenter from your classmates? ______________

What is your teacher's rating? ____

If you have the same rating as your teacher, you earn a  .

Choose TWO areas from the checklist where you ticked 'no' or 'unsure' and make ONE recommendation to the presenters on how they could have improved in those areas.

Selected area 1: ____

Recommendation: ____

____

____

Selected area 2: ____

Recommendation 1: ____

____

____

Elements of Poetry in "My Parents"

Your classmates will present their analysis of "My Parents". In this analysis, they will identify, explain and discuss the historical background, literary elements, form and literary devices used in the poem. You will be expected to critically assess the analysis being presented. This will be done in a step-by-step process.

Step 1: Listen for Information – While you listen to the analysis, complete the different activities with information presented in the analysis.

Step 2: Consult Your Peers – Share with a peer to see if he/she heard anything you might have missed or if you heard anything, he/she missed.

Step 3: Rate the Analysis – Look at the number of answered and unanswered activities you have and rate the overall analysis.

Historical Background

Directions. In this section, the presenters are expected to provide relevant information for all the areas in the picture below. However, you are only expected to write the ***poet's name, birthday, country of birth, quick facts and other works by the poet*** from the presenters' analysis. Complete the other sections based on your own feelings about the poet.

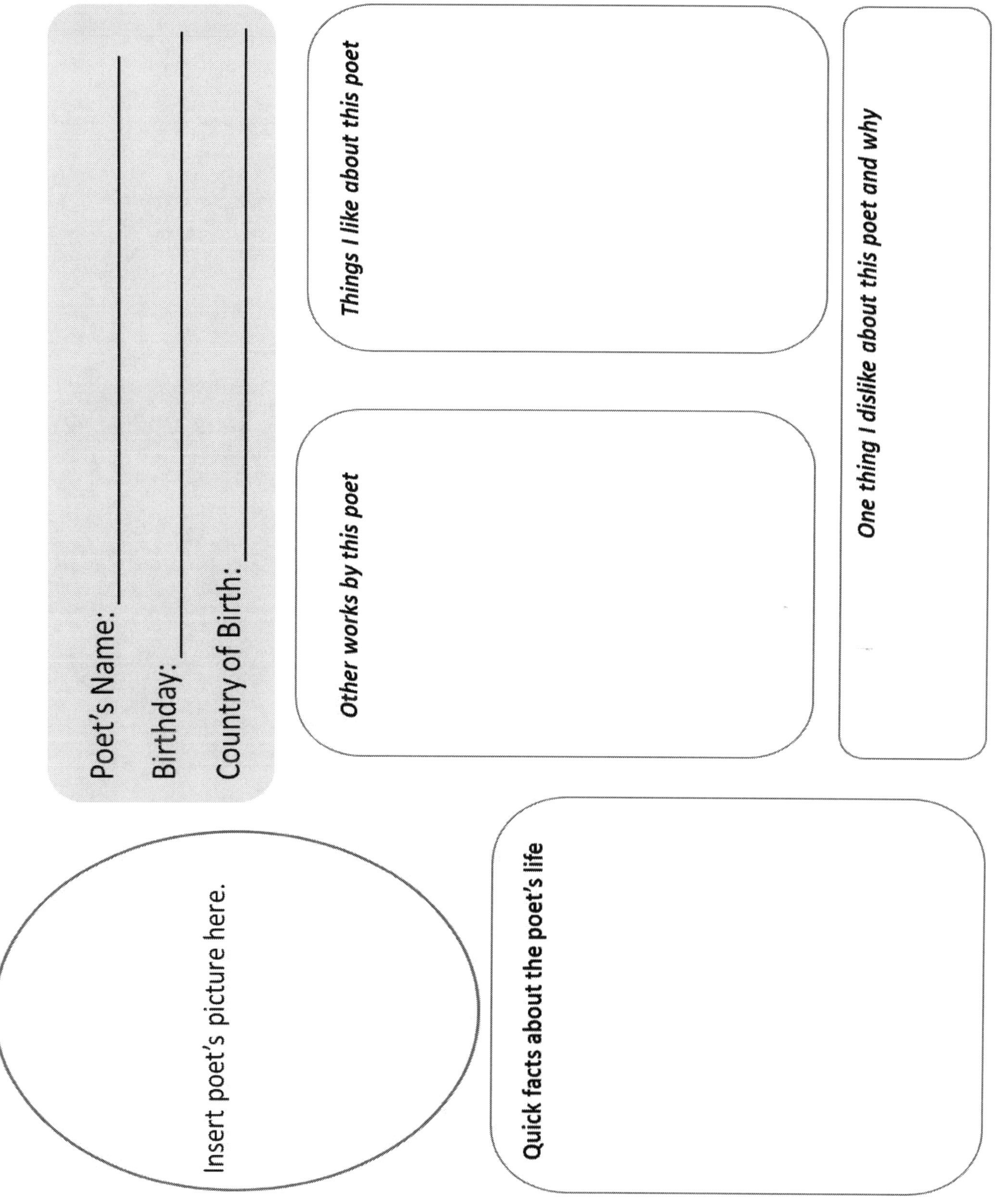

Literary Elements in "My Parents"

Directions. Write the literary elements identified by the presenter(s). After the presentation, you will be allowed time to identify these elements for yourself and compare your answers to the presenters' answers. Revise your notes on each element if you are unsure. Complete the table as follows:

1. Write the presenters' identifications.
2. Tick whether you agree or disagree with each identification.
3. Whether you agree or disagree, write one piece of evidence from the poem to support your decision.

Characters		
Persona:	**Agree**	**Disagree**
Evidence:		
Tone:	**Agree**	**Disagree**
Evidence:		
Other characters:	**Agree**	**Disagree**
Evidence:		
Type of Narration:	**Agree**	**Disagree**
Evidence:		

Setting		
Time and Place:	**Agree**	**Disagree**
Evidence:		
Mood:	**Agree**	**Disagree**
Evidence:		

Theme		
1st Theme Category: **Message** ***(one sentence):***	**Agree**	**Disagree**
Evidence		
2nd Theme Category: **Message** ***(one sentence):***	**Agree**	**Disagree**
Evidence		

Plot in "My Parents"

Directions. Summarize each stanza in a single sentence. Then, combine the sentences into a paragraph. Use suitable transition words and phrases to make the paragraph more coherent. Remember to use your own words.

Stanza 1:

Stanza 2:

Stanza 3:

____

____

____

____

____

____

____

____

____

Stylistics in "My Parents"

We will look at the form of the poem and the literary devices used.

Form of "My Parents"

Directions. Fill in the blanks with information from "My Parents"

"My Parents" is a ____________________ (*Type of poem*). The poem consists of ____________ (*Number of lines*) lines which are divided into ______________________ (*Number and type of stanza*). The poem has ________________ (*Type of rhythm*) and is written in __________________ (*Type of rhyme scheme*).

Literary Devices in "My Parents"

Activity 1: Identifying the Devices

Directions. Write the names of FOUR literary devices used in the poem. Then, write an example of each of the listed devices from the poem. Ensure you write the line number(s) for each example given.

Literary Devices	Examples
1. ______________________:	______________________________________
	______________________________________
2. ______________________:	______________________________________
	______________________________________
3. ______________________:	______________________________________
	______________________________________
4. ______________________:	______________________________________
	______________________________________

If you have identified a simile or metaphor, explain it by using the formula.

____

____

____

____

____

____

____

____

____

____

____

____

____

____

____

____

____

____

Activity 2: Effect and Effectiveness

Directions. Choose TWO devices identified in "My Parents" and comment on their effect and effectiveness. If you need to remind yourself of what is required when you are asked to examine or comment on the use of a literary device, read the notes presented of **pages 52 – 53** of this Workbook.

Device	Evidence
Effect:	
Effectiveness:	

Device	Evidence
Effect:	
Effectiveness:	

Assessing Your Peers' Presentation

Directions. Compare the information your peers provided with your own analysis and rate your classmates' analysis of "My Parents" by shading the stars below. Five stars mean you believe the analysis was excellent. Then, justify your rating.

Your Rating	Your Justification
☆☆☆☆☆	

What is the most common rating received by the presenter from your classmates? ____________

What is your teacher's rating? ____________

If you have the same rating as your teacher, you earn a  .

Choose ONE element of poetry that you think the presenters need to make improvement in analyzing and make TWO recommendations to the presenters on how they can improve in analyzing that element.

Selected area: ____________

Recommendation 1: ____________

Recommendation 2: ____________

Now that you have finished analyzing “My Parents”, look back at the predictions you made before you analyzed the poem and answer the following questions.

1. To what extent were your predictions right?

   Not at all ☐ A small extent ☐ Somewhat ☐ To a large extent ☐ Spot on ☐

2. Explain your selection for question 1.

   ____

   ____

   ____

   ____

3. How did the boys treat the persona? Give evidence from the poem to support your answer.

   ____

   ____

   ____

   ____

   ____

4. How did the persona respond to the treatment of the boys?

   ____

   ____

   ____

5. What would you have done?

   ____

   ____

6. “My Parents” and ‘Little Boy Crying” deal with the theme of love and family relationship.”

   Write an essay in which you describe the relationship between the parent(s) and the child in EACH poem. In this essay, you must also discuss how the parents demonstrate their love for the child in EACH poem and examine ONE device that is used to present the theme of love and family relationship in EACH poem.

Checking My Progress

You have just finished the activities on "My Parents". Before we move to the activities on the next poem, review what you have learnt or are still uncertain about. Do so by first checking the objectives you have accomplished so far.

Directions. Go back to the objectives at the beginning of the activities on "My Parents". If you think you have accomplished an objective, without looking back at your notes, put a tick in the box ☐ before the objective. If you are unsure you have accomplished the objective, put a question mark (?) and if you are sure you have not accomplished the objective, leave it unchecked (blank). Ensure you pay more attention to your unchecked boxes and the boxes with your question marks as you study. Also, ensure that you can perform the number indicated in each objective (e.g., list **three** genres). You have accomplished the objective when you can list the indicated number (three).

Now complete the 3-2-1 activity below. It works as follows:

Three – **W**rite **three** things you learned from the activities on "My Parents".

Two – **W**rite **two** things you found interesting or about which you would like to learn more.

One – **W**rite **one** question you still have about the material.

Share your question with your classmates and listen to their responses. Did they clarify things? If not, maybe it is time you did some independent research.

Finally, record ONE question from one of your classmates and provide an answer to that classmate.

Checking What I Know!!!

3. ____

____

____

2. ____

____

1. ____

Helping My Peers!!!

Peer's question: ______________________________________

____

My answer: ____

____

____

"Birdshooting Season" by Olive Senior

Objectives

After completing the activities on "Birdshooting Season", you should be able to accurately:

- ☐ make predictions based on the title of the poem;
- ☐ identify the elements of poetry in the poem;
- ☐ critically assess your peers' presentation and analysis of the poem;
- ☐ examine the effect and effectiveness of literary devices used in the poem;
- ☐ discuss diction in poetry;
- ☐ discuss gender roles in your society.

Getting Started

Activity 1: Before you begin …

Before you begin to read any piece of writing, it is usually a good idea to think of what you already know about the topic. Write down what you know about the title of the poem by completing the table below. The table should be completed as follows:

It says … - Write the title of the poem.

I know … - Write what you know about the title. In this case, what do you know about 'seasons'? What happens in birdshooting season?

And so … - Make a prediction about what you think the poem will be about based on the stated title and what you know about the title.

It says …	
I know …	
And so …	

Activity 2: If I Were

Directions. In our society, males and females are usually expected to play different roles. These roles are called gender roles because it is the individual's gender that determines what role(s) he/she should play. In this activity, you will be expected to think about the gender roles of the opposite sex and write a poem or song depicting the roles society expects the **opposite sex** to play in the household, sports and drinking alcohol. You should also include the attitude of the opposite sex towards the killing of small animals.

Earn a 

for creating the best piece.

Use the **If I Were Checklist** to ensure you have the best piece. After you are finished putting a tick beside each statement, make recommendations to yourself about how you may improve your performance. Ask your peers and teacher for their recommendations as well.

Checklist for "If I Were" Song or Poem

Directions. The checklist below consists of a list of statements highlighting important things to consider when preparing for your piece and three emojis. If your answer to the statement is yes, put a tick beside the statement and under the happy face. If your answer to the statement is no, put a tick beside the statement and under the sad face. If you are unsure, put a tick beside the statement and under the unsure face.

Checklist for "If I Were" Song or Poem			
1. Piece includes at least ONE example of opposite sex's role in sports.			
2. Piece includes at least ONE example of opposite sex's role in the household.			
3. Piece includes at least ONE example of opposite sex's role in drinking alcohol.			
4. Piece includes the attitude of the opposite sex towards the killing of small animals.			
5. Piece includes at least ONE simile.			
6. Simile is effectively used.			
7. Piece includes at least one metaphor.			
8. Metaphor is effectively used.			
9. Piece includes at least TWO types of conflict.			
10. Performance is entertaining.			

Activity 3: The Featured Presentation

Use the checklist below to assess your peers' recitation of "Birdshooting Season".

Checklist for the Poetry Recitation

Directions. The checklist below consists of a list of statements highlighting important things to consider when reciting a poem and three emojis. If your answer to the statement is yes, put a tick beside the statement and under the happy face. If your answer to the statement is no, put a tick beside the statement and under the sad face. If you are unsure, put a tick beside the statement and under the unsure face.

Checklist for Poetry Recitation	(happy face)	(unsure face)	(sad face)
1. Performance is no longer than three minutes.			
2. The words of the poem are said exactly as presented in the text.			
3. The performer adapts the role of the persona in movement, posture and general demeanour.			
4. Performer conveys the appropriate emotion.			
5. Performer makes appropriate use of facial expression, gestures, tone etc. to convey the meaning of the poem.			
6. Performer makes appropriate use of stage.			
7. Performance is audible and confident.			
8. Performance is entertaining.			

Directions. Based on your ticks in the checklist, rate your classmates' recitation of "Birdshooting Season" by shading the stars below. Five stars mean you believe the recitation was excellent. Then justify your rating.

Your Rating	Your Justification
☆☆☆☆☆	

What is the most common rating received by the presenter from your classmates? ____________________

What is your teacher's rating? ____________________

If you have the same rating as your teacher, you earn a  .

Choose TWO areas from the checklist where you ticked 'no' or 'unsure' and make ONE recommendation to the presenters on how they could have improved in those areas.

Selected area 1: ____________________

Recommendation: ____________________

____

____

Selected area 2: ____________________

Recommendation: ____________________

____

____

Elements of Poetry "Birdshooting Season"

Your classmates will present their analysis of "Birdshooting Season". In this analysis, they will identify, explain and discuss the historical background, literary elements, form and literary devices used in the poem. You will be expected to critically assess the analysis being presented. This will be done in a step-by-step process.

Step 1: Listen for Information – While you listen to the analysis, complete the different activities with information presented in the analysis.

Step 2: Consult Your Peers – Share with a peer to see if he/she heard anything you might have missed or if you heard anything, he/she missed.

Step 3: Rate the Analysis – Look at the number of answered and unanswered activities you have and rate the overall analysis.

Historical Background

Directions. In this section, the presenters are expected to provide relevant information for all the areas in the picture below. However, you are only expected to write the ***poet's name, birthday, country of birth, quick facts and other works by the poet*** from the presenters' analysis. Complete the other sections based on your own feelings about the poet.

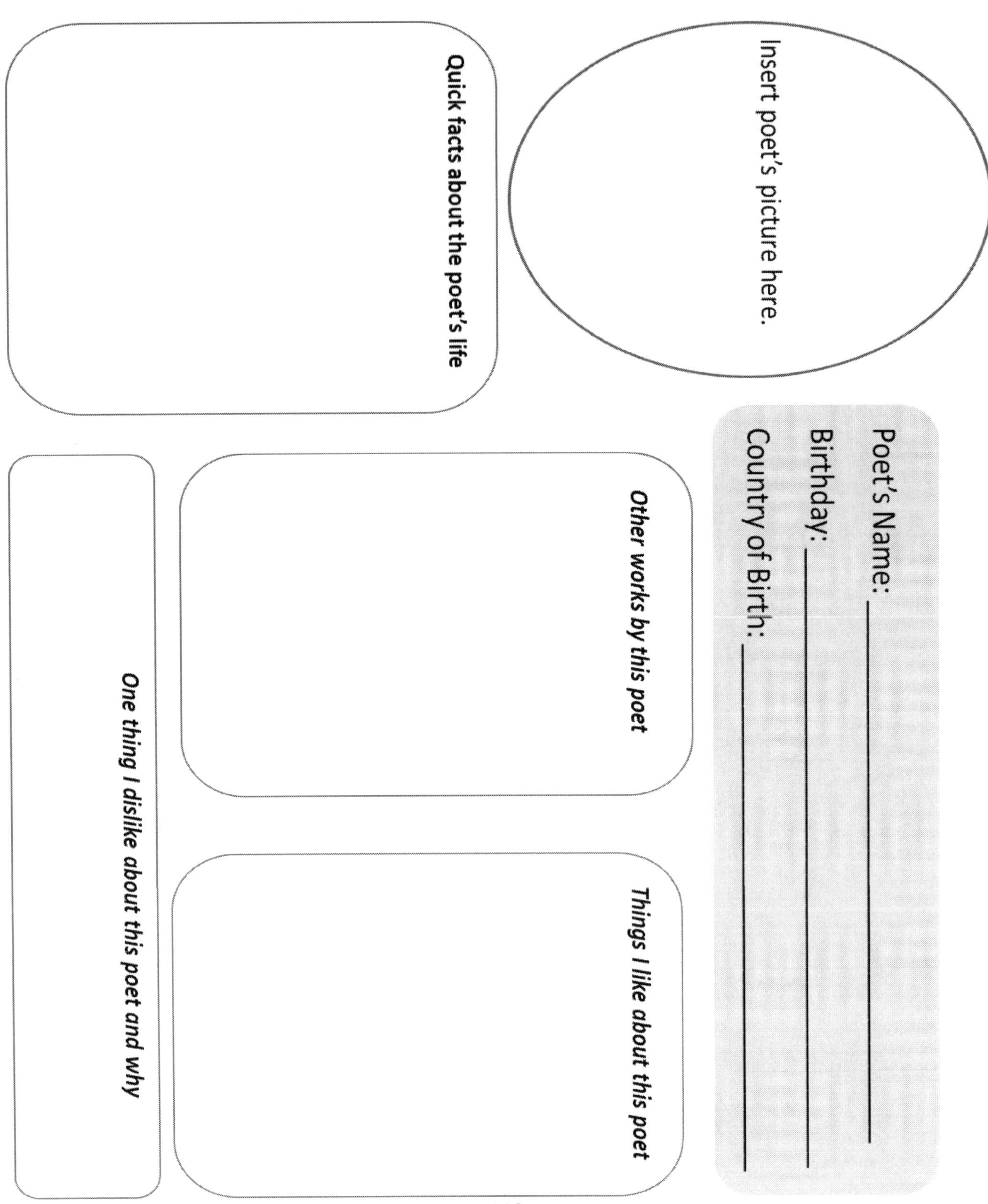

Literary Elements in "Birdshooting Season"

Directions. Write the literary elements identified by the presenter(s). After the presentation, you will be allowed time to identify these elements for yourself and compare your answers to the presenters' answers. Revise your notes on each element if you are unsure. Complete the table as follows:

1. Write the presenters' identifications.
2. Tick whether you agree or disagree with each identification.
3. Whether you agree or disagree, write one piece of evidence from the poem to support your decision.

Characters		
Persona:	**Agree**	**Disagree**
Evidence:		
Tone:	**Agree**	**Disagree**
Evidence:		
Other characters:	**Agree**	**Disagree**
Evidence:		
Type of Narration:	**Agree**	**Disagree**
Evidence:		

Setting		
Time and Place:	**Agree**	**Disagree**
Evidence:		
Mood:	**Agree**	**Disagree**
Evidence:		

Theme		
1st Theme Category: **Message *(one sentence):***	**Agree**	**Disagree**
Evidence		
2nd Theme Category: **Message *(one sentence):***	**Agree**	**Disagree**
Evidence		

Plot in "Birdshooting Season"

Directions. Summarize each stanza in a single sentence. Then, combine the sentences into a paragraph. Use suitable transition words and phrases to make the paragraph more coherent. Remember to use your own words.

Stanza 1:

Stanza 2:

Stanza 3:

Stanza 4:

Stylistics in "Birdshooting Season"

We will look at the form of the poem and the literary devices used.

Form of "Birdshooting Season"

Directions. Fill in the blanks with information from "Birdshooting Season".

"Birdshooting Season" is a ___________________ (*Type of poem*). The poem consists of ___________ (*Number of lines*) lines which are divided into ________ (*Number of stanzas*) stanzas. Each stanza is a different type of stanza with first being a ___________ (*Type of stanzas*), the second being a __________________ (*Type of stanza*) the third being a _________________ (*Type of stanza*) and the fourth being a _______________ (*Type of stanza*). The poem has _______________ (*Type of rhyme scheme*) and is written in _________________________ (*Type of rhythm*).

Answer the following questions.

1. Look at the words of the poem as they appear in the World of Poetry. Which stanza stands out and why?

   ____

   ____

   ____

2. What does the inconsistent number of lines in the stanzas contribute to the poem?

   ____

   ____

   ____

   ____

   ____

3. What does the rhyme scheme or the absence of a rhyme scheme contribute to the poem?

   ____

   ____

   ____

   ____

   ____

   ____

Literary Devices in "Birdshooting Season"

Activity 1: Identifying the Devices

Directions. Write the names of FOUR literary devices used in the poem. Then, write an example of each of the listed devices from the poem. Ensure you write the line number(s) for each example given.

Literary Devices	Examples
1. ______________________:	______________________________
	______________________________
2. ______________________:	______________________________
	______________________________
3. ______________________:	______________________________
	______________________________
4. ______________________:	______________________________
	______________________________

Identify and explain TWO contrasts made in the poem.

Activity 2: Effect and Effectiveness

Directions. Choose TWO devices identified in "Birdshooting Season" and comment on their effect and effectiveness. If you need to remind yourself of what is required when you are asked to examine or comment on the use of a literary device, read the notes presented of **pages 52 – 53** of this Workbook.

Device	**Evidence**
Effect:	
Effectiveness:	

Device	**Evidence**
Effect:	
Effectiveness:	

Diction

Diction refers to the choice of words. Writers choose to use specific words to achieve a desired effect or to communicate additional meaning to the readers.

Activity 1: Powerful Words

Directions. Examine the use of the following words as used in "Birdshooting Season". Then, find a suitable synonym to replace the words without changing the meaning of the poem. When examining each word, state the meaning of the word, and explain why the poet chose to use that specific word.

1. 'marriages' (L2) - ____________________

   ____

   ____

   Synonym - ____________________

2. 'macho' (L3) - ____________________

   ____

   ____

   Synonym - ____________________

3. 'contentless' (L5) - ____________________

   ____

   ____

   Synonym - ____________________

4. 'sport' (L9) - ____________________

   ____

   ____

   Synonym - ____________________

5. 'shivering' (L14) - ____________________

   ____

   ____

   Synonyms - ____________________

Assessing Your Peers' Presentation

Directions. Compare the information your peers provided with your own analysis and rate your classmates' analysis of "Birdshooting Season" by shading the stars below. Five stars mean you believe the analysis was excellent. Then, justify your rating.

Your Rating	Your Justification
☆☆☆☆☆	

What is the most common rating received by the presenter from your classmates? ____________

What is your teacher's rating? ____________

If you have the same rating as your teacher, you earn a ⚖ .

Choose ONE element of poetry that you think the presenters need to make improvement in analyzing and make TWO recommendations to the presenters on how they can improve in analyzing that element.

Selected area: ____________

Recommendation 1: ____________

Recommendation 2: ____________

Now that you have finished analyzing "Birdshooting Season", look back at the predictions you made before you analyzed the poem and answer the following questions.

1. To what extent were your predictions right?

   Not at all ☐ A small extent ☐ Somewhat ☐ To a large extent ☐ Spot on ☐

2. Explain your selection for question 1.____

   ____

   ____

   ____

3. Compare the gender roles identified in the poem or song you wrote at the beginning of the activities on "Birdshooting Season" to those highlighted in the poem, "Birdshooting Season".

   ____

   ____

   ____

   ____

   ____

4. Compare the men's attitude to their prescribed roles to the women's attitude to their prescribed roles. ____

   ____

   ____

   ____

   ____

   ____

5. Choose TWO poems that you have studied from the prescribed list which focus on conflict between man and his society.

   Write an essay in which you describe the aspect of society with which EACH persona is in conflict. In this essay, you must discuss EACH persona's response to the aspect of society described and examine ONE device that is used to highlight the conflict in EACH poem.

Use the rubric for poetry essays in the CXC English syllabus to assess your essay writing skills. Then, ask your classmate to use the same rubric to assess your essay while you do the same for him/her. Revise your essay before presenting it to your teacher.

Checking My Progress

You have just finished the activities on "Birdshooting Season". Before we move to the activities on the next poem, review what you have learnt or are still uncertain about. Do so by first checking the objectives you have accomplished so far.

Directions. Go back to the objectives at the beginning of the activities on "Birdshooting Season". If you think you have accomplished an objective, without looking back at your notes, put a tick in the box ☐ before the objective. If you are unsure you have accomplished the objective, put a question mark (?) and if you are sure you have not accomplished the objective, leave it unchecked (blank). Ensure you pay more attention to your unchecked boxes and the boxes with your question marks as you study. Also, ensure that you can perform the number indicated in each objective (e.g., list **three** genres). You have accomplished the objective when you can list the indicated number (three).

Now complete the 3-2-1 activity below. It works as follows:

Three – Write three things you learned from the activities on "Birdshooting Season".

Two – Write two things you found interesting or about which you would like to learn more.

One – Write one question you still have about the material.

Share your question with your classmates and listen to their responses. Did they clarify things? If not, maybe it is time you did some independent research.

Finally, record ONE question from one of your classmates and provide an answer to that classmate.

Checking What I Know!!!

3. ____

____

____

2. ____

____

1. ____

Helping My Peers!!!

Peer's question: __________________________________

____

My answer: __________________________________

____

____

"An African Thunderstorm" by David Rubdiri

Objectives

After completing the activities on "An African Thunderstorm", you should be able to accurately:

- ☐ make predictions based on the title of the poem;
- ☐ identify the elements of poetry in the poem;
- ☐ critically assess your peers' presentation and analysis of the poem;
- ☐ examine the relationship between literary devices and imagery;
- ☐ discuss preparations for natural disasters.

Getting Started

Activity 1: Before you begin …

Before you begin to read any piece of writing, it is usually a good idea to think of what you already know about the topic. Write down what you know about the title of the poem by completing the table below. The table should be completed as follows:

It says … - Write the title of the poem.

I know … - Write what you know about the title. In this case, what are some of the things that usually happen in a thunderstorm? What does the word, "African" tell you about the setting of the poem?

And so … - Make a prediction about what you think the poem will be about based on the stated title and what you know about the title.

It says …	
I know …	
And so …	

Activity 2: Preparing for Natural Disasters

Directions. Answer the following questions.

1. What is the name of the organization in your country that is responsible for providing information on natural disasters in your country?

    ____

    ____

2. Record the contact information for this organization

    Chief Executive Officer: ______________________________

    Head Office (Address): ______________________________

    ____

    Head Office (Telephone): ______________________________

    Head Office (Email): ______________________________

3. Find a newspaper article or video that provides guidelines for preparing for an identified natural disaster. Record the source information of the article below.

    Title: ______________________________________

    ____

    Date: ____________________ **Writer:** ____________________

4. List at least THREE guidelines for preparing for the natural disaster as outlined in the article/video.

    ____

    ____

    ____

    ____

    ____

5. Have you ever experienced a natural disaster? Use THREE adjectives to describe how you or people around you felt before the disaster struck. Explain each selected adjective.

    ____

    ____

    ____

Activity 3: The Featured Presentation

Use the checklist below to assess your peers' recitation of "An African Thunderstorm".

Checklist for the Poetry Recitation

Directions. The checklist below consists of a list of statements highlighting important things to consider when reciting a poem and three emojis. If your answer to the statement is yes, put a tick beside the statement and under the happy face. If your answer to the statement is no, put a tick beside the statement and under the sad face. If you are unsure, put a tick beside the statement and under the unsure face.

Checklist for Poetry Recitation	Happy face	Unsure face	Sad face
1. Performance is no longer than three minutes.			
2. The words of the poem are said exactly as presented in the text.			
3. The performer adapts the role of the persona in movement, posture and general demeanour.			
4. Performer conveys the appropriate emotion.			
5. Performer makes appropriate use of facial expression, gestures, tone etc. to convey the meaning of the poem.			
6. Performer makes appropriate use of stage.			
7. Performance is audible and confident.			
8. Performance is entertaining.			

Directions. Based on your ticks in the checklist, rate your classmates' recitation of "An African Thunderstorm" by shading the stars below. Five stars mean you believe the recitation was excellent. Then, justify your rating.

Your Rating	Your Justification
☆☆☆☆☆	

What is the most common rating received by the presenter from your classmates? ____________________

What is your teacher's rating? ____

If you have the same rating as your teacher, you earn a .

Choose TWO areas from the checklist where you ticked 'no' or 'unsure' and make ONE recommendation to the presenters on how they could have improved in those areas.

Selected area 1: ____

Recommendation 1: ____

____

____

Selected area 2: ____

Recommendation 1: ____

____

____

Elements of Poetry in "An African Thunderstorm"

Your classmates will present their analysis of "An African Thunderstorm". In this analysis, they will identify, explain and discuss the historical background, literary elements, form and literary devices used in the poem. You will be expected to critically assess the analysis being presented. This will be done in a step-by-step process.

Step 1: Listen for Information – While you listen to the analysis, complete the different activities with information presented in the analysis.

Step 2: Consult Your Peers – Share with a peer to see if he/she heard anything you might have missed or if you heard anything, he/she missed.

Step 3: Rate the Analysis – Look at the number of answered and unanswered activities you have and rate the overall analysis.

Historical Background

Directions. In this section, the presenters are expected to provide relevant information for all the areas in the picture below. However, you are only expected to write the ***poet's name, birthday, country of birth, quick facts and other works by the poet*** from the presenters' analysis. Complete the other sections based on your own feelings about the poet.

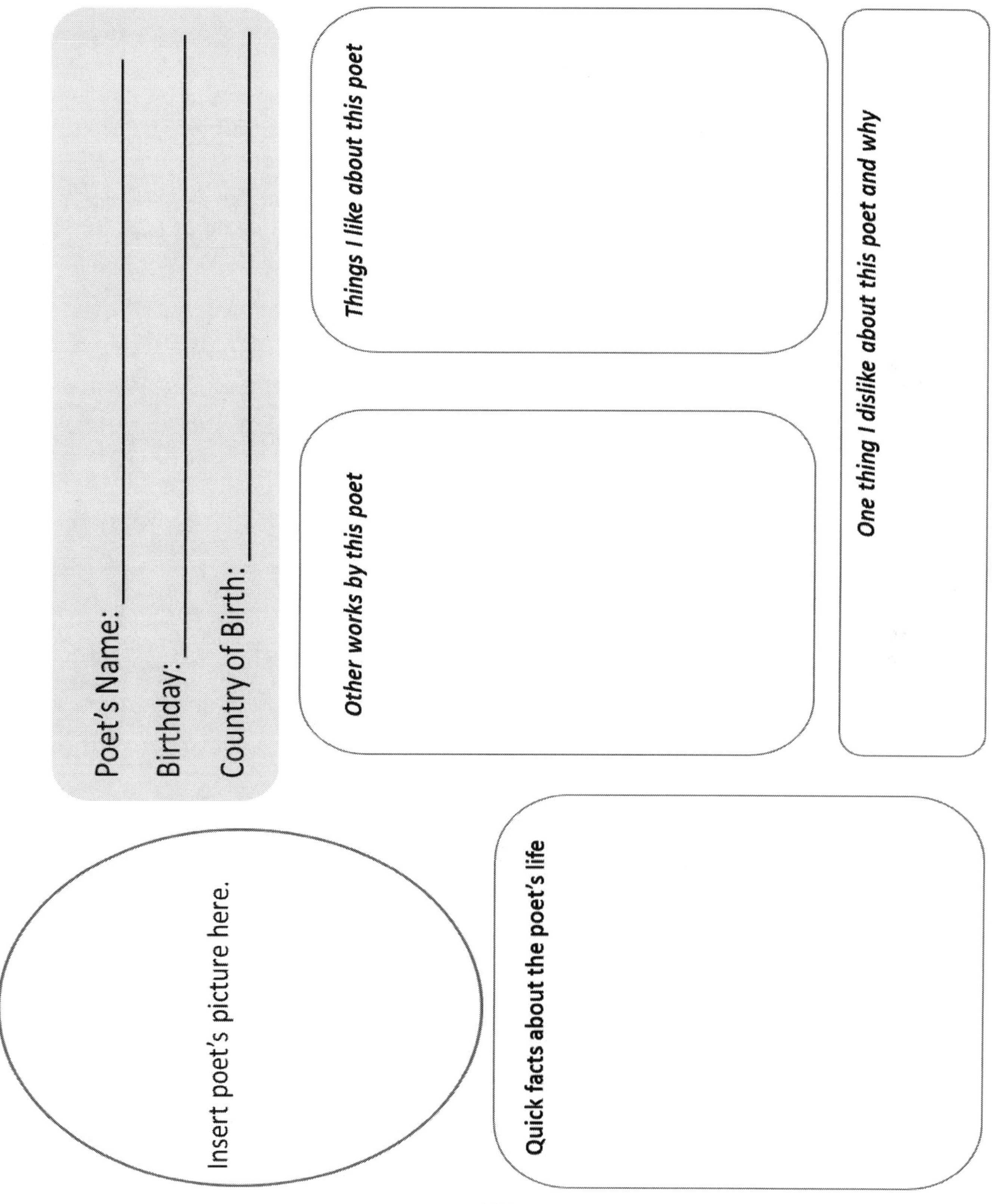

Literary Elements in "An African Thunderstorm"

Directions. Write the literary elements identified by the presenter(s). After the presentation, you will be allowed time to identify these elements for yourself and compare your answers to the presenters' answers. Revise your notes on each element if you are unsure. Complete the table as follows:

1. Write the presenters' identifications.
2. Tick whether you agree or disagree with each identification.
3. Whether you agree or disagree, write one piece of evidence from the poem to support your decision.

Characters		
Persona:	**Agree**	**Disagree**
Evidence:		
Tone:	**Agree**	**Disagree**
Evidence:		
Other characters:	**Agree**	**Disagree**
Evidence:		
Type of Narration:	**Agree**	**Disagree**
Evidence:		

Setting		
Time and Place:	**Agree**	**Disagree**
Evidence:		
Mood:	**Agree**	**Disagree**
Evidence:		

Theme		
1st Theme Category: **Message *(one sentence):***	**Agree**	**Disagree**
Evidence		
2nd Theme Category: **Message *(one sentence):***	**Agree**	**Disagree**
Evidence		

Plot in "An African Thunderstorm"

Directions. Summarize each stanza in a single sentence. Then, combine the sentences into a paragraph. Use suitable transition words and phrases to make the paragraph more coherent. Remember to use your own words.

Stanza 1:

Stanza 2:

Stylistics in "An African Thunderstorm"

We will look at the form of the poem and the literary devices used.

Form of "An African Thunderstorm"

Directions. Fill in the blanks with information from "An African Thunderstorm"

"An African Thunderstorm" is a ________________ (*Type of poem*). The poem consists of ________ (*Number of lines*) lines which are divided into _____ (*Number of stanzas*) stanzas. The poem has ________________ (*Type of rhyme scheme*) and is written in ________________ (*Type of rhythm*).

Answer the following questions.

1. There are many lines in the poem that consists of only one word. Choose any TWO and explain the contribution of the word as a line in the poem.

____

____

____

____

____

Literary Devices in "An African Thunderstorm"

Activity 1: Identifying the Devices

Directions. Write the names of FOUR literary devices used in the poem. Then, write an example of each of the listed devices from the poem. Ensure you write the line number(s) for each example given.

	Literary Devices	Examples
1.	____________________:	______________________________
		______________________________
2.	____________________:	______________________________
		______________________________
3.	____________________:	______________________________
		______________________________
4.	____________________:	______________________________
		______________________________

If you have identified a simile or metaphor, explain it by using the formula.

Activity 3: Effect and Effectiveness

Directions. Choose THREE devices identified in "An African Thunderstorm" and comment on their effect and effectiveness. If you need to remind yourself of what is required when you are asked to examine or comment on the use of a literary device, read the notes presented of **pages 52 – 53** of this Workbook.

Device	Evidence
Effect:	
Effectiveness:	

Device	Evidence
Effect:	
Effectiveness:	

Device	Evidence
Effect:	
Effectiveness:	

Imagery

All the devices in the poem are used to create images that appeal to our senses. So, we will spend some time taking a closer look at imagery. In poetry, imagery refers to the use of words, phrases or devices to appeal to our different senses: hearing, smelling, seeing, tasting and touching. There are different types of imagery: gustatory, tactile, auditory, visual and olfactory. Each type of imagery appeals to a different sense. Match the types of imagery to the sense organ in the picture below. Then, give an example of something you can see, taste, touch, smell or hear as appropriate for each type of imagery.

Activity 2: Team Challenge – Words and Senses

Directions: For this activity, you will need your dream team, your favourite snack and a wide vocabulary.

Step 1 – After selecting or being assigned to groups of five, you should select the snack that is most suitable for all the senses. As a group, taste, touch, look at, smell or listen to the snack and make a list of adjectives that appropriately describe the snack based on each sense.

The group with the most adjectives for an assigned sense earns a 

.

Step 2 – Then as a group, create a poem about the selected snack using as many of the words in your list as possible. Your poem should contain:

- ✓ FIVE quatrains each focused on a different sense
- ✓ FIVE types of imagery
- ✓ an alternate rhyme scheme
- ✓ at least ONE simile, ONE metaphor AND ONE personification
- ✓ an oxymoron, euphemism OR alliteration
- ✓ input from ALL members of your team.

Earn a 

and a for creating the best poem.

Step 3 – This step you should complete individually. Paste a picture of yourself in the box in the middle. Then, match each literary device identified in Activity 1 with its appropriate sense. For example, "pregnant clouds" is a personification which could be matched to your eyes (sense of sight) as it helps you to see how engorged the clouds were.

Earn a BRILLIANT for adding at least TWO other literary devices.

Based on the activity, make ONE observation about the relationship between imagery and literary devices

Assessing Your Peers' Presentation

Directions. Compare the information your peers provided with your own analysis and rate your classmates' analysis of "An African Thunderstorm" by shading the stars below. Five stars mean you believe the analysis was excellent. Then, justify your rating.

Your Rating	Your Justification
☆☆☆☆☆	

What is the most common rating received by the presenter from your classmates? ___________________

What is your teacher's rating? ____

If you have the same rating as your teacher, you earn a  .

Choose ONE element of poetry that you think the presenters need to make improvement in analyzing and make TWO recommendations to the presenters on how they can improve in analyzing that element.

Selected area: ____

Recommendation 1: ____

____

____

____

Recommendation 2: ____

____

____

____

____

Now that you have finished analyzing "An African Thunderstorm", look back at the predictions you made before you analyzed the poem and answer the following questions.

1. To what extent were your predictions right?

   Not at all ☐ A small extent ☐ Somewhat ☐ To a large extent ☐ Spot on ☐

2. Explain your selection for question 1.

   ____

   ____

   ____

   ____

   ____

2. Why does the poet begin the word 'wind' with a capital letter?

   ____

   ____

3. In what way did the historical background of the poem contribute to your understanding of the poem?

   ____

   ____

   ____

   ____

4. Choose TWO poems that you have studied from the prescribed list which focus on childhood experiences.

   Write an essay in which you outline the childhood experience in EACH poem. In this essay, you must also compare the child's perspective of the experience with an adult perspective presented in EACH poem and examine ONE device that is used to present the child's perspective in EACH poem.

Use the rubric for poetry essays in the CXC English syllabus to assess your essay writing skills. Then, ask your classmate to use the same rubric to assess your essay while you do the same for him/her. Revise your essay before presenting it to your teacher.

Checking My Progress

You have just finished the activities on "An African Thunderstorm". Before we move to the activities on the next poem, review what you have learnt or are still uncertain about. Do so by first checking the objectives you have accomplished so far.

Directions. Go back to the objectives at the beginning of the activities on "An African Thunderstorm". If you think you have accomplished an objective, without looking back at your notes, put a tick in the box ☐ before the objective. If you are unsure you have accomplished the objective, put a question mark (?) and if you are sure you have not accomplished the objective, leave it unchecked (blank). Ensure you pay more attention to your unchecked boxes and the boxes with your question marks as you study. Also, ensure that you can perform the number indicated in each objective (e.g., list **three** genres). You have accomplished the objective when you can list the indicated number (three).

Now complete the 3-2-1 activity below. It works as follows:

Three – Write **three** things you learned from the activities on "An African Thunderstorm".

Two – Write **two** things you found interesting or about which you would like to learn more.

One – Write **one** question you still have about the material.

Share your question with your classmates and listen to their responses. Did they clarify things? If not, maybe it is time you did some independent research.

Finally, record ONE question from one of your classmates and provide an answer to that classmate.

Checking What I Know!!!

3. ____

____

____

2. ____

____

1. ____

Helping My Peers!!!

Peer's question: ____

____

My answer: ____

____

____

"This is the dark time, my love" by Martin Carter

Objectives

After completing the activities on "This is the dark time, my love", you should be able to accurately:

- ☐ make predictions based on the title of the poem;
- ☐ identify the elements of poetry in the poem;
- ☐ critically assess your peers' presentation and analysis of the poem;
- ☐ examine the effect and effectiveness of literary devices used in the poem;
- ☐ examine the relationship between literary devices and imagery.

Getting Started

Activity 1: Before you begin …

Before you begin to read any piece of writing, it is usually a good idea to think of what you already know about the topic. Write down what you know about the title of the poem by completing the table below. The table should be completed as follows:

It says … - Write the title of the poem.

I know … - Write what you know about the title. In this case, to what does the phrase 'dark time' refer and why is there a comma (,) before the words "my love"?

And so … - Make a prediction about what you think the poem will be about based on the stated title and what you know about the title.

It says …	
I know …	
And so …	

Activity 2: My Dark Time

Directions. Think about a 'dark time' in your life as a student, member of your family, member of your community or in your country and write about it. After ten minutes, volunteers will be asked to share.

Based on the experience you shared, write THREE adjectives to describe how you felt. Use your mood list to help you to find the right words to describe your feelings. Then, briefly explain why or when you felt each emotion.

Emotions	**Why/When**
1. ____________________:	____
	____
2. ____________________:	____
	____
3. ____________________:	____
	____

How did you overcome this 'dark time'?

____

____

____

____

____

____

____

____

____

____

____

After sharing the experience with your classmates and teachers, ask for suggestions on other ways you could have dealt with your 'dark time'. List TWO of their suggestions below.

____

____

____

____

____

Activity 3: The Featured Presentation

Use the checklist below to assess your peers' recitation of "This is the dark time, my love".

Checklist for the Poetry Recitation

Directions. The checklist below consists of a list of statements highlighting important things to consider when reciting a poem and three emojis. If your answer to the statement is yes, put a tick beside the statement and under the happy face. If your answer to the statement is no, put a tick beside the statement and under the sad face. If you are unsure, put a tick beside the statement and under the unsure face.

Checklist for Poetry Recitation	(happy face)	(unsure face)	(sad face)
1. Performance is no longer than three minutes.			
2. The words of the poem are said exactly as presented in the text.			
3. The performer adapts the role of the persona in movement, posture and general demeanour.			
4. Performer conveys the appropriate emotion.			
5. Performer makes appropriate use of facial expression, gestures, tone etc. to convey the meaning of the poem.			
6. Performer makes appropriate use of stage.			
7. Performance is audible and confident.			
8. Performance is entertaining.			

Directions. Based on your ticks in the checklist, rate your classmates' recitation of "This is the dark time, my love" by shading the stars below. Five stars mean you believe the recitation was excellent. Then, justify your rating.

Your Rating	Your Justification
☆☆☆☆☆	

What is the most common rating received by the presenter from your classmates? ____________________

What is your teacher's rating? ____

If you have the same rating as your teacher, you earn a  .

Choose TWO areas from the checklist where you ticked 'no' or 'unsure' and make ONE recommendation to the presenters on how they could have improved in those areas.

Selected area 1: ____

Recommendation: ____

____

____

Selected area 2: ____

Recommendation: ____

____

____

Elements of Poetry in "This is the dark time, my love"

Your classmates will present their analysis of "This is the dark time, my love". In this analysis, they will identify, explain and discuss the historical background, literary elements, form and literary devices used in the poem. You will be expected to critically assess the analysis being presented. This will be done in a step-by-step process.

Step 1: Listen for Information – While you listen to the analysis, complete the different activities with information presented in the analysis.

Step 2: Consult Your Peers – Share with a peer to see if he/she heard anything you might have missed or if you heard anything, he/she missed.

Step 3: Rate the Analysis – Look at the number of answered and unanswered activities you have and rate the overall analysis.

Historical Background

Directions. In this section, the presenters are expected to provide relevant information for all the areas in the picture below. However, you are only expected to write the ***poet's name, birthday, country of birth, quick facts and other works by the poet*** from the presenters' analysis. Complete the other sections based on your own feelings about the poet.

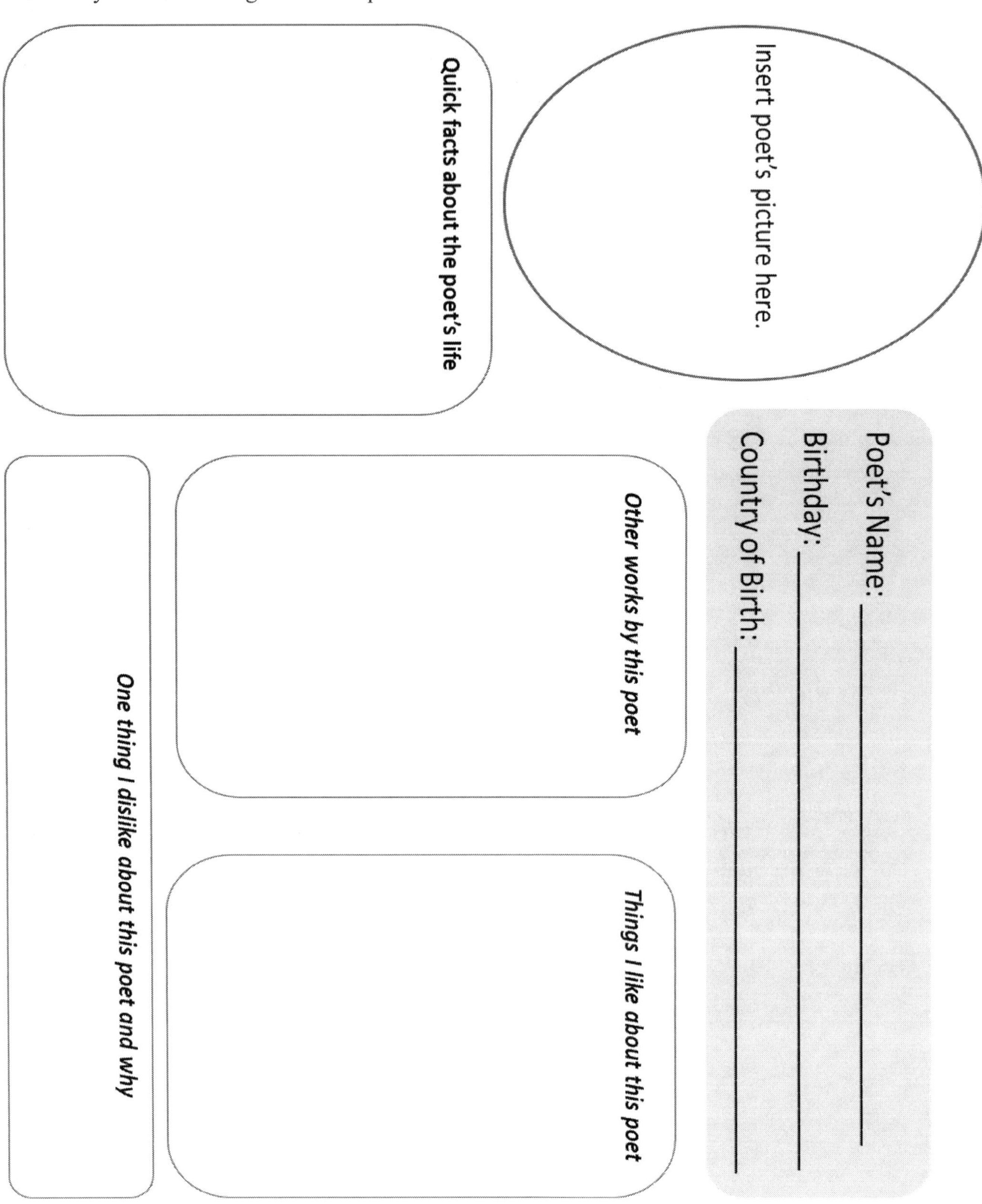

Literary Elements in "This is the dark time, my love"

Directions. Write the literary elements identified by the presenter(s). After the presentation, you will be allowed time to identify these elements for yourself and compare your answers to the presenters' answers. Revise your notes on each element if you are unsure. Complete the table as follows:

1. Write the presenters' identifications.
2. Tick whether you agree or disagree with each identification.
3. Whether you agree or disagree, write one piece of evidence from the poem to support your decision.

Characters		
Persona:	**Agree**	**Disagree**
Evidence:		
Tone:	**Agree**	**Disagree**
Evidence:		
Other characters:	**Agree**	**Disagree**
Evidence:		
Type of Narration:	**Agree**	**Disagree**
Evidence:		

Setting		
Time and Place:	**Agree**	**Disagree**
Evidence:		
Mood:	**Agree**	**Disagree**
Evidence:		

Theme		
1st Theme Category: **Message *(one sentence):***	**Agree**	**Disagree**
Evidence		
2nd Theme Category: **Message *(one sentence):***	**Agree**	**Disagree**
Evidence		

Plot in "This is the dark time, my love"

Directions. Summarize each stanza in a single sentence. Then, combine the sentences into a paragraph. Use suitable transition words and phrases to make the paragraph more coherent. Remember to use your own words.

Stanza 1:

Stanza 2:

Stanza 3:

____

____

____

____

____

____

____

Stylistics in "This is the dark time, my love"

We will look at the form of the poem and the literary devices used.

Form of "This is the dark time, my love"

Directions. Fill in the blanks with information from "This is the dark time, my love".

"This is the dark time, my love" is a ____________________ (*Type of poem*). The poem consists of ____ (*Number of lines*) lines which are divided into ____________________________ (*Number and type of stanzas*). The poem has ____________________ (*Type of rhyme scheme*) and is written in ________________________________ (*Type of rhythm*).

Answer the following questions.

1. What does the consistent number of lines and stanzas contribute to the poem?

____

____

____

____

2. What does the rhyme scheme or the absence of a rhyme scheme contribute to the poem?

____

____

____

____

Literary Devices in "This is the dark time, my love"

For each poem, you should be able to:

- ✓ list the main devices used;
- ✓ explain each device used;
- ✓ comment on the effect and effectiveness of each device used.

Activity 1: Identifying the Devices

Directions. Write the names of FOUR literary devices used in the poem. Then, write an example of each of the listed devices from the poem. Ensure you write the line number(s) for each example given.

	Literary Devices	**Examples**
1.	____________________:	______________________________ ______________________________
2.	____________________:	______________________________ ______________________________
3.	____________________:	______________________________ ______________________________
4.	____________________:	______________________________ ______________________________

If you have identified a simile or metaphor, explain it by using the formula.

"This is the dark time, my love" also makes extensive use of images. Identify the different types of imagery used in the poem.

Earn a  ***for accurately identifying the most images.***

Symbols

A symbol is a thing that represents or stands for something else. For example, red symbolizes danger and gold is a symbol of wealth. Poets use symbols to heighten the poetic experience, to appeal to emotions and to add meaning. Oftentimes, symbols are created when a concrete object is used to represent something abstract. Concrete objects are things you can physically see, touch, hear, taste and smell (e.g., flowers, house and dog). On the other hand, abstract things are ideas or qualities that cannot be seen, touched, heard, tasted or smelt (e.g., honesty, freedom and courage). Identify each of the following as abstract or concrete.

a. Orchid ___________
b. Patience ___________
c. Truth ___________
d. Box _____________
e. Flowers __________
f. Poetry ____________
g. Memory __________
h. Litter ____________
i. Resilience ________

Activity 2: Symbolism of "This is the dark time, my love"

Directions. Find a picture of each of the abstract objects mentioned in the poem. Then explain the abstract message that it is sending.

Brown beetles	
The shining sun hidden in the sky	
Red flowers bend their heads	

Directions. Identify THREE other symbols used in the poem. Insert a picture of EACH and explain their meanings.

Activity 3: Effect and Effectiveness

Directions. Choose TWO devices identified in "This is the dark time, my love" and comment on their effect and effectiveness. If you need to remind yourself of what is required when you are asked to examine or comment on the use of a literary device, read the notes presented of **pages 52 – 53** of this Workbook.

Device	**Evidence**
Effect:	
Effectiveness:	

Device	**Evidence**
Effect:	
Effectiveness:	

Assessing Your Peers' Presentation

Directions. Compare the information your peers provided with your own analysis and rate your classmates' analysis of "This is the dark time, my love" by shading the stars below. Five stars mean you believe the analysis was excellent. Then justify your rating.

Your Rating	Your Justification
☆☆☆☆☆	

What is the most common rating received by the presenter from your classmates? ________________

What is your teacher's rating? ____

If you have the same rating as your teacher, you earn a .

Choose ONE element of poetry that you think the presenters need to make improvement in analyzing and make TWO recommendations to the presenters on how they can improve in analyzing that element.

Selected area: ____

Recommendation 1: ____

____

____

____

Recommendation 2: ____

____

____

____

____

Now that you have finished analyzing "This is the dark time, my love", look back at the predictions you made before you analyzed the poem and answer the following questions.

1. To what extent were your predictions right?

   Not at all ☐ A small extent ☐ Somewhat ☐ To a large extent ☐ Spot on ☐

2. Explain your selection for question 1.

   ____
   ____
   ____
   ____
   ____

3. To whom or what is the poet referring as "my love"? Justify your answer.

   ____
   ____
   ____
   ____
   ____

4. In what way did the historical background of the poem contribute to your understanding of the poem?

   ____
   ____
   ____
   ____
   ____

5. Would you add this poem to your list of favourite poems? Why or Why not?

   ____
   ____
   ____
   ____
   ____

Checking My Progress

You have just finished the activities on "This is the dark time, my love". Before we move to the activities on the next poem, review what you have learnt or are still uncertain about. Do so by first checking the objectives you have accomplished so far.

Directions. Go back to the objectives at the beginning of the activities on "This is the dark time, my love". If you think you have accomplished an objective, without looking back at your notes, put a tick in the box ☐ before the objective. If you are unsure you have accomplished the objective, put a question mark (?) and if you are sure you have not accomplished the objective, leave it unchecked (blank). Ensure you pay more attention to your unchecked boxes and the boxes with your question marks as you study. Also, ensure that you can perform the number indicated in each objective (e.g., list **three** genres). You have accomplished the objective when you can list the indicated number (three).

Now complete the 3-2-1 activity below. It works as follows:

Three – **W**rite **three** things you learned from the activities on "This is the dark time, my love".

Two – **W**rite **two** things you found interesting or about which you would like to learn more.

One – **W**rite **one** question you still have about the material.

Share your question with your classmates and listen to their responses. Did they clarify things? If not, maybe it is time you did some independent research.

Finally, record ONE question from one of your classmates and provide an answer to that classmate.

Checking What I Know!!!

3. ____

____

____

2. ____

____

1. ____

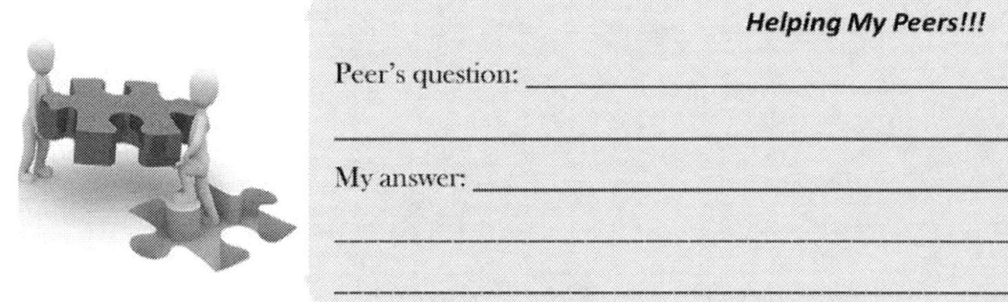

Helping My Peers!!!

Peer's question: ____

____

My answer: ____

____

____

"Dulce et Decorum Est" by Wilfred Owen

Objectives

After completing the activities on "Dulce et Decorum Est", you should be able to accurately:

- ☐ make predictions based on the title of the poem;
- ☐ identify the elements of poetry in the poem;
- ☐ critically assess your peers' presentation and analysis of the poem;
- ☐ examine the effect and effectiveness of literary devices used in the poem;
- ☐ compare perspectives on war.

Getting Started

Activity 1: Before you begin …

Before you begin to read any piece of writing, it is usually a good idea to think of what you already know about the topic. Write down what you know about the title of the poem by completing the table below. The table should be completed as follows:

It says … - Write the title of the poem.

I know … - Write what you know about the title. In this case, in which language is the title written? What is the English translation of the title?

And so … - Make a prediction about what you think the poem will be about based on the stated title and what you know about the title.

It says …	
I know …	
And so …	

Activity 2: For the Love of Country

Directions. Answer the following questions.

1. List TWO things you will do to improve or protect your country.

___

___

___

2. List TWO things you would NOT do even if it meant your country would be destroyed.

___

___

___

3. "It is sweet and proper to die for one's country". Do you agree or disagree with this statement? Give TWO reasons to support your position.

___

___

___

___

___

Activity 3: Perceptions of War

Directions. Answer the following questions after watching each of videos. Read the questions before watching the videos.

1. **https://www.youtube.com/watch?v=i5ufp07bmuw**
2. **https://www.youtube.com/watch?v=P4Lzo_EXXOQ**
3. **https://www.youtube.com/watch?v=SgQhH67oPgY**

1. Whose perspective of war is presented in the video?
2. How do you feel after watching the video? Use your mood list to help you find the most appropriate emotion(s).
3. Would you join the army after watching this video? Why or Why not?
4. Explain ONE difference between the perspectives of war presented in the videos.

Activity 4: The Featured Presentation

Use the checklist below to assess your peers' recitation of "Dulce et Decorum Est".

Checklist for the Poetry Recitation

Directions. The checklist below consists of a list of statements highlighting important things to consider when reciting a poem and three emojis. If your answer to the statement is yes, put a tick beside the statement and under the happy face. If your answer to the statement is no, put a tick beside the statement and under the sad face. If you are unsure, put a tick beside the statement and under the unsure face.

Checklist for Poetry Recitation			
1. Performance is no longer than three minutes.			
2. The words of the poem are said exactly as presented in the text.			
3. The performer adapts the role of the persona in movement, posture and general demeanour.			
4. Performer conveys the appropriate emotion.			
5. Performer makes appropriate use of facial expression, gestures, tone etc. to convey the meaning of the poem.			
6. Performer makes appropriate use of stage.			
7. Performance is audible and confident.			
8. Performance is entertaining.			

Directions. Based on your ticks in the checklist, rate your classmates' recitation of "Dulce et Decorum Est" by shading the stars below. Five stars mean you believe the recitation was excellent. Then justify your rating.

Your Rating	Your Justification
☆☆☆☆☆	

What is the most common rating received by the presenter from your classmates? ____________________

What is your teacher's rating? ____________________

If you have the same rating as your teacher, you earn a  .

Choose TWO areas from the checklist where you ticked 'no' or 'unsure' and make ONE recommendation to the presenter on how he or she could have improved in those areas.

Selected area 1: ____________________

Recommendation: ____________________

____

____

Selected area 2: ____________________

Recommendation: ____________________

____

____

Elements of Poetry in "Dulce et Decorum Est"

Your classmates will present their analysis of "Dulce et Decorum Est". In this analysis, they will identify, explain and discuss the historical background, literary elements, form and literary devices used in the poem. You will be expected to critically assess the analysis being presented. This will be done in a step-by-step process.

Step 1: Listen for Information – While you listen to the analysis, complete the different activities with information presented in the analysis.

Step 2: Consult Your Peers – Share with a peer to see if he/she heard anything you might have missed or if you heard anything, he/she missed.

Step 3: Rate the Analysis – Look at the number of answered and unanswered activities you have and rate the overall analysis.

Historical Background

Directions. In this section, the presenters are expected to provide relevant information for all the areas in the picture below. However, you are only expected to write the ***poet's name, birthday, country of birth, quick facts and other works by the poet*** from the presenters' analysis. Complete the other sections based on your own feelings about the poet.

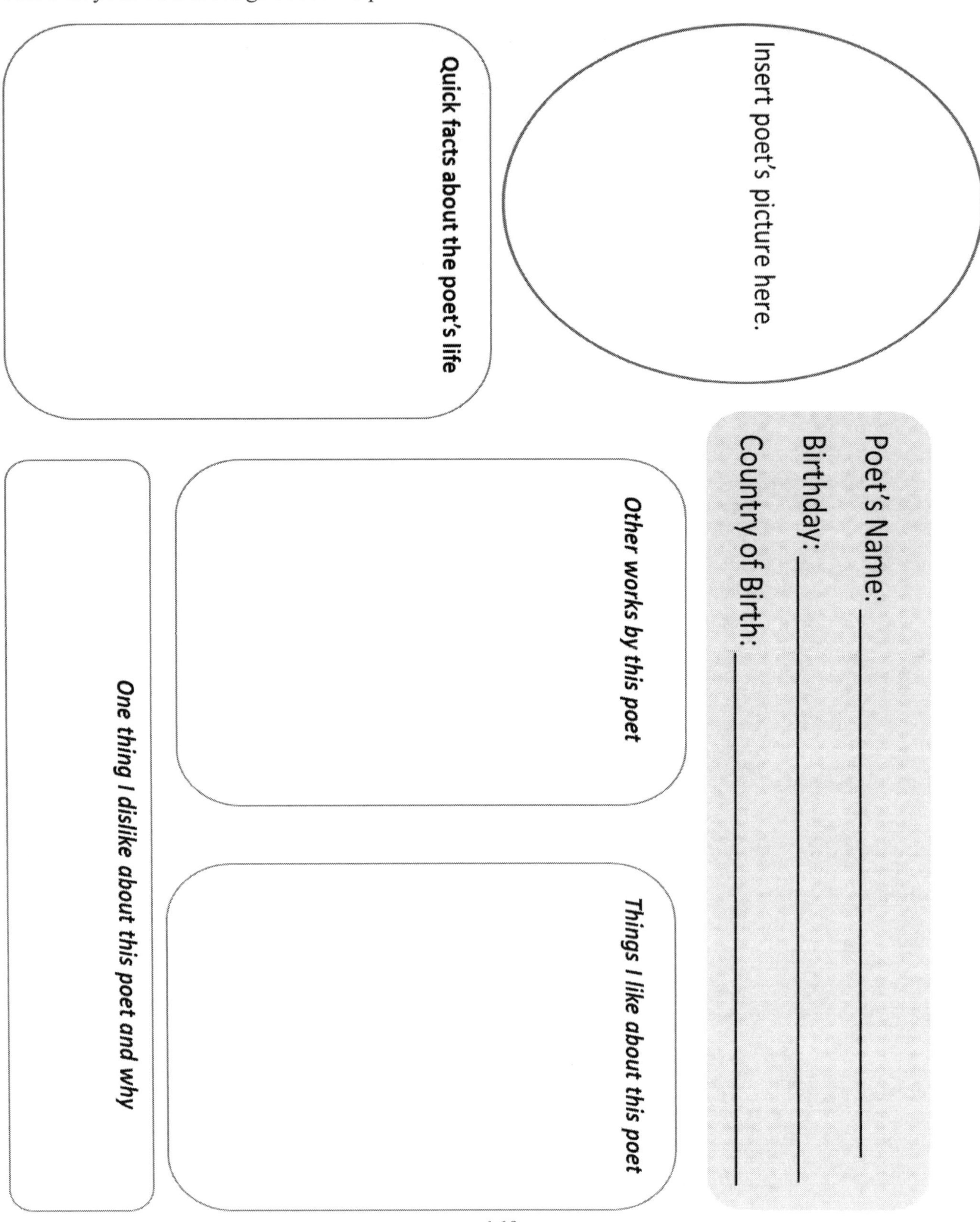

Literary Elements in "Dulce et Decorum Est"

Directions. Write the literary elements identified by the presenter(s). After the presentation, you will be allowed time to identify these elements for yourself and compare your answers to the presenters' answers. Revise your notes on each element if you are unsure. Complete the table as follows:

1. Write the presenters' identifications.
2. Tick whether you agree or disagree with each identification.
3. Whether you agree or disagree, write one piece of evidence from the poem to support your decision.

Characters		
Persona:	**Agree**	**Disagree**
Evidence:		
Tone:	**Agree**	**Disagree**
Evidence:		
Other characters:	**Agree**	**Disagree**
Evidence:		
Type of Narration:	**Agree**	**Disagree**
Evidence:		

Setting		
Time and Place:	**Agree**	**Disagree**
Evidence:		
Mood:	**Agree**	**Disagree**
Evidence:		

Theme		
1st Theme Category: **Message *(one sentence):***	**Agree**	**Disagree**
Evidence		
2nd Theme Category: **Message *(one sentence):***	**Agree**	**Disagree**
Evidence		

Plot in "Dulce et Decorum Est"

Directions. Summarize each stanza in a single sentence. Then, combine the sentences into a paragraph. Use suitable transition words and phrases to make the paragraph more coherent. Remember to use your own words.

Stanza 1:

Stanza 2:

Stanza 3:

Stanza 4:

Stylistics in "Dulce et Decorum Est"

We will look at the form of the poem and the literary devices used.

Form of "Dulce et Decorum Est"

Directions. Fill in the blanks with information from "Dulce et Decorum Est".

"Dulce et Decorum Est" is a ____________________ (*Type of poem*). The poem consists of __________ (*Number of lines*) lines which are divided into _________ (*Number of stanzas*) stanzas. Each stanza is a different type of stanza with first being a ___________ (*Type of stanza*), the second being a _____________ (*Type of stanza*) the third being a _____________ (*Type of stanza*) and the fourth being a _______________ (*Type of stanza*). The poem has ________________ (*Type of rhyme scheme*) and is written in ___________________________ (*Type of rhythm*).

Answer the following questions.

1. Look at the words of the poem as they appear in the <u>World of Poetry</u>. Which stanza stands out and why?

   ____

   ____

   ____

2. What does the inconsistent number of lines in the stanzas contribute to the poem?

   ____

   ____

   ____

   ____

   ____

3. What does the rhyme scheme or the absence of a rhyme scheme contribute to the poem?

   ____

   ____

   ____

   ____

   ____

Literary Devices in "Dulce et Decorum Est"

For each poem, you should be able to:

- ✓ list the main devices used;
- ✓ explain each device used;
- ✓ comment on the effect and effectiveness of each device used.

Activity 1: Identifying the Devices

Directions. Write the names of FOUR literary devices used in the poem. Then, write an example of each of the listed devices from the poem. Ensure you write the line number(s) for each example given.

Literary Devices	Examples
1. ________________:	________________________________
	________________________________
2. ________________:	________________________________
	________________________________
3. ________________:	________________________________
	________________________________
4. ________________:	________________________________
	________________________________

If you have identified a simile or metaphor, explain it by using the formula.

____

____

____

____

____

____

____

____

____

____

____

____

____

____

Activity 2: Imagery

"Dulce et Decorum Est" also makes extensive use of imagery to convey the sound and sense of the poem. Many of these images are also created by the literary devices used in the poem. Complete the table below by putting in the missing information. The first one is done for you.

Devices	Evidence	Type of Imagery
Simile	*Bent double, like old beggars under sacks*	*Visual*
	Knock-kneed, coughing like hags	
Alliteration		
Simile		
	The blood come gargling from the froth-corrupted lungs, (L21-22)	Auditory
	And watch the white eyes writhing in his face, (L19)	Visual
Onomatopoeia	Deaf even to the hoots of tired, outstripped Five-Nines (L7-8)	
Simile	Blood bitter as the cud of vile, incurable sores on innocent tongues, (L21–24)	
Assonance		

To which senses do these images mostly appeal? ____________________

Activity 3: Effect and Effectiveness

Directions. Choose TWO devices identified in "Dulce et Decorum Est" and comment on their effect and effectiveness. If you need to remind yourself of what is required when you are asked to examine or comment on the use of a literary device, read the notes presented of **pages 52 – 53** of this Workbook.

<table>
<tr><td>Device</td><td>Evidence</td></tr>
<tr><td></td><td></td></tr>
<tr><td colspan="2">Effect:</td></tr>
<tr><td colspan="2">Effectiveness:</td></tr>
</table>

<table>
<tr><td>Device</td><td>Evidence</td></tr>
<tr><td></td><td></td></tr>
<tr><td colspan="2">Effect:</td></tr>
<tr><td colspan="2">Effectiveness:</td></tr>
</table>

Assessing Your Peers' Presentation

Directions. Compare the information your peers provided with your own analysis and rate your classmates' analysis of "Dulce et Decorum Est" by shading the stars below. Five stars mean you believe the analysis was excellent. Then justify your rating.

Your Rating	Your Justification
☆☆☆☆☆	

What is the most common rating received by the presenter from your classmates? ___________________

What is your teacher's rating? ____

If you have the same rating as your teacher, you earn a .

Choose ONE element of poetry that you think the presenters need to make improvement in analyzing and make TWO recommendations to the presenters on how they can improve in analyzing that element.

Selected area: ____

Recommendation 1: ____

____

____

____

Recommendation 2: ____

____

____

____

____

Now that you have finished analyzing "Dulce et Decorum Est", look back at the predictions you made before you analyzed the poem and answer the following questions.

1. To what extent were your predictions right?

   Not at all ☐ A small extent ☐ Somewhat ☐ To a large extent ☐ Spot on ☐

2. Explain your selection for question 1.

   ____

   ____

   ____

   ____

   ____

3. Does the poet believe it is sweet and proper to die for one's country? Explain your answer.

   ____

   ____

   ____

   ____

   ____

4. In what way did the historical background of the poem contribute to your understanding of the poem?

   ____

   ____

   ____

   ____

   ____

5. "Dulce et Decorum Est" and 'This is the dark time, my love" share experiences with war."

   Write an essay in which you describe the experience of EACH persona. In this essay, you must also discuss how the persona in EACH poem feels about war and examine ONE device that is used to present the persona's perspective of war in EACH poem.

Checking My Progress

You have just finished the activities on "Dulce et Decorum Est". Before we move to the activities on the next poem, review what you have learnt or are still uncertain about. Do so by first checking the objectives you have accomplished so far.

Directions. Go back to the objectives at the beginning of the activities on "Dulce et Decorum Est". If you think you have accomplished an objective, without looking back at your notes, put a tick in the box ☐ before the objective. If you are unsure you have accomplished the objective, put a question mark (?) and if you are sure you have not accomplished the objective, leave it unchecked (blank). Ensure you pay more attention to your unchecked boxes and the boxes with your question marks as you study. Also, ensure that you can perform the number indicated in each objective (e.g., list **three** genres). You have accomplished the objective when you can list the indicated number (three).

Now complete the 3-2-1 activity below. It works as follows:

Three – Write **three** things you learned from the activities on "Dulce et Decorum Est".

Two – Write **two** things you found interesting or about which you would like to learn more.

One – Write **one** question you still have about the material.

Share your question with your classmates and listen to their responses. Did they clarify things? If not, maybe it is time you did some independent research.

Finally, record ONE question from one of your classmates and provide an answer to that classmate.

Checking What I Know!!!

3. ____

____

____

2. ____

____

1. ____

Helping My Peers!!!

Peer's question: ____

____

My answer: ____

____

____

"Death, be not proud ..." by John Donne

Objectives

After completing the activities on "Death, be not proud ...", you should be able to accurately:

- ☐ make predictions based on the title of the poem;
- ☐ identify the elements of poetry in the poem;
- ☐ critically assess your peers' presentation and analysis of the poem;
- ☐ examine the effect and effectiveness of literary devices used in the poem;
- ☐ examine the use of apostrophes in literature.

Getting Started

Activity 1: Before you begin ...

Before you begin to read any piece of writing, it is usually a good idea to think of what you already know about the topic. Write down what you know about the title of the poem by completing the table below. The table should be completed as follows:

It says ... - Write the title of the poem.

I know ... - Write what you know about the title. In this case, what is death? How do people usually feel about death? What does the comma in the title indicate? How does the persona feel about death?

And so ... - Make a prediction about what you think the poem will be about based on the stated title and what you know about the title.

It says ...	
I know ...	
And so ...	

Activity 2: Dear Death

Directions. If you could speak to death, what would you say? Write an informal letter to death expressing your thoughts and emotions about it.

Dear Death,

Activity 3: The Featured Presentation

Use the checklist below to assess your peers' recitation of "Death, be not proud ...".

Checklist for the Poetry Recitation

Directions. The checklist below consists of a list of statements highlighting important things to consider when reciting a poem and three emojis. If your answer to the statement is yes, put a tick beside the statement and under the happy face. If your answer to the statement is no, put a tick beside the statement and under the sad face. If you are unsure, put a tick beside the statement and under the unsure face.

Checklist for Poetry Recitation			
1. Performance is no longer than three minutes.			
2. The words of the poem are said exactly as presented in the text.			
3. The performer adapts the role of the persona in movement, posture and general demeanour.			
4. Performer conveys the appropriate emotion.			
5. Performer makes appropriate use of facial expression, gestures, tone etc. to convey the meaning of the poem.			
6. Performer makes appropriate use of stage.			
7. Performance is audible and confident.			
8. Performance is entertaining.			

Directions. Based on your ticks in the checklist, rate your classmates' recitation of "Death, be not proud ..." by shading the stars below. Five stars mean you believe the recitation was excellent. Then, justify your rating.

Your Rating	**Your Justification**
☆☆☆☆☆	

What is the most common rating received by the presenter from your classmates? ____________________

What is your teacher's rating? ____

If you have the same rating as your teacher, you earn a  .

Choose TWO areas from the checklist where you ticked 'no' or 'unsure' and make ONE recommendation to the presenters on how they could have improved in those areas.

Selected area 1: ____

Recommendation: ____

____

____

____

Selected area 2: ____

Recommendation: ____

____

____

____

Elements of Poetry in "Death, be not proud ..."

Your classmates will present their analysis of "Death, be not proud ...". In this analysis, they will identify, explain and discuss the historical background, literary elements, form and literary devices used in the poem. You will be expected to critically assess the analysis being presented. This will be done in a step-by-step process.

Step 1: Listen for Information – While you listen to the analysis, complete the different activities with information presented in the analysis.

Step 2: Consult Your Peers – Share with a peer to see if he/she heard anything you might have missed or if you heard anything, he/she missed.

Step 3: Rate the Analysis – Look at the number of answered and unanswered activities you have and rate the overall analysis.

Historical Background

Directions. In this section, the presenters are expected to provide relevant information for all the areas in the picture below. However, you are only expected to write the ***poet's name, birthday, country of birth, quick facts and other works by the poet*** from the presenters' analysis. Complete the other sections based on your own feelings about the poet.

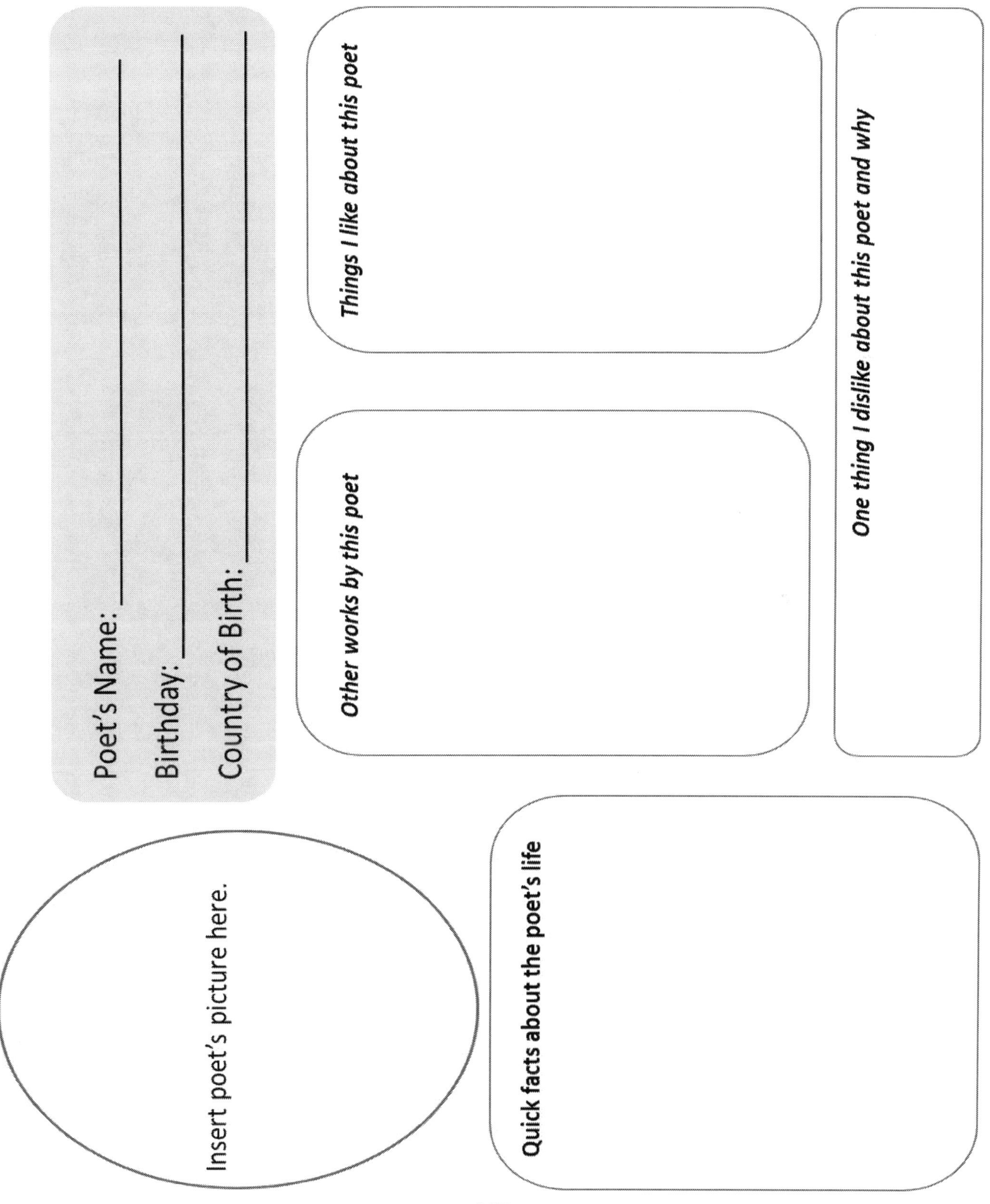

Literary Elements in "Death, be not proud ..."

Directions. Write the literary elements identified by the presenter(s). After the presentation, you will be allowed time to identify these elements for yourself and compare your answers to the presenters' answers. Revise your notes on each element if you are unsure. Complete the table as follows:

1. Write the presenters' identifications.
2. Tick whether you agree or disagree with each identification.
3. Whether you agree or disagree, write one piece of evidence from the poem to support your decision.

Characters		
Persona:	**Agree**	**Disagree**
Evidence:		
Tone:	**Agree**	**Disagree**
Evidence:		
Other characters:	**Agree**	**Disagree**
Evidence:		
Type of Narration:	**Agree**	**Disagree**
Evidence:		

Setting		
Time and Place:	**Agree**	**Disagree**
Evidence:		
Mood:	**Agree**	**Disagree**
Evidence:		

Theme		
1st Theme Category: **Message *(one sentence):***	**Agree**	**Disagree**
Evidence		
2nd Theme Category: **Message *(one sentence):***	**Agree**	**Disagree**
Evidence		

Plot in "Death, be not proud ..."

Directions. In no more than ONE paragraph, summarize the poem. Use suitable transitional words and phrases to make the paragraph more coherent. Remember to use your own words.

List THREE reasons why the poet is telling Death it should not be proud.

If Death should not be proud, how should it feel? Give ONE reason to support your answer. Your reason should be supported by evidence from the poem.

Stylistics in "Death, be not proud ..."

We will look at the form of the poem and the literary devices used.

Form of "Death, be not proud ..."

Directions. Fill in the blanks with information from "Death, be not proud ...".

"Death, be not proud ..." is a ____________________ which consists of ____________ lines.
Type of poem *Number of lines*

The poem is divided into an ____________ in which the poet ______________________________
Name of the first eight lines *Main idea in this section*

____,

and a ____________ in which the poet ______________________________
Name of the last six lines

____.
Main idea in this section

The poem has ______________________ and is written in ____________________.
Type of rhyme scheme *Type of rhythm*

Answer the following questions.

1. Why is Death capitalised throughout the poem?

____

____

____

____

____

____

2. Why are lines 13 and 14 indented?

____

____

____

____

____

Literary Devices in "Death, be not proud ..."

Activity 1: Identifying the Devices

Directions. Write the names of FOUR literary devices used in the poem. Then, write an example of each of the listed devices from the poem. Ensure you write the line number(s) for each example given.

Literary Devices	**Examples**
1. ______________________:	______________________________
	______________________________
2. ______________________:	______________________________
	______________________________
3. ______________________:	______________________________
	______________________________
4. ______________________:	______________________________
	______________________________

If you have identified a simile or metaphor, explain it by using the formula.

____

____

____

____

____

____

____

____

____

Explain a sound device used in the poem.

____

____

____

____

____

____

____

Apostrophe

An apostrophe is a type of poem in which the speaker addresses a person, thing or idea that is unable to respond. When the speaker addresses a person, he/she may be unable to respond because the person is not physically present or dead. Apostrophes allow the speaker the freedom to honestly express his/her inner thoughts without interruption or discussion. They are also frequently used to highlight the importance or significance of the person, thing or idea being addressed. An example of an apostrophe is *Twinkle Twinkle Little Star*. In this nursery rhyme, the speaker is talking to an inanimate object – a star – which is unable to respond because stars do not speak. The speaker also highlights the importance of the star by comparing it to a diamond (a precious jewel). Can you find another song that is an apostrophe? Insert the lyrics below

Answer the following questions.

1. What person/thing/idea that is unable to respond is being addressed in the song?

   ____

2. How do you know he/she/it is unable to respond? ____________________________

   ____

   ____

3. How does the singer feel about the person/thing/idea being addressed? Give evidence from the song to support your answer.

   ____

   ____

   ____

Activity 2: Use of Apostrophe in "Death, be not proud …"

Directions. Answer the following questions,

1. What person/thing/idea that is unable to respond is being addressed in the poem?

   ____

2. How do you know he/she/it is unable to respond? ____________________________

   ____

   ____

3. How does the writer feel about the person/thing/idea being addressed? Give evidence from the poem to support your answer.

   ____

   ____

   ____

   ____

4. What is the effect of using an apostrophe to highlight this attitude towards the addressee?

   ____

   ____

   ____

   ____

   ____

   ____

   ____

Activity 3: Effect and Effectiveness

Directions. Choose TWO devices identified in "Death, be not proud ..." and comment on their effect and effectiveness.

Device	**Evidence**
Effect:	
Effectiveness:	

Device	**Evidence**
Effect:	
Effectiveness:	

Assessing Your Peers' Presentation

Directions. Compare the information your peers provided with your own analysis and rate your classmates' analysis of "Death, be not proud ..." by shading the stars below. Five stars mean you believe the analysis was excellent. Then, justify your rating.

Your Rating	Your Justification
☆☆☆☆☆	

What is the most common rating received by the presenters from your classmates? ____________

What is your teacher's rating? ____________

If you have the same rating as your teacher, you earn a ____________.

Choose ONE element of poetry that you think the presenters need to make improvement in analyzing and make TWO recommendations to the presenters on how they can improve in analyzing that element.

Selected area: ____________

Recommendation 1: ____________

Recommendation 2: ____________

Now that you have finished analyzing "Death, be not proud ...", look back at the predictions you made before you analyzed the poem and answer the following questions.

1. To what extent were your predictions right?

   Not at all ☐ A small extent ☐ Somewhat ☐ To a large extent ☐ Spot on ☐

2. Explain your selection for question 1. ______________________________

   ____
   ____
   ____
   ____
   ____

3. Compare the persona's attitude towards death to your own as presented in your letter to death?

   ____
   ____
   ____
   ____
   ____
   ____
   ____
   ____

4. "Death, be not proud ..." and "This is the dark time, my love" both focus on death.

   Write an essay in which you describe the causes of death in EACH poem. In this essay, you must also compare EACH persona's attitude towards death in EACH poem and examine ONE device that is used to present death in EACH poem.

Use the rubric for poetry essays in the CXC English syllabus to assess your essay writing skills. Then, ask your classmate to use the same rubric to assess your essay while you do the same for him/her. Revise your essay before presenting it to your teacher.

Checking My Progress

You have just finished the activities on "Death, be not proud ...". Before we move to the activities on the next poem, review what you have learnt or are still uncertain about. Do so by first checking the objectives you have accomplished so far.

Directions. Go back to the objectives at the beginning of the activities on "Death, be not proud ...". If you think you have accomplished an objective, without looking back at your notes, ☐ put a tick in the box before the objective. If you are unsure you have accomplished the objective, put a question mark (?) and if you are sure you have not accomplished the objective, leave it unchecked (blank). Ensure you pay more attention to your unchecked boxes and the boxes with your question marks as you study. Also, ensure that you can perform the number indicated in each objective (e.g., list **three** genres). You have accomplished the objective when you can list the indicated number (three).

Now complete the 3-2-1 activity below. It works as follows:

Three – Write **three** things you learned from the activities on "Death, be not proud ...".

Two – Write **two** things you found interesting or about which you would like to learn more.

One – Write **one** question you still have about the material.

Share your question with your classmates and listen to their responses. Did they clarify things? If not, maybe it is time you did some independent research.

Finally, record ONE question from one of your classmates and provide an answer to that classmate.

Checking What I Know!!!

3. ____

____

____

2. ____

____

1. ____

Helping My Peers!!!

Peer's question: ____

____

My answer: ____

____

____

"South" by Kamau Brathwaite

Objectives

After completing the activities on "South", you should be able to accurately:

- ☐ make predictions based on the title of the poem;
- ☐ identify the elements of poetry in the poem;
- ☐ critically assess your peers' presentation and analysis of the poem;
- ☐ examine the effect and effectiveness of literary devices used in the poem;
- ☐ compare northern and southern countries.

Getting Started

Activity 1: Before you begin …

Before you begin to read any piece of writing, it is usually a good idea to think of what you already know about the topic. Write down what you know about the title of the poem by completing the table below. The table should be completed as follows:

It says … - Write the title of the poem.

I know … - Write what you know about the title. In this case, what does the word 'south' bring to your mind? What are some characteristics of countries in the 'south'?

And so … - Make a prediction about what you think the poem will be about based on the stated title and what you know about the title.

It says …	
I know …	
And so …	

Activity 2: No Place Like Home

Directions. Have you ever spent any extended time away from your home? Maybe you spent a holiday in another part of your country or in another country. If you have never spent any extended period away from home, imagine you could spend a holiday in any place of your choosing.

1. How did/would you feel before you went on your holiday? Why?

   ____

   ____

   ____

2. After some time, what are some things you missed/would have missed about your home?

   ____

   ____

   ____

   ____

3. How did/would you feel when you returned home? Why?

   ____

   ____

   ____

   ____

Activity 3: North and South

Directions. On the globe below, colour the north in blue and the south in red. Then, answer the questions that follow.

Answer the following questions.

1. List FIVE countries in the north. List your own country if it is located in the north.

   ____

   ____

2. List FIVE countries in the south. List your own country if it is located in the south.

   ____

   ____

Fill in the necessary information in the table below.

Characteristics	**North**	**South**
Climate		
Bodies of Water		
Disposition of the People		
Advantages of living in the …		
Disadvantages of living in the …		
Place you prefer		

Activity 4: The Featured Presentation

Use the checklist below to assess your peers' recitation of "South".

Checklist for the Poetry Recitation

Directions. The checklist below consists of a list of statements highlighting important things to consider when reciting a poem and three emojis. If your answer to the statement is yes, put a tick beside the statement and under the happy face. If your answer to the statement is no, put a tick beside the statement and under the sad face. If you are unsure, put a tick beside the statement and under the unsure face.

Checklist for Poetry Recitation			
1. Performance is no longer than three minutes.			
2. The words of the poem are said exactly as presented in the text.			
3. The performer adapts the role of the persona in movement, posture and general demeanour.			
4. Performer conveys the appropriate emotion.			
5. Performer makes appropriate use of facial expression, gestures, tone etc. to convey the meaning of the poem.			
6. Performer makes appropriate use of stage.			
7. Performance is audible and confident.			
8. Performance is entertaining.			

Directions. Based on your ticks in the checklist, rate your classmates' recitation of "South" by shading the stars below. Five stars mean you believe the recitation was excellent. Then, justify your rating.

Your Rating	Your Justification
☆☆☆☆☆	

What is the most common rating received by the presenter from your classmates? ______________

What is your teacher's rating? ____

If you have the same rating as your teacher, you earn a  .

Choose TWO areas from the checklist where you ticked 'no' or 'unsure' and make ONE recommendation to the presenter on how he or she could have improved in those areas.

Selected area 1: ____

Recommendation: ____

____

____

Selected area 2: ____

Recommendation: ____

____

____

Elements of Poetry in "South"

Your classmates will present their analysis of "South". In this analysis, they will identify, explain and discuss the historical background, literary elements, form and literary devices used in the poem. You will be expected to critically assess the analysis being presented. This will be done in a step-by-step process.

Step 1: Listen for Information – While you listen to the analysis, complete the different activities with information presented in the analysis.

Step 2: Consult Your Peers – Share with a peer to see if he/she heard anything you might have missed or if you heard anything, he/she missed.

Step 3: Rate the Analysis – Look at the number of answered and unanswered activities you have and rate the overall analysis.

Historical Background

Directions. In this section, the presenters are expected to provide relevant information for all the areas in the picture below. However, you are only expected to write the ***poet's name, birthday, country of birth, quick facts and other works by the poet*** from the presenters' analysis. Complete the other sections based on your own feelings about the poet.

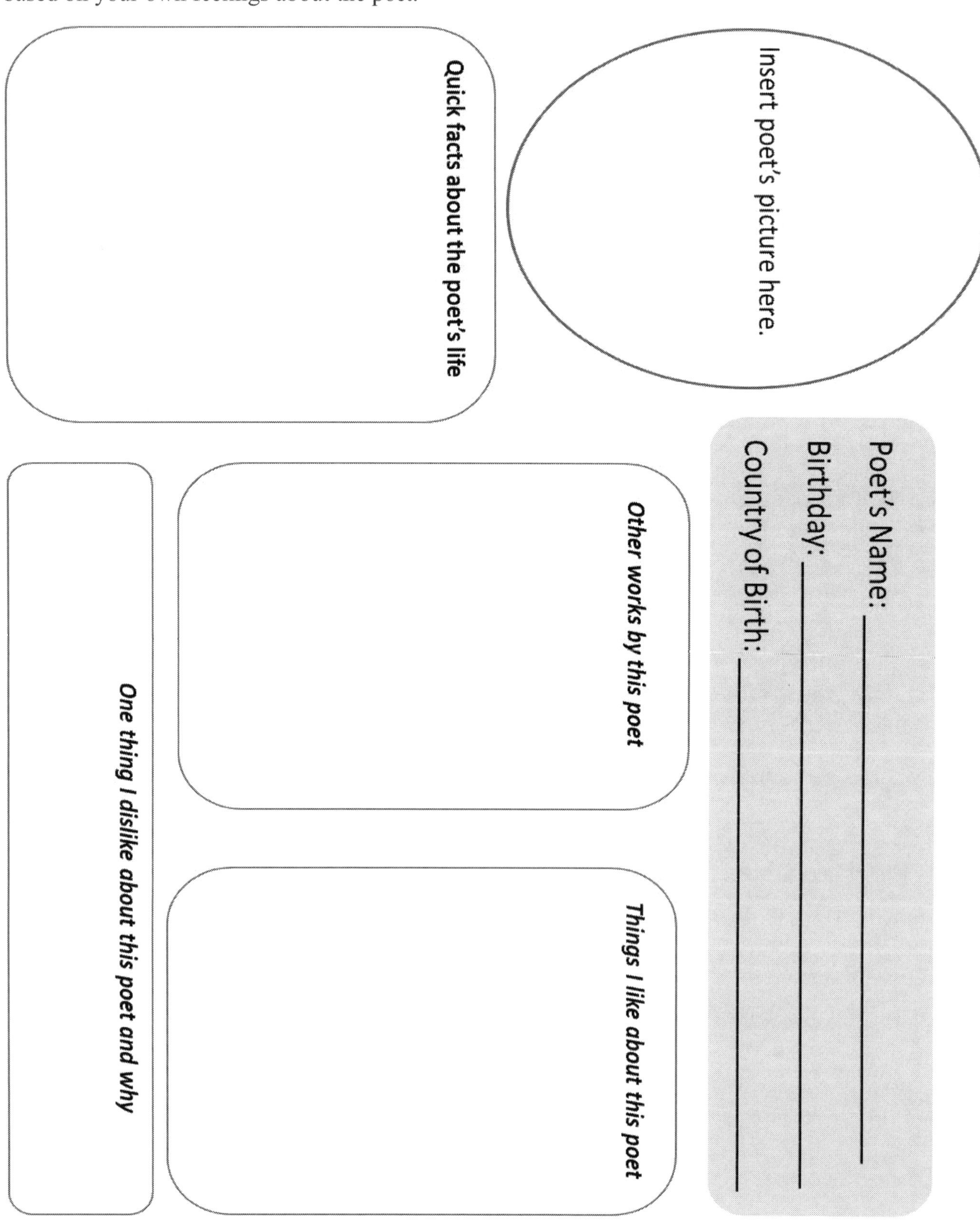

Literary Elements in "South"

Directions. Write the literary elements identified by the presenter(s). After the presentation, you will be allowed time to identify these elements for yourself and compare your answers to the presenters' answers. Revise your notes on each element if you are unsure. Complete the table as follows:

1. Write the presenters' identifications.
2. Tick whether you agree or disagree with each identification.
3. Whether you agree or disagree, write one piece of evidence from the poem to support your decision.

Characters		
Persona:	**Agree**	**Disagree**
Evidence:		
Tone:	**Agree**	**Disagree**
Evidence:		
Other characters:	**Agree**	**Disagree**
Evidence:		
Type of Narration:	**Agree**	**Disagree**
Evidence:		

Setting		
Time and Place:	**Agree**	**Disagree**
Evidence:		
Mood:	**Agree**	**Disagree**
Evidence:		

Theme		
1st Theme Category: **Message** ***(one sentence):***	**Agree**	**Disagree**
Evidence		
2nd Theme Category: **Message** ***(one sentence):***	**Agree**	**Disagree**
Evidence		

Plot in "South"

Directions. Summarize each stanza in a single sentence. Then, combine the sentences into a paragraph. Use suitable transition words and phrases to make the paragraph more coherent. Remember to use your own words.

Stanza 1:

Stanza 2:

Stanza 3:

Stanza 4:

Stanza 5:

Stanza 6:

Stylistics in "South"

We will look at the form of the poem and the literary devices used.

Form of "South"

Directions. Fill in the blanks with information from "South".

"South" is a ____________________ (*Type of poem*). The poem consists of ___________ (*Number of lines*) lines which are divided into ________________ (*Number of stanzas*) stanzas. There are three types of stanzas in the poem. The first four stanzas are ___________ (*Type of stanza*), the fifth is a _____________ (*Type of stanza*) and the sixth is a _____________ (*Type of stanza*). The poem has ___________________ (*Type of rhyme scheme*) and is written in ____________________________ (*Type of rhythm*).

Literary Devices in "South"

Activity 1: Identifying the Devices

Directions. Write the names of FOUR literary devices used in the poem. Then, write an example of each of the listed devices from the poem. Ensure you write the line number(s) for each example given.

Literary Devices	**Examples**
1. ________________________:	____ ____
2. ________________________:	____ ____
3. ________________________:	____ ____
4. ________________________:	____ ____

If you have identified a simile or metaphor, explain it by using the formula.

____

____

____

Activity 2: Contrast – North vs South

Directions. In the poem, the persona contrasts his experiences living in the north with those he had while living in the south. Complete the table below with the information presented in the poem.

Characteristics	North	South
Weather		
Bodies of Water		
Disposition of the People		
Features of the place		
Emotions the Persona felt in each place		

Activity 3: Effect and Effectiveness

Directions. Choose TWO devices identified in "South" and comment on their effect and effectiveness. If you need to remind yourself of what is required when you are asked to examine or comment on the use of a literary device, read the notes presented of **pages 52 – 53** of this Workbook.

Device	**Evidence**
Effect:	
Effectiveness:	

Device	**Evidence**
Effect:	
Effectiveness:	

Assessing Your Peers' Presentation

Directions. Compare the information your peers provided with your own analysis and rate your classmates' analysis of "South" by shading the stars below. Five stars mean you believe the analysis was excellent. Then, justify your rating.

Your Rating	Your Justification
☆☆☆☆☆	

What is the most common rating received by the presenter from your classmates? ___________________

What is your teacher's rating? ___________________

If you have the same rating as your teacher, you earn a .

Choose ONE element of poetry that you think the presenters need to make improvement in analyzing and make TWO recommendations to the presenters on how they can improve in analyzing that element.

Selected area: ___________________

Recommendation 1: ___________________

Recommendation 2: ___________________

Now that you have finished analyzing "South", look back at the predictions you made before you analyzed the poem and answer the following questions.

1. To what extent were your predictions right?

   Not at all ☐ A small extent ☐ Somewhat ☐ To a large extent ☐ Spot on ☐

2. Explain your selection for question 1.

   ____

   ____

   ____

   ____

   ____

3. In what way did the historical background of the poem contribute to your understanding of the poem?

   ____

   ____

   ____

   ____

   ____

   ____

   ____

4. "South" and "Once Upon A Time" present personas who are longing for the past".

   Write an essay in which you describe an aspect of their past life EACH persona wants to reclaim. In this essay, you must also discuss the likelihood the persona in EACH poem will achieve what he longs for and examine ONE device that is used to explore the theme of desire in EACH poem.

Use the rubric for poetry essays in the CXC English syllabus to assess your essay writing skills. Then, ask your classmate to use the same rubric to assess your essay while you do the same for him/her. Revise your essay before presenting it to your teacher.

Checking My Progress

You have just finished the activities on "South". Before we move to the activities on the next poem, review what you have learnt or are still uncertain about. Do so by first checking the objectives you have accomplished so far.

Directions. Go back to the objectives at the beginning of the activities on "South". If you think you have accomplished an objective, without looking back at your notes, put a tick in the box ☐ before the objective. If you are unsure you have accomplished the objective, put a question mark (?) and if you are sure you have not accomplished the objective, leave it unchecked (blank). Ensure you pay more attention to your unchecked boxes and the boxes with your question marks as you study. Also, ensure that you can perform the number indicated in each objective (e.g., list **three** genres). You have accomplished the objective when you can list the indicated number (three).

Now complete the 3-2-1 activity below. It works as follows:

Three – Write three things you learned from the activities on "South".

Two – Write two things you found interesting or about which you would like to learn more.

One – Write one question you still have about the material.

Share your question with your classmates and listen to their responses. Did they clarify things? If not, maybe it is time you did some independent research.

Finally, record ONE question from one of your classmates and provide an answer to that classmate.

Checking What I Know!!!

3. ______________________________

____

____

2. ______________________________

____

1. ______________________________

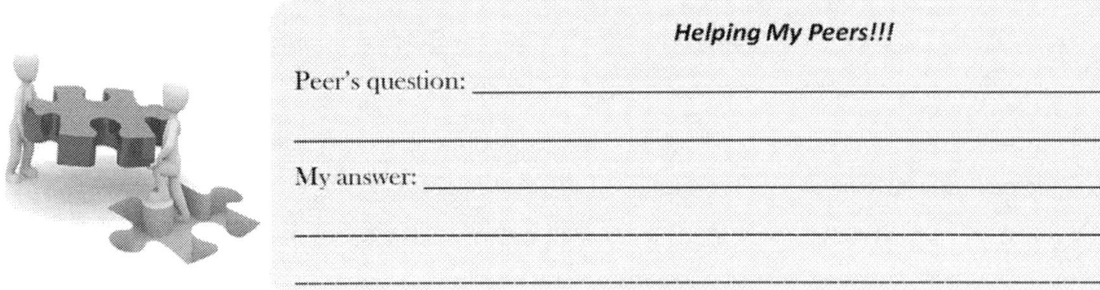

Helping My Peers!!!

Peer's question: ______________________________

____

My answer: ______________________________

____

____

"Sonnet Composed Upon Westminster Bridge" by William Wordsworth

Objectives

After completing the activities on "Sonnet Composed Upon Westminster Bridge", you should be able to accurately:

- ☐ make predictions based on the title of the poem;
- ☐ identify the elements of poetry in the poem;
- ☐ identify the features of a sonnet;
- ☐ critically assess your peers' presentation and analysis of the poem;
- ☐ examine the effect and effectiveness of literary devices used in the poem;
- ☐ write sonnets.

Getting Started

Activity 1: Before you begin …

Before you begin to read any piece of writing, it is usually a good idea to think of what you already know about the topic. Write down what you know about the title of the poem by completing the table below. The table should be completed as follows:

It says … - Write the title of the poem.

I know … - Write what you know about the title. In this case, what is a sonnet? Where is Westminster Bridge? What do you think a sonnet that is composed upon Westminster Bridge would include?

And so … - Make a prediction about what you think the poem will be about based on the stated title and what you know about the title.

It says …	
I know …	
And so …	

Activity 2: The Most Beautiful Place on Earth

Directions. Write the name and insert a picture of a place you consider to be the most beautiful place on earth.

Insert picture here.

____

1. List TWO things you admire the most in this place.

____

____

2. List TWO emotions you feel while being in or looking at this place.

____

____

3. When is this place most beautiful? At what time of the day/year? Explain your answer.

____

____

____

____

____

____

____

Activity 3: City Views

Directions. Write the name and insert a picture of a town or a city near you.

Insert picture here.

____

In column A below, make a list of things that are unattractive, or you dislike about this city. In column B, make a list of things you find attractive, or you like about this city.

Column A	Column B

When is this place most beautiful? At what time of the day/year? Explain your answer.

Activity 4: The Featured Presentation

Directions. Use the checklist below to assess your peers' recitation of "Sonnet Composed Upon Westminster Bridge".

Checklist for the Poetry Recitation

Directions. The checklist below consists of a list of statements highlighting important things to consider when reciting a poem and three emojis. If your answer to the statement is yes, put a tick beside the statement and under the happy face. If your answer to the statement is no, put a tick beside the statement and under the sad face. If you are unsure, put a tick beside the statement and under the unsure face.

Checklist for Poetry Recitation	(happy face)	(unsure face)	(sad face)
1. Performance is no longer than three minutes.			
2. The words of the poem are said exactly as presented in the text.			
3. The performer adapts the role of the persona in movement, posture and general demeanour.			
4. Performer conveys the appropriate emotion.			
5. Performer makes appropriate use of facial expression, gestures, tone etc. to convey the meaning of the poem.			
6. Performer makes appropriate use of stage.			
7. Performance is audible and confident.			
8. Performance is entertaining.			

Directions. Based on your ticks in the checklist, rate your classmates' recitation of "Sonnet Composed Upon Westminster Bridge" by shading the stars below. Five stars mean you believe the recitation was excellent. Then, justify your rating.

Your Rating	**Your Justification**
☆☆☆☆☆	

What is the most common rating received by the presenters from your classmates? ________________

What is your teacher's rating? ____

If you have the same rating as your teacher, you earn a .

Choose TWO areas from the checklist where you ticked 'no' or 'unsure' and make ONE recommendation to the presenter on how he or she could have improved in those areas.

Selected area 1: ____

Recommendation: ____

____

____

Selected area 2: ____

Recommendation: ____

____

____

Elements of Poetry in "Sonnet Composed Upon Westminster Bridge"

Your classmates will present their analysis of "Sonnet Composed Upon Westminster Bridge". In this analysis, they will identify, explain and discuss the historical background, literary elements, form and literary devices used in the poem. You will be expected to critically assess the analysis being presented. This will be done in a step-by-step process.

Step 1: Listen for Information – While you listen to the analysis, complete the different activities with information presented in the analysis.

Step 2: Consult Your Peers – Share with a peer to see if he/she heard anything you might have missed or if you heard anything, he/she missed.

Step 3: Rate the Analysis – Look at the number of answered and unanswered activities you have and rate the overall analysis.

Historical Background

Directions. In this section, the presenters are expected to provide relevant information for all the areas in the picture below. However, you are only expected to write the ***poet's name, birthday, country of birth, quick facts and other works by the poet*** from the presenters' analysis. Complete the other sections based on your own feelings about the poet.

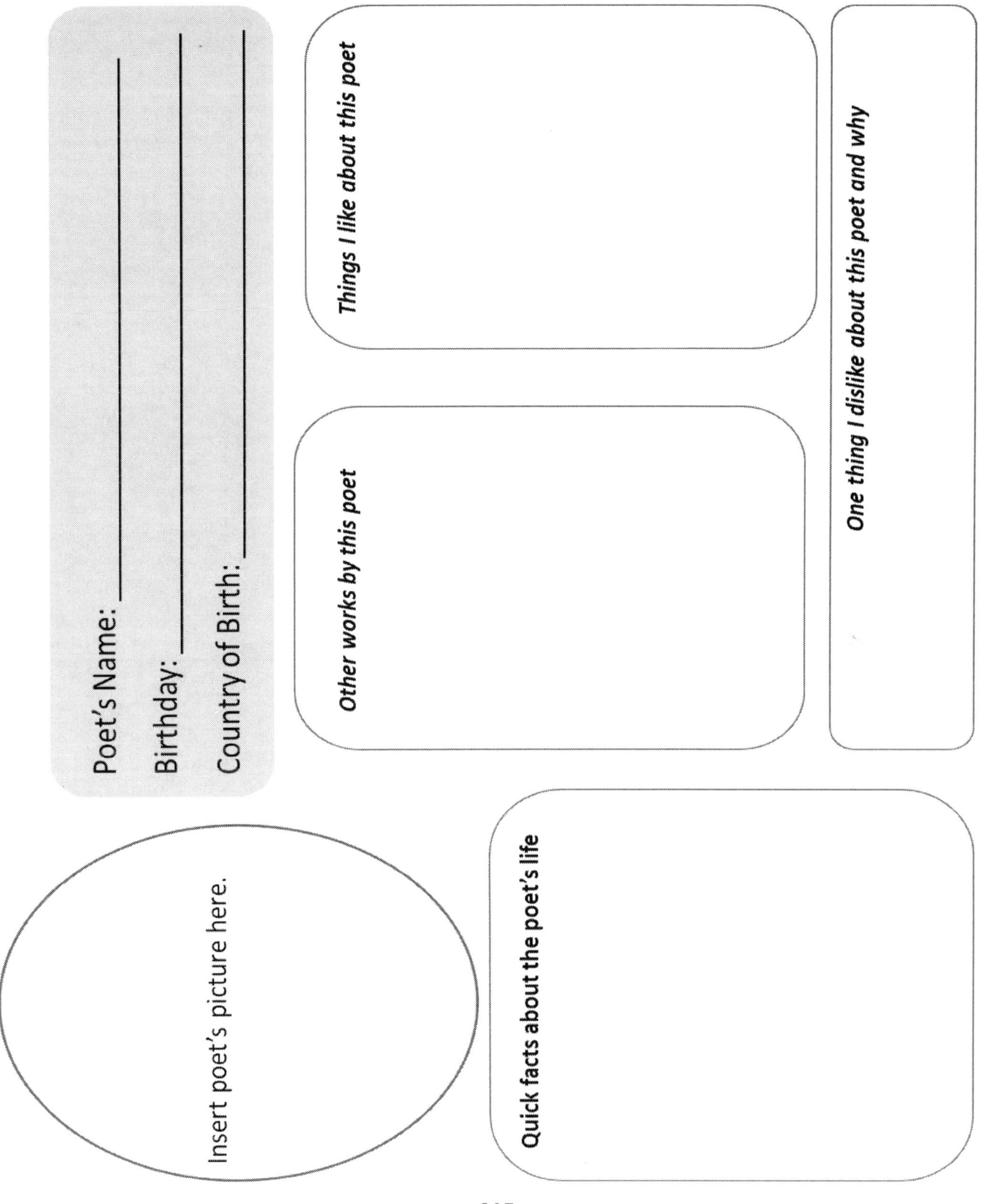

Literary Elements in "Sonnet Composed Upon Westminster Bridge"

Directions. Write the literary elements identified by the presenter(s). After the presentation, you will be allowed time to identify these elements for yourself and compare your answers to the presenters' answers. Revise your notes on each element if you are unsure. Complete the table as follows:

1. Write the presenters' identifications.
2. Tick whether you agree or disagree with each identification.
3. Whether you agree or disagree, write one piece of evidence from the poem to support your decision.

Characters		
Persona:	**Agree**	**Disagree**
Evidence:		
Tone:	**Agree**	**Disagree**
Evidence:		
Other characters:	**Agree**	**Disagree**
Evidence:		
Type of Narration:	**Agree**	**Disagree**
Evidence:		

Setting		
Time and Place:	**Agree**	**Disagree**
Evidence:		
Mood:	**Agree**	**Disagree**
Evidence:		

Theme		
1st Theme Category: **Message *(one sentence):***	**Agree**	**Disagree**
Evidence		
2nd Theme Category: **Message *(one sentence):***	**Agree**	**Disagree**
Evidence		

Plot in "Sonnet Composed Upon Westminster Bridge"

Directions. Summarize the poem in ONE paragraph. Use suitable transition words and phrases to make the paragraph more coherent. Remember to use your own words.

____

____

____

____

____

____

____

____

____

____

____

____

____

Stylistics in "Sonnet Composed Upon Westminster Bridge"

We will look at the form of the poem and the literary devices used.

Form of "Sonnet Composed Upon Westminster Bridge"

Directions. Fill in the blanks with information from "Sonnet Composed Upon Westminster Bridge".

"Sonnet Composed Upon Westminster Bridge" is a ________________ (*Type of poem*) which consists of ___________ (*Number of lines*) lines. The poem is divided into an _______________ (*Name of the first eight lines*) in which the poet __________________________ (*Main idea in this section*) ______________________________, and a ________________ (*Name of the last six lines*) in which the poet ________________ ____ (*Main idea in this section*).

The poem has ______________________________ (*Type of rhyme scheme*) and is written in _________________________ (*Type of rhythm*).

Literary Devices in "Sonnet Composed Upon Westminster Bridge"

Activity 1: Identifying the Devices

Directions. Write the names of FOUR literary devices used in the poem. Then, write an example of each of the listed devices from the poem. Ensure you write the line number(s) for each example given.

Literary Devices	**Examples**
1. ____________________:	______________________________
2. ____________________:	______________________________
3. ____________________:	______________________________
4. ____________________:	______________________________

If you have identified a simile or metaphor, explain it by using the formula.

Identify TWO types of imagery used in the poem.

Activity 2: Effect and Effectiveness

Directions. Choose TWO devices identified in "Sonnet Composed Upon Westminster Bridge" and comment on their effect and effectiveness. If you need to remind yourself of what is required when you are asked to examine or comment on the use of a literary device, read the notes presented of pages 52 – 53 of this Workbook.

Device	**Evidence**
Effect:	
Effectiveness:	

Device	**Evidence**
Effect:	
Effectiveness:	

Assessing Your Peers' Presentation

Directions. Compare the information your peers provided with your own analysis and rate your classmates' analysis of "Sonnet Composed Upon Westminster Bridge" by shading the stars below. Five stars mean you believe the analysis was excellent. Then justify your rating.

Your Rating	Your Justification
☆☆☆☆☆	

What is the most common rating received by the presenter from your classmates? ______________

What is your teacher's rating? ______________

If you have the same rating as your teacher, you earn a .

Choose ONE element of poetry that you think the presenters need to make improvement in analyzing and make TWO recommendations to the presenters on how they can improve in analyzing that element.

Selected area: ______________

Recommendation 1: ______________

Recommendation 2: ______________

Now that you have finished analyzing "Sonnet Composed Upon Westminster Bridge" look back at the predictions you made before you analyzed the poem and answer the following questions.

1. To what extent were your predictions right?

   Not at all ☐ A small extent ☐ Somewhat ☐ To a large extent ☐ Spot on ☐

2. Explain your selection for question 1.

   ____

   ____

   ____

   ____

3. Critics have argued that Wordworth's view of London, as presented in this poem is unrealistic. Do you agree with this statement? Why or Why not?

   ____

   ____

   ____

   ____

   ____

4. Use thc attractive and unattractive features of your city or town to create a sonnet. Your sonnet should include:
   - ✓ 14 lines
   - ✓ a contrast between the octave and the sestet
   - ✓ ONE simile, ONE metaphor and ONE personification
   - ✓ at least THREE types of imagery

Earn a 

for creating the best sonnet

Checking My Progress

You have just finished the activities on "Sonnet Composed Upon Westminster Bridge". Before we move to the activities on the next poem, review what you have learnt or are still uncertain about. Do so by first checking the objectives you have accomplished so far.

Directions. Go back to the objectives at the beginning of the activities on "Sonnet Composed Upon Westminster Bridge". If you think you have accomplished an objective, without looking back at your notes, put a tick in the box ☐ before the objective. If you are unsure you have accomplished the objective, put a question mark (?) and if you are sure you have not accomplished the objective, leave it unchecked (blank). Ensure you pay more attention to your unchecked boxes and the boxes with your question marks as you study. Also, ensure that you can perform the number indicated in each objective (e.g., list **three** genres). You have accomplished the objective when you can list the indicated number (three).

Now complete the 3-2-1 activity below. It works as follows:

Three – Write **three** things you learned from the activities on "Sonnet Composed Upon Westminster Bridge".

Two – Write **two** things you found interesting or about which you would like to learn more.

One – Write **one** question you still have about the material.

Share your question with your classmates and listen to their responses. Did they clarify things? If not, maybe it is time you did some independent research.

Finally, record ONE question from one of your classmates and provide an answer to that classmate.

Checking What I Know!!!

3. ____

____

____

2. ____

____

1. ____

Helping My Peers!!!

Peer's question: ____

____

My answer: ____

____

____

"Landscape Painter, Jamaica" by Vivian Virtue

Objectives

After completing the activities on "Landscape Painter, Jamaica", you should be able to accurately:

- ☐ make predictions based on the title of the poem;
- ☐ identify the elements of poetry in the poem;
- ☐ critically assess your peers' presentation and analysis of the poem;
- ☐ examine the effect and effectiveness of literary devices used in the poem;
- ☐ examine odes in poetry.

Getting Started

Activity 1: Before you begin …

Before you begin to read any piece of writing, it is usually a good idea to think of what you already know about the topic. Write down what you know about the title of the poem by completing the table below. The table should be completed as follows:

It says … - Write the title of the poem.

I know … - Write what you know about thc title. In this case, who is a landscape painter? What does the comma in the title indicate? What do the italicised words "*for Albert Huie*" suggest?

And so … - Make a prediction about what you think the poem will be about based on the stated title and what you know about the title.

It says …	
I know …	
And so …	

Activity 2: Team Challenge – Our View of the Landscape

Directions. In groups of five (try to ensure one group member is a visual artist), make a presentation describing your view of the landscape. This will be done in a step-by-step process.

Step 1: Find a spot – As a group, go outside, observe the landscape, and find a view the group agrees is worth painting. Ensure you can see the mountains and the sky.

Step 2: Identify your feelings – Individually, record how looking at the spot makes you feel and/or imagine how you would feel if you were in the spot. Record emotions that are stirred by your different senses. What do you see? How does it make your feel? What do you hear? How does that make you feel and so on? Use the table below to record your feelings. Do not worry if you do not have the same feelings as your group members. This part is just about you and the scenery.

Senses	Elements in the scenery that caused your feeling	Feelings/Emotions
Sight		
Hearing		
Smelling		
Tasting		
Feeling		

Step 3: Put it all together – On a sheet of paper, combine your individual tables into one group table. This table will be presented to the artist who will try to capture the different emotions in the painting of your selected scene. After all, landscape painting is not just about recreating a picture of the landscape. It is also about demonstrating and creating and emotional appeal through colours, sizes, depth of the brush stroke and so on.

Step 4: Take a picture – Take a picture of your selected scenery.

Step 5: Painting the landscape – Paint a landscape recreating the picture you had taken and capturing the varying emotions on your group emotions sheet. If there are no visual artists in your group, ask your art teacher or another student artist to paint the picture for your group. Ensure you observe the artist and record your impressions of how he/she paints the picture. Each group member should make his/her own notes, so the group will have more information to use when making your presentation. Individually, record the artist's actions, sounds/words, what you think he/she is thinking in the table.

The Artist at Work

Actions	
Sounds/Words	
Artist's Possible Thoughts	
Your overall impression of the artist:	
Your overall impression of the painting of a landscape:	

Step 5: Describing your experience – Using the notes and impressions of all the group members, make a descriptive and creative presentation about the artist painting a landscape. Be sure to capture the process, actions, sounds and possible thoughts of the artist. Also ensure that the dominant impression you had is communicated to your audience. Your presentation may be in a form (poem, story, song, dramatization, video etc.). It should include:

- ✓ the picture of the landscape that the group had taken. (The picture must include the mountains and the sky.)
- ✓ the painting in which the artist recreated the group's picture;
- ✓ your description of the artist at work;
- ✓ images that appeal to at least THREE senses;
- ✓ at least THREE literary devices (one of which must be a sound device);
- ✓ lively verbs and adjectives;
- ✓ appeal to at least ONE dominant emotion

Use the **Landscape Painting Checklist** to ensure you have the best presentation.

Landscape Painting Checklist

Directions. The checklist below consists of a list of statements highlighting important things to consider when preparing for your presentation and three emojis. If your answer to the statement is yes, put a tick beside the statement and under the happy face. If your answer to the statement is no, put a tick beside the statement and under the sad face. If you are unsure, put a tick beside the statement and under the unsure face.

Landscape Painting Checklist	Happy face	Unsure face	Sad face
1. The presentation is no more than FIVE minutes long.			
2. The picture of the landscape that the group had taken is included.			
3. The picture includes the mountains and the sky.			
4. The artist's recreation of the scenery is included.			
5. A description of the artist at work is included.			
6. The description includes the process the artist engaged in to create the painting.			
7. The description includes the actions of the artist as he/she painted the scenery.			
8. The description includes sounds the artist made as he/she painted the scenery.			
9. The description includes possible thoughts of the artist as he/she painted the scenery.			
10. The description includes images that appeal to at least THREE senses.			
11. The description included at least THREE literary devices.			
12. At least ONE of the literary devices included is a sound device.			
13. The description includes lively verbs, adverbs and adjectives.			
14. The description appeals to at least ONE dominant emotion.			
15. The description is creative.			
16. The description is free from grammatical errors.			

After you are finished putting a tick beside each statement, make recommendations to yourself about how you may improve your performance. Ask your peers and teacher for their recommendations as well.

Earn a SUPERB! for making the best presentation.

Activity 3: The Featured Presentation

Use the checklist below to assess your peers' recitation of "Landscape Painter, Jamaica".

Checklist for the Poetry Recitation

Directions. The checklist below consists of a list of statements highlighting important things to consider when reciting a poem and three emojis. If your answer to the statement is yes, put a tick beside the statement and under the happy face. If your answer to the statement is no, put a tick beside the statement and under the sad face. If you are unsure, put a tick beside the statement and under the unsure face.

Checklist for Song Performance			
1. Performance is no longer than three minutes.			
2. The words of the poem are said exactly as presented in the text.			
3. The performer adapts the role of the persona in movement, posture and general demeanour.			
4. Performer conveys the appropriate emotion.			
5. Performer makes appropriate use of facial expression, gestures, tone etc. to convey the meaning of the poem.			
6. Performer makes appropriate use of stage.			
7. Performance is audible and confident.			
8. Performance is entertaining.			

Directions. Based on your ticks in the checklist, rate your classmates' recitation of "Landscape Painter, Jamaica" by shading the stars below. Five stars mean you believe the recitation was excellent. Then justify your rating.

Your Rating	**Your Justification**
☆☆☆☆☆	

What is the most common rating received by the presenter from your classmates? ____________________

What is your teacher's rating? ____

If you have the same rating as your teacher, you earn a  .

Choose TWO areas from the checklist where you ticked 'no' or 'unsure' and make ONE recommendation to the presenters on how they could have improved in those areas.

Selected area 1: ____

Recommendation: ____

____

____

____

Selected area 2: ____

Recommendation: ____

____

____

____

Elements of Poetry in "Landscape Painter, Jamaica"

Your classmates will present their analysis of "Landscape Painter, Jamaica". In this analysis, they will identify, explain and discuss the historical background, literary elements, form and literary devices used in the poem. You will be expected to critically assess the analysis being presented. This will be done in a step-by-step process.

Step 1: Listen for Information – While you listen to the analysis, complete the different the activities with information presented in the analysis.

Step 2: Consult Your Peers – Share with a peer to see if he/she heard anything you might have missed or if you heard anything, he/she missed.

Step 3: Rate the Analysis – Look at the number of answered and unanswered activities you have and rate the overall analysis.

Historical Background

Directions. In this section, the presenters are expected to provide relevant information for all the areas in the picture below. However, you are only expected to write the ***poet's name, birthday, country of birth, quick facts and other works by the poet*** from the presenters' analysis. Complete the other sections based on your own feelings about the poet.

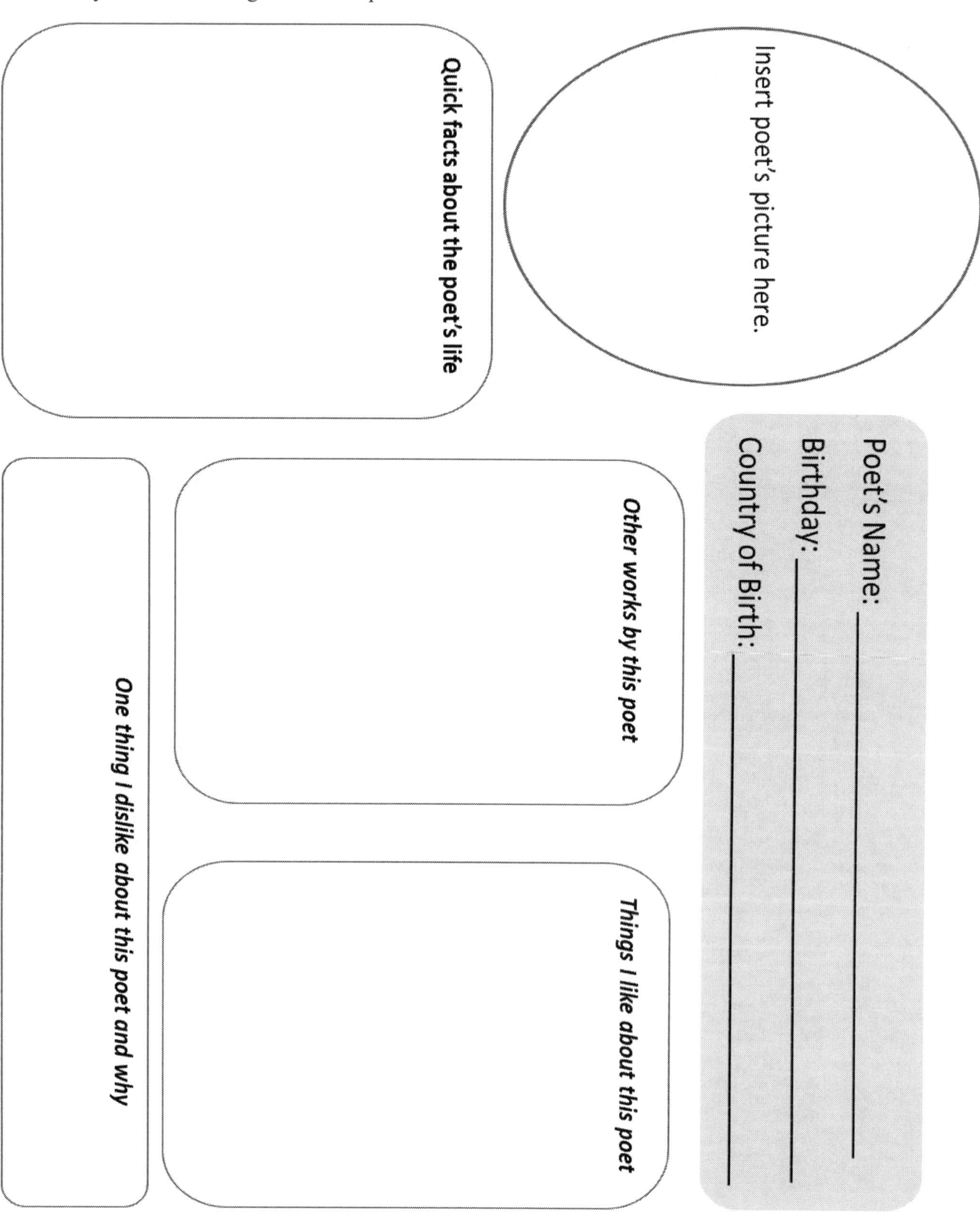

Literary Elements in "Landscape Painter, Jamaica"

Directions. Write the literary elements identified by the presenter(s). After the presentation, you will be allowed time to identify these elements for yourself and compare your answers to the presenters' answers. Revise your notes on each element if you are unsure. Complete the table as follows:

1. Write the presenters' identifications.
2. Tick whether you agree or disagree with each identification.
3. Whether you agree or disagree, write one piece of evidence from the poem to support your decision.

Characters		
Persona:	**Agree**	**Disagree**
Evidence:		
Tone:	**Agree**	**Disagree**
Evidence:		
Other characters:	**Agree**	**Disagree**
Evidence:		
Type of Narration:	**Agree**	**Disagree**
Evidence:		

Setting		
Time and Place:	**Agree**	**Disagree**
Evidence:		
Mood:	**Agree**	**Disagree**
Evidence:		

Theme		
1st Theme Category: **Message** ***(one sentence):***	**Agree**	**Disagree**
Evidence		
2nd Theme Category: **Message** ***(one sentence):***	**Agree**	**Disagree**
Evidence		

Plot in "Landscape Painter, Jamaica"

Directions. Summarize each stanza in a single sentence. Then, combine the sentences into a paragraph. Use suitable transition words and phrases to make the paragraph more coherent. Remember to use your own words.

Stanza 1:

Stanza 2:

Stanza 3:

Stanza 4:

Stanza 5:

Stylistics in “Landscape Painter, Jamaica”

We will look at the form of the poem and the literary devices used.

Form of “Landscape Painter, Jamaica”

Directions. Fill in the blanks with information from “Landscape Painter, Jamaica”

“Landscape Painter, Jamaica” is an __________________ (*Type of poem*). The poem consists of ______________ (*Number of lines*) lines which are divided into _________ (*Number of stanzas*) stanzas. The first and second stanzas are ____________________ (*Type of stanza*).

The third stanza is an ________________ (*Type of stanza*), and the fourth and fifth stanzas are _____________________ (*Type of stanza*).

The poem has __________________________ (*Type of rhythm*) and is written in ____________________________ (*Type of rhyme scheme*).

Answer the following questions.

1. Turn your text in the landscape orientation (rotate 90° left) and use a pencil to connect the ends of each line. What is the image created? ____

   ____

2. Why is the effect of having the third stanza and especially line 11 being noticeably longer?

   ____

   ____

   ____

   ____

   ____

   ____

   ____

   ____

   ____

   ____

   ____

   ____

   ____

3. Odes are poems that are written in praise, celebration or dedication to someone, something or some event. Would you consider "Landscape Painter, Jamaica" an ode?

   ____

   a. Who/What is being celebrated or praised? ______________________________

   b. Why is he/she/it being praised or celebrated? ___________________________

   c. What words and phrases in the poem highlight the praise being given to the person/thing/event?

   ____

   ____

   ____

   ____

   ____

   ____

   ____

   ____

   ____

   ____

   ____

Literary Devices in "Landscape Painter, Jamaica"

Activity 1: Identifying the Devices

Directions. Write the names of FOUR literary devices used in the poem. Then, write an example of each of the listed devices from the poem. Ensure you write the line number(s) for each example given.

Literary Devices	Examples
1. ____________________:	______________________________
	______________________________
2. ____________________:	______________________________
	______________________________
3. ____________________:	______________________________
	______________________________
4. ____________________:	______________________________
	______________________________

If you have identified a simile or metaphor, explain it by using the formula.

Explain ONE device with contradiction used in the poem.

Assessing Your Peers' Presentation

Directions. Compare the information your peers provided with your own analysis and rate your classmates' analysis of "Landscape Painter, Jamaica" by shading the stars below. Five stars mean you believe the analysis was excellent. Then justify your rating.

Your Rating	Your Justification
☆☆☆☆☆	

What is the most common rating received by the presenter from your classmates? ___________________

What is your teacher's rating? ___________________

If you have the same rating as your teacher, you earn a .

Choose ONE element of poetry that you think the presenters need to make improvement in analyzing and make TWO recommendations to the presenters on how they can improve in analyzing that element.

Selected area: ___________________

Recommendation 1: ___________________

Recommendation 2: ___________________

Now that you have finished analyzing "Landscape Painter, Jamaica", look back at the predictions you made before you analyzed the poem and answer the following questions.

1. To what extent were your predictions right?

   Not at all ☐ A small extent ☐ Somewhat ☐ To a large extent ☐ Spot on ☐

2. Explain your selection for question 1.

   ____

   ____

   ____

3. Create a Twitter page for the Albert Huie as presented in "Landscape Painter, Jamaica". The page should include:
   - ✓ Name
   - ✓ Handle
   - ✓ Biography
   - ✓ Location
   - ✓ FIVE celebrities the persona is following. (TWO of these persons should come from any poem/play/short story you have studied and THREE you should choose based on what you know about him.
   - ✓ FIVE persons who are following the persona. (THREE should be characters from any poem/story/play you have studied who you think would share similar interest as Albert Huie, and TWO should be actual people you know who share similar interest as he does.)
   - ✓ TWO tweets by the persona. ONE should be on how he feels about the painting he has created in the poem and THE OTHER should be about how he views painting, landscapes, or Jamaica

Earn a 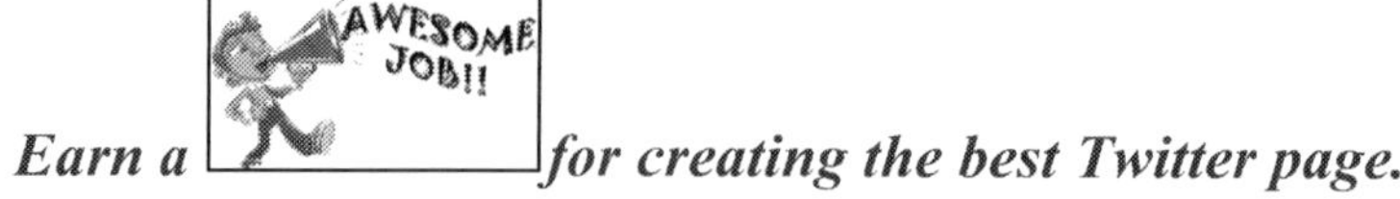

for creating the best Twitter page.

4. Choose TWO poems that you have studied from the prescribed list which focus on elements of nature.

   Write an essay in which you describe the incident in which the persona noticed a NAMED element of nature. In this essay, you must also discuss EACH persona's attitude towards the element of nature in EACH poem and examine ONE device that is used to present the natural world in EACH poem.

Checking My Progress

You have just finished the activities on "Landscape Painter, Jamaica". Before we move to the activities on the next poem, review what you have learnt or are still uncertain about. Do so by first checking the objectives you have accomplished so far.

Directions. Go back to the objectives at the beginning of the activities on "Landscape Painter, Jamaica". If you think you have accomplished an objective, without looking back at your notes, put a tick in the ☐ box before the objective. If you are unsure you have accomplished the objective, put a question mark (?) and if you are sure you have not accomplished the objective, leave it unchecked (blank). Ensure you pay more attention to your unchecked boxes and the boxes with your question marks as you study. Also, ensure that you can perform the number indicated in each objective (e.g., list **three** genres). You have accomplished the objective when you can list the indicated number (three).

Now complete the 3-2-1 activity below. It works as follows:

Three – Write three things you learned from the activities on "Landscape Painter, Jamaica".

Two – Write two things you found interesting or about which you would like to learn more.

One – Write one question you still have about the material.

Share your question with your classmates and listen to their responses. Did they clarify things? If not, maybe it is time you did some independent research.

Finally, record ONE question from one of your classmates and provide an answer to that classmate.

Checking What I Know!!!

3. ____

____

____

2. ____

____

1. ____

Helping My Peers!!!

Peer's question: ____

____

My answer: ____

____

____

"West Indies, U.S.A." by Stewart Brown

Objectives

After completing the activities on "West Indies, U.S.A.", you should be able to accurately:

- ☐ make predictions based on the title of the poem;
- ☐ identify the elements of poetry in the poem;
- ☐ critically assess your peers' presentation and analysis of the poem;
- ☐ examine the effect and effectiveness of literary devices used in the poem;
- ☐ examine the relationship between The U.S.A. and Caribbean territories.

Getting Started

Activity 1: Before you begin …

Before you begin to read any piece of writing, it is usually a good idea to think of what you already know about the topic. Write down what you know about the title of the poem by completing the table below. The table should be completed as follows:

It says … - Write the title of the poem.

I know … - Write what you know about the title. In this case, when you see or write an address with Jamaica, West Indies or Barbados, W.I., what is suggested about the location of the country?

And so … - Make a prediction about what you think the poem will be about based on the stated title and what you know about the title.

It says …	
I know …	
And so …	

Activity 2: Flying in the Caribbean

Directions. Answer the following questions.

1. Name ONE international airport and one distinctive feature of EACH of the following countries.

Antigua and Barbuda
Airport:
Distinguishing Feature:

Haiti
Airport:
Distinguishing Feature:

Puerto Rico
Airport:
Distinguishing Feature:

Trinidad and Tobago
Airport:
Distinguishing Feature:

2. Is Puerto Rico in the West Indies or the United States of America (U.S.A). Justify your selection.

____

____

____

____

____

____

____

____

____

Activity 3: The Featured Presentation

Use the checklist below to assess your peers' recitation of "West Indies, U.S.A.".

Checklist for the Poetry Recitation

Directions. The checklist below consists of a list of statements highlighting important things to consider when reciting a poem and three emojis. If your answer to the statement is yes, put a tick beside the statement and under the happy face. If your answer to the statement is no, put a tick beside the statement and under the sad face. If you are unsure, put a tick beside the statement and under the unsure face.

Checklist for Poetry Recitation	Happy face	Unsure face	Sad face
1. Performance is no longer than three minutes.			
2. The words of the poem are said exactly as presented in the text.			
3. The performer adapts the role of the persona in movement, posture and general demeanour.			
4. Performer conveys the appropriate emotion.			
5. Performer makes appropriate use of facial expression, gestures, tone etc. to convey the meaning of the poem.			
6. Performer makes appropriate use of stage.			
7. Performance is audible and confident.			
8. Performance is entertaining.			

Directions. Based on your ticks in the checklist, rate your classmates' recitation of "West Indies, U.S.A." by shading the stars below. Five stars mean you believe the recitation was excellent. Then justify your rating.

Your Rating	Your Justification
☆☆☆☆☆	

What is the most common rating received by the presenter from your classmates? ____________

What is your teacher's rating? ______________________________

If you have the same rating as your teacher, you earn a  .

Choose TWO areas from the checklist where you ticked 'no' or 'unsure' and make ONE recommendation to the presenter on how he or she could have improved in those areas.

Selected area 1: ______________________________

Recommendation: ______________________________

____

____

____

Selected area 2: ______________________________

Recommendation: ______________________________

____

____

____

Elements of Poetry in "West Indies, U.S.A."

Your classmates will present their analysis of "West Indies, U.S.A." In this analysis, they will identify, explain and discuss the historical background, literary elements, form and literary devices used in the poem. You will be expected to critically assess the analysis being presented. This will be done in a step-by-step process.

Step 1: Listen for Information – While you listen to the analysis, complete the different activities with information presented in the analysis.

Step 2: Consult Your Peers – Share with a peer to see if he/she heard anything you might have missed or if you heard anything, he/she missed.

Step 3: Rate the Analysis – Look at the number of answered and unanswered activities you have and rate the overall analysis.

Historical Background

Directions. In this section, the presenters are expected to provide relevant information for all the areas in the picture below. However, you are only expected to write the ***poet's name, birthday, country of birth, quick facts and other works by the poet*** from the presenters' analysis. Complete the other sections based on your own feelings about the poet.

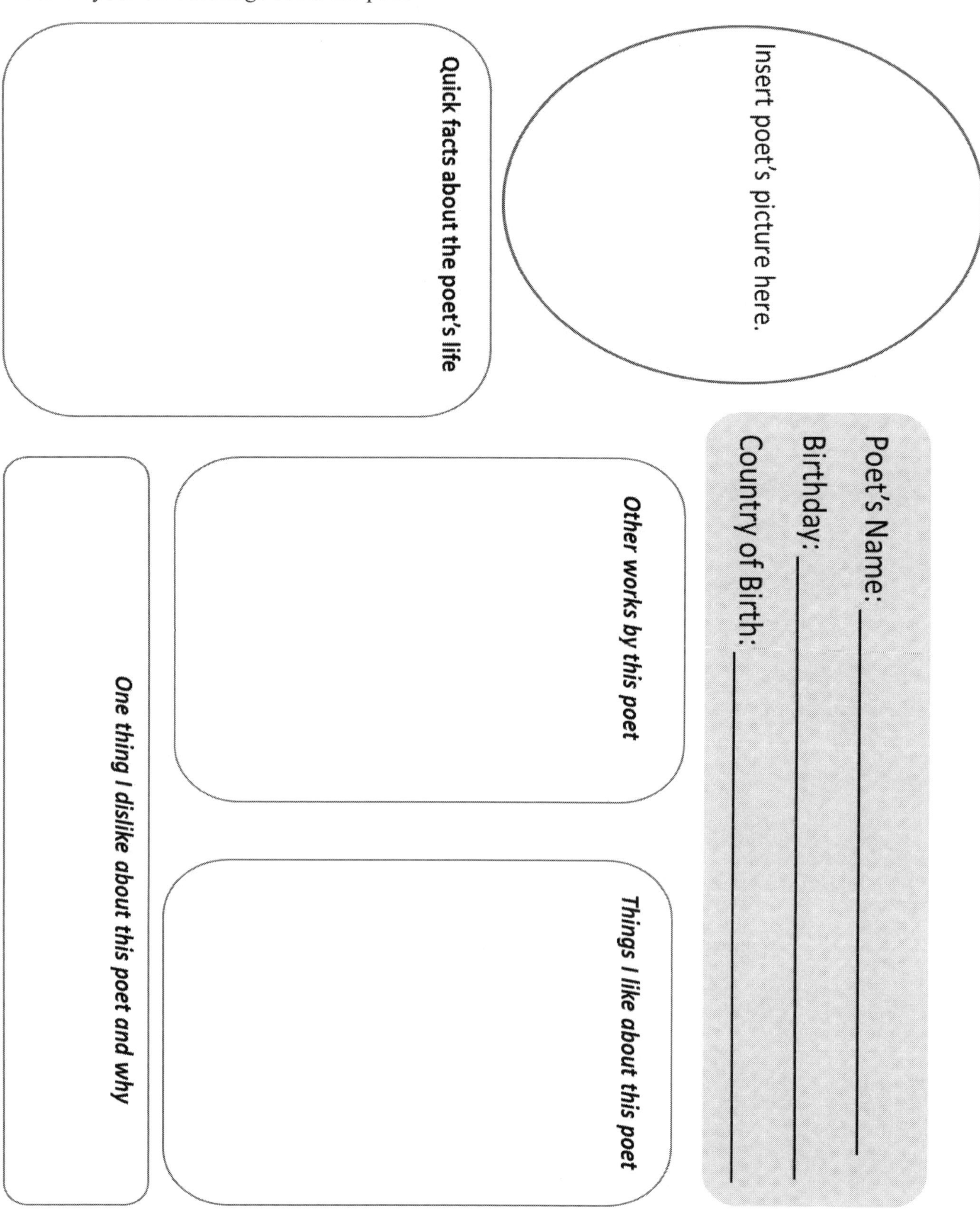

Literary Elements in "West Indies, U.S.A."

Directions. Write the literary elements identified by the presenter(s). After the presentation, you will be allowed time to identify these elements for yourself and compare your answers to the presenters' answers. Revise your notes on each element if you are unsure. Complete the table as follows:

1. Write the presenters' identifications.
2. Tick whether you agree or disagree with each identification.
3. Whether you agree or disagree, write one piece of evidence from the poem to support your decision.

Characters		
Persona:	**Agree**	**Disagree**
Evidence:		
Tone:	**Agree**	**Disagree**
Evidence:		
Other characters:	**Agree**	**Disagree**
Evidence:		
Type of Narration:	**Agree**	**Disagree**
Evidence:		

<table>
<tr><td colspan="3">Setting</td></tr>
<tr><td>Time and Place:</td><td>Agree</td><td>Disagree</td></tr>
<tr><td colspan="3">Evidence:</td></tr>
<tr><td>Mood:</td><td>Agree</td><td>Disagree</td></tr>
<tr><td colspan="3">Evidence:</td></tr>
<tr><td colspan="3">Theme</td></tr>
<tr><td>1st Theme Category:
Message (one sentence):</td><td>Agree</td><td>Disagree</td></tr>
<tr><td colspan="3">Evidence</td></tr>
<tr><td>2nd Theme Category:
Message (one sentence):</td><td>Agree</td><td>Disagree</td></tr>
<tr><td colspan="3">Evidence</td></tr>
</table>

Plot in "West Indies, U.S.A."

Directions. Summarize each stanza in a single sentence. Then, combine the sentences into a paragraph. Use suitable transition words and phrases to make the paragraph more coherent. Remember to use your own words.

Stanza 1:

Stanza 2:

Stanza 3:

Stanza 4:

Stanza 5:

Stanza 6:

Stylistics in "West Indies, U.S.A."

We will look at the form of the poem and the literary devices used.

Form of "West Indies, U.S.A."

Directions. Fill in the blanks with information from "West Indies, U.S.A.".

"West Indies, U.S.A." is a ______________________ (*Type of poem*). The poem consists of _________ (*Number of lines*) lines which are divided into ______ (*Number of stanza*) stanzas. The first two stanzas are ___________ (*Type of stanza*), and the third is a _____________ (*Type of stanza*). The fourth stanza is also a _____________ (*Type of stanza*), the fifth is a _____________ (*Type of stanza*) while the sixth stanza is a _____________ (*Type of stanza*). The poem has __________________ (*Type of rhyme scheme*) and is written in __________________________ (*Type of rhythm*).

Answer the following questions.

1. Look at the words of the poem as they appear in the World of Poetry. Which stanza stands out and why?

   ____

   ____

   ____

2. Why do you think the second to sixth stanza begin almost half-way across the page?

   ____

   ____

   ____

3. What does the inconsistent number of lines in the stanzas contribute to the poem?

   ____

   ____

   ____

4. What does the rhyme scheme or the absence of a rhyme scheme contribute to the poem?

   ____

   ____

   ____

Literary Devices in "West Indies, U.S.A."

Activity 1: Identifying the Devices

Directions. Write the names of FOUR literary devices used in the poem. Then, write an example of each of the listed devices from the poem. Ensure you write the line number(s) for each example given.

Literary Devices	Examples
1. ______________________:	____
	____
2. ______________________:	____
	____
3. ______________________:	____
	____
4. ______________________:	____
	____

Reference Devices

Reference devices refer to, mention, or hint at a person, place, thing or significant historical, political, biblical, cultural, literary event or idea. When these devices are used, the writer or poet does not give many details about the person or thing. It is the left up to the reader to find out what is being referred to and how is it connected to the poem. In examining reference devices, you should:

- ✓ identify the device;
- ✓ identify the person, place, thing, event or idea being referred to;
- ✓ describe at least one significant characteristic of the person, place, event or idea that was referenced;
- ✓ connect the described characteristic to the poem (theme, mood, setting, characterization etc.)
- ✓ comment on the effect and/or effectiveness of the reference.

The reference device we will be focused on is **allusion.** An allusion is a reference device that allows writers and especially poets to expand the context of the poem and add meaning, depth and greater significance to the poem. It allows the poet to communicate more than what is actually written on the page. Allusions are oftentimes found within similes and metaphors. An easy way to spot allusions is by the mention of a specific name of a person, group, place or event. The poet may mention the name of a person and leave it up to you to find out who the person is and how he/she is related to the poem. Therefore, once you see a specific name being mentioned in a poem, do some research to tap into the greater meaning or importance the poet is trying to communicate.

Activity 1: Everyday Allusions

Directions. We sometimes use allusions in our everyday speech. Examine the examples below. Be sure to go through all the steps listed on pages 210 – 211.

1. After we had decided how we were planning to complete our assignment, he came with the same idea like a real Christopher Columbus.
2. Some people are real house slaves.
3. My aunt is a Delilah.

Activity 2: Creating Allusions

Directions. Create TWO allusions. One should refer to a place and the other should make reference to another literary text, story or poem on the prescribed list.

Explain TWO allusions made in "West Indies, U.S.A".

Activity 3: Effect and Effectiveness

Directions. Choose TWO devices identified in "West Indies, U.S.A." and comment on their effect and effectiveness. If you need to remind yourself of what is required when you are asked to examine or comment on the use of a literary device, read the notes presented of **pages 52 – 53** of this Workbook.

Device	**Evidence**
Effect:	
Effectiveness:	

Device	**Evidence**
Effect:	
Effectiveness:	

Assessing Your Peers' Presentation

Directions. Compare the information your peers provided with your own analysis and rate your classmates' analysis of "West Indies, U.S.A." by shading the stars below. Five stars mean you believe the analysis was excellent. Then justify your rating.

Your Rating	Your Justification
☆☆☆☆☆	

What is the most common rating received by the presenter from your classmates? ____________________

What is your teacher's rating? ____________________

If you have the same rating as your teacher, you earn a .

Choose ONE element of poetry that you think the presenters need to make improvement in analyzing and make TWO recommendations to the presenters on how they can improve in analyzing that element.

Selected area: ____________________

Recommendation 1: ____________________

____

____

____

____

Recommendation 2: ____________________

____

____

____

____

Now that you have finished analyzing "West Indies, U.S.A.", look back at the predictions you made before you analyzed the poem and answer the following questions.

1. To what extent were your predictions right?

   Not at all ☐ A small extent ☐ Somewhat ☐ To a large extent ☐ Spot on ☐

2. Explain your selection for question 1.

   ____

   ____

   ____

3. In stanza two, the persona highlights distinguishing features of the islands visited based on activities at the airports. What are these features? How do these features compare to the ones you had identified at the beginning?

   ____

   ____

   ____

   ____

   ____

4. The title, "West Indies, U.S.A" suggests that the U.S.A. is very influential in the West Indies. To what extent is this true for your own country?

   ____

   ____

   ____

   ____

   ____

5. "West Indies, U.S.A." and "Sonnet Composed Upon Westminster Bridge" share the personas' impressions of places they have visited."

   Write an essay in which you describe the places visited by EACH persona. In this essay, you must also discuss the attitude of the persona towards the place in EACH poem and examine ONE device used to convey the persona's impression of the place in EACH poem.

Checking My Progress

You have just finished the activities on "West Indies, U.S.A.". Before we move to the activities on the next poem, review what you have learnt or are still uncertain about. Do so by first checking the objectives you have accomplished so far.

Directions. Go back to the objectives at the beginning of the activities on "West Indies, U.S.A.". If you think you have accomplished an objective, without looking back at your notes, put a tick in the box ☐ before the objective. If you are unsure you have accomplished the objective, put a question mark (?) and if you are sure you have not accomplished the objective, leave it unchecked (blank). Ensure you pay more attention to your unchecked boxes and the boxes with your question marks as you study. Also, ensure that you can perform the number indicated in each objective (e.g., list **three** genres). You have accomplished the objective when you can list the indicated number (three).

Now complete the 3-2-1 activity below. It works as follows:

Three – Write three things you learned from the activities on "West Indies, U.S.A.".

Two – Write two things you found interesting or about which you would like to learn more.

One – Write one question you still have about the material.

Share your question with your classmates and listen to their responses. Did they clarify things? If not, maybe it is time you did some independent research.

Finally, record ONE question from one of your classmates and provide an answer to that classmate.

Checking What I Know!!!

3. ____

____

____

2. ____

____

1. ____

Helping My Peers!!!

Peer's question: ____

____

My answer: ____

____

____

"It is the Constant Image of your Face" by Dennis Brutus

Objectives
After completing the activities on "It is the Constant Image of your Face", you should be able to accurately:

- ☐ make predictions based on the title of the poem;
- ☐ identify the elements of poetry in the poem;
- ☐ critically assess your peers' presentation and analysis of the poem;
- ☐ examine the effect and effectiveness of literary devices used in the poem;
- ☐ discuss the theme of patriotism.

Getting Started

Activity 1: Before you begin …

Before you begin to read any piece of writing, it is usually a good idea to think of what you already know about the topic. Write down what you know about the title of the poem by completing the table below. The table should be completed as follows:

It says … - Write the title of the poem.

I know … - Write what you know about the title. In this case, why would the image of the face be constant? How does the constant image of the face impact the persona?

And so … - Make a prediction about what you think the poem will be about based on the stated title and what you know about the title.

It says …	
I know …	
And so …	

Activity 2: The Face of All Faces

Directions. Insert a picture of the face of someone you love.

Insert your picture here.

1. List TWO things you love about this face.

___

___

___

2. List TWO things about the person that you love.

___

___

___

3. Name ONE thing (place, object, animal, aspiration) that you love more than anything in the world. ___

4. If you had to choose between this person and another person or thing, who would you choose? Why? How would you feel about choosing?

___

___

___

Activity 3: The Featured Presentation

Use the checklist below to assess your peers' recitation of "It is the Constant Image of your Face".

Checklist for the Poetry Recitation

Directions. The checklist below consists of a list of statements highlighting important things to consider when reciting a poem and three emojis. If your answer to the statement is yes, put a tick beside the statement and under the happy face. If your answer to the statement is no, put a tick beside the statement and under the sad face. If you are unsure, put a tick beside the statement and under the unsure face.

Checklist for Poetry Recitation			
1. Performance is no longer than three minutes.			
2. The words of the poem are said exactly as presented in the text.			
3. The performer adapts the role of the persona in movement, posture and general demeanour.			
4. Performer conveys the appropriate emotion.			
5. Performer makes appropriate use of facial expression, gestures, tone etc. to convey the meaning of the poem.			
6. Performer makes appropriate use of stage.			
7. Performance is audible and confident.			
8. Performance is entertaining.			

Directions. Based on your ticks in the checklist, rate your classmates' recitation of "It is the Constant Image of your Face" by shading the stars below. Five stars mean you believe the recitation was excellent. Then justify your rating.

Your Rating	**Your Justification**
☆☆☆☆☆	

What is the most common rating received by the presenter from your classmates? ____________________

What is your teacher's rating? ____

If you have the same rating as your teacher, you earn a .

Choose TWO areas from the checklist where you ticked 'no' or 'unsure' and make ONE recommendation to the presenter on how he or she could have improved in those areas.

Selected area 1: ____

Recommendation: ____

____

____

____

Selected area 2: ____

Recommendation: ____

____

____

____

Elements of Poetry in "It is the Constant Image of your Face"

Your classmates will present their analysis of "It is the Constant Image of your Face". In this analysis, they will identify, explain and discuss the historical background, literary elements, form and literary devices used in the poem. You will be expected to critically assess the analysis being presented. This will be done in a step-by-step process.

Step 1: Listen for Information – While you listen to the analysis, complete the different activities with information presented in the analysis.

Step 2: Consult Your Peers – Share with a peer to see if he/she heard anything you might have missed or if you heard anything, he/she missed.

Step 3: Rate the Analysis – Look at the number of answered and unanswered activities you have and rate the overall analysis.

Historical Background

Directions. In this section, the presenters are expected to provide relevant information for all the areas in the picture below. However, you are only expected to write the ***poet's name, birthday, country of birth, quick facts and other works by the poet*** from the presenters' analysis. Complete the other sections based on your own feelings about the poet.

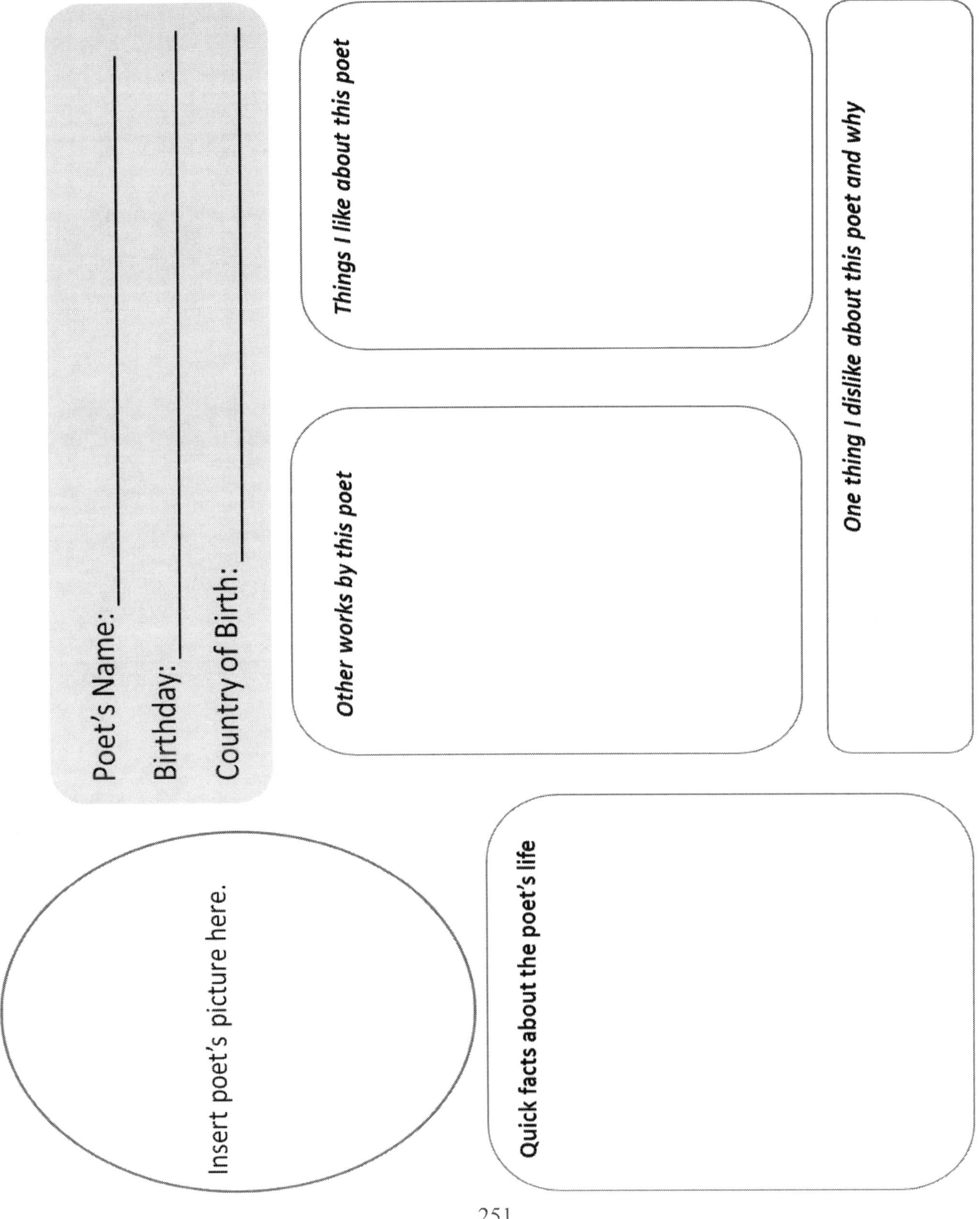

Literary Elements in "It is the Constant Image of your Face".

Directions. Write the literary elements identified by the presenter(s). After the presentation, you will be allowed time to identify these elements for yourself and compare your answers to the presenters' answers. Revise your notes on each element if you are unsure. Complete the table as follows:

1. Write the presenters' identifications.
2. Tick whether you agree or disagree with each identification.
3. Whether you agree or disagree, write one piece of evidence from the poem to support your decision.

Characters		
Persona:	**Agree**	**Disagree**
Evidence:		
Tone:	**Agree**	**Disagree**
Evidence:		
Other characters:	**Agree**	**Disagree**
Evidence:		
Type of Narration:	**Agree**	**Disagree**
Evidence:		

Setting		
Time and Place:	**Agree**	**Disagree**
Evidence:		
Mood:	**Agree**	**Disagree**
Evidence:		

Theme		
1st Theme Category: **Message *(one sentence):***	**Agree**	**Disagree**
Evidence		
2nd Theme Category: **Message *(one sentence):***	**Agree**	**Disagree**
Evidence		

Plot in "It is the Constant Image of your Face"

Directions. Summarize each stanza in a single sentence. Then, combine the sentences into a paragraph. Use suitable transition words and phrases to make the paragraph more coherent. Remember to use your own words.

Stanza 1:

Stanza 2:

____

____

____

____

____

____

____

____

____

Stylistics in "It is the Constant Image of your Face"

We will look at the form of the poem and the literary devices used.

Form of "It is the Constant Image of your Face"

Directions. Fill in the blanks with information from "It is the Constant Image of your Face".

"It is the Constant Image of your Face" is a ____________________ (*Type of poem*). The poem consists of ________ (*Number of lines*) lines which are divided into ________________________ (*Number and type of stanzas*). The poem has ____________________ (*Type of rhythm*) and is written in ______________________________ (*Type of rhyme scheme*).

Answer the following questions.

1. The poet has TWO great loves in the poem. What are they?

____

2. What is the main conflict in the poem?

____

____

____

3. How does the form of the poem contribute to the presentation of the conflict in the poem?

____

____

____

____

____

Literary Devices in "It is the Constant Image of your Face"

Activity 1: Identifying the Devices

Directions. Write the names of FOUR literary devices used in the poem. Then, write an example of each of the listed devices from the poem. Ensure you write the line number(s) for each example given.

Literary Devices	Examples
1. ____________________:	______________________________
	______________________________
2. ____________________:	______________________________
	______________________________
3. ____________________:	______________________________
	______________________________
4. ____________________:	______________________________
	______________________________

If you have identified a simile or metaphor, explain it by using the formula.

Examine the different types of images present in this poem.

Identify FIVE words or phrases from the poem that are related to law or crime. What does the use of these words suggest about the persona's attitude towards his love(s).

Activity 2: Effect and Effectiveness

Directions. Choose TWO devices identified in "It is the Constant Image of your Face" and comment on their effect and effectiveness. If you need to remind yourself of what is required when you are asked to examine or comment on the use of a literary device, read the notes presented of **pages 52 – 53** of this Workbook.

Device	Evidence
Effect:	
Effectiveness:	

Device	Evidence
Effect:	
Effectiveness:	

Assessing Your Peers' Presentation

Directions. Compare the information your peers provided with your own analysis and rate your classmates' analysis of "It is the Constant Image of your Face" by shading the stars below. Five stars mean you believe the analysis was excellent. Then justify your rating.

Your Rating	Your Justification
☆☆☆☆☆	

What is the most common rating received by the presenter from your classmates? ___________

What is your teacher's rating? ___________

If you have the same rating as your teacher, you earn a ⚖.

Choose ONE element of poetry that you think the presenters need to make improvement in analyzing and make TWO recommendations to the presenters on how they can improve in analyzing that element.

Selected area: ___________

Recommendation 1: ___________

Recommendation 2: ___________

Now that you have finished analyzing "It is the Constant Image of your Face", look back at the predictions you made before you analyzed the poem and answer the following questions.

1. To what extent were your predictions right?

   Not at all ☐ A small extent ☐ Somewhat ☐ To a large extent ☐ Spot on ☐

2. Explain your selection for question 1.

   ____

   ____

   ____

   ____

   ____

3. "It is the Constant Image of your Face" and 'This is the dark time, my love" are both set in countries in difficult situations."

   Write an essay in which you describe the difficult situation in EACH country. In this essay, you must also discuss the speaker's attitude to the difficult situation the country is in and examine ONE device that is used to present the persona's perspective of the situation in EACH poem.

4. Choose TWO poems that you have studied from the prescribed list which focuses on the relationship between a person and his/her country.

   Write an essay in which you outline how EACH persona feels about his country. In this essay, you must discuss an obstacle that affects the relationship between the persona and his country in EACH poem and examine ONE device that is used to explore the theme of patriotism in EACH poem.

Use the rubric for poetry essays in the CXC English syllabus to assess your essay writing skills. Then, ask your classmate to use the same rubric to assess your essay while you do the same for him/her. Revise your essay before presenting it to your teacher.

Checking My Progress

You have just finished the activities on "It is the Constant Image of your Face". Before we move to the activities on the next poem, review what you have learnt or are still uncertain about. Do so by first checking the objectives you have accomplished so far.

Directions. Go back to the objectives at the beginning of the activities on "It is the Constant Image of your Face". If you think you have accomplished an objective, without looking back at your notes, put a tick in the box ☐ before the objective. If you are unsure you have accomplished the objective, put a question mark (?) and if you are sure you have not accomplished the objective, leave it unchecked (blank). Ensure you pay more attention to your unchecked boxes and the boxes with your question marks as you study. Also, ensure that you can perform the number indicated in each objective (e.g., list **three** genres). You have accomplished the objective when you can list the indicated number (three).

Now complete the 3-2-1 activity below. It works as follows:

Three – Write **three** things you learned from the activities on "It is the Constant Image of your Face".

Two – Write **two** things you found interesting or about which you would like to learn more.

One – Write **one** question you still have about the material.

Share your question with your classmates and listen to their responses. Did they clarify things? If not, maybe it is time you did some independent research.

Finally, record ONE question from one of your classmates and provide an answer to that classmate.

Checking What I Know!!!

3. ______________________________

____

____

2. ______________________________

____

1. ______________________________

Helping My Peers!!!

Peer's question: ______________________________

____

My answer: ______________________________

____

____

"Dreaming Black Boy" by James Berry

Objectives

After completing the activities on "Dreaming Black Boy", you should be able to accurately:

- ☐ make predictions based on the title of the poem;
- ☐ identify the elements of poetry in the poem;
- ☐ critically assess your peers' presentation and analysis of the poem;
- ☐ examine the effect and effectiveness of literary devices used in the poem;
- ☐ evaluate the impact of racism.

Getting Started

Activity 1: Before you begin …

Before you begin to read any piece of writing, it is usually a good idea to think of what you already know about the topic. Write down what you know about the title of the poem by completing the table below. The table should be completed as follows:

It says … - Write the title of the poem.

I know … - Write what you know about the title. In this case, why is 'Black' used to describe the dreaming boy? What does a black boy dream about?

And so … - Make a prediction about what you think the poem will be about based on the stated title and what you know about the title.

It says …	
I know …	
And so …	

Activity 2: My Dream and Desires

Directions. Answer the following questions.

1. List TWO different meanings for the word 'dream'.

   ____

   ____

   ____

2. List TWO dreams you have for yourself, your school and your country.

   Yourself: ____

   ____

   Your school: ____

   ____

   Your country: ____

   ____

3. Have you ever been treated unfairly because of a personal trait you have no control over (your hair, height, skin colour, home address, gender, the school you attend etc.? Share an experience.

   ____

   ____

   ____

   ____

   ____

   ____

   ____

   ____

   ____

4. How did you feel in the situation? Use your mood list to help you to find the right words.

   ____

5. What is ONE thing you wish would have been different in that situation?

   ____

   ____

Activity 3: The Featured Presentation

Use the checklist below to assess your peers' recitation of "Dreaming Black Boy".

Checklist for the Poetry Recitation

Directions. The checklist below consists of a list of statements highlighting important things to consider when reciting a poem and three emojis. If your answer to the statement is yes, put a tick beside the statement and under the happy face. If your answer to the statement is no, put a tick beside the statement and under the sad face. If you are unsure, put a tick beside the statement and under the unsure face.

Checklist for Poetry Recitation	(happy face)	(unsure face)	(sad face)
1. Performance is no longer than three minutes.			
2. The words of the poem are said exactly as presented in the text.			
3. The performer adapts the role of the persona in movement, posture and general demeanour.			
4. Performer conveys the appropriate emotion.			
5. Performer makes appropriate use of facial expression, gestures, tone etc. to convey the meaning of the poem.			
6. Performer makes appropriate use of stage.			
7. Performance is audible and confident.			
8. Performance is entertaining.			

Directions. Based on your ticks in the checklist, rate your classmates' recitation of "Dreaming Black Boy" by shading the stars below. Five stars mean you believe the recitation was excellent. Then, justify your rating.

Your Rating	Your Justification
☆☆☆☆☆	

What is the most common rating received by the presenter from your classmates? ____________________

What is your teacher's rating? ____

If you have the same rating as your teacher, you earn a  .

Choose TWO areas from the checklist where you ticked 'no' or 'unsure' and make ONE recommendation to the presenters on how they could have improved in those areas.

Selected area 1: ____

Recommendation: ____

____

____

Selected area 2: ____

Recommendation: ____

____

____

Elements of Poetry in "Dreaming Black Boy"

Your classmates will present their analysis of "Dreaming Black Boy". In this analysis, they will identify, explain and discuss the historical background, literary elements, form and literary devices used in the poem. You will be expected to critically assess the analysis being presented. This will be done in a step-by-step process.

Step 1: Listen for Information – While you listen to the analysis, complete the different activities with information presented in the analysis.

Step 2: Consult Your Peers – Share with a peer to see if he/she heard anything you might have missed or if you heard anything, he/she missed.

Step 3: Rate the Analysis – Look at the number of answered and unanswered activities you have and rate the overall analysis.

Historical Background

Directions. In this section, the presenters are expected to provide relevant information for all the areas in the picture below. However, you are only expected to write the ***poet's name, birthday, country of birth, quick facts and other works by the poet*** from the presenters' analysis. Complete the other sections based on your own feelings about the poet.

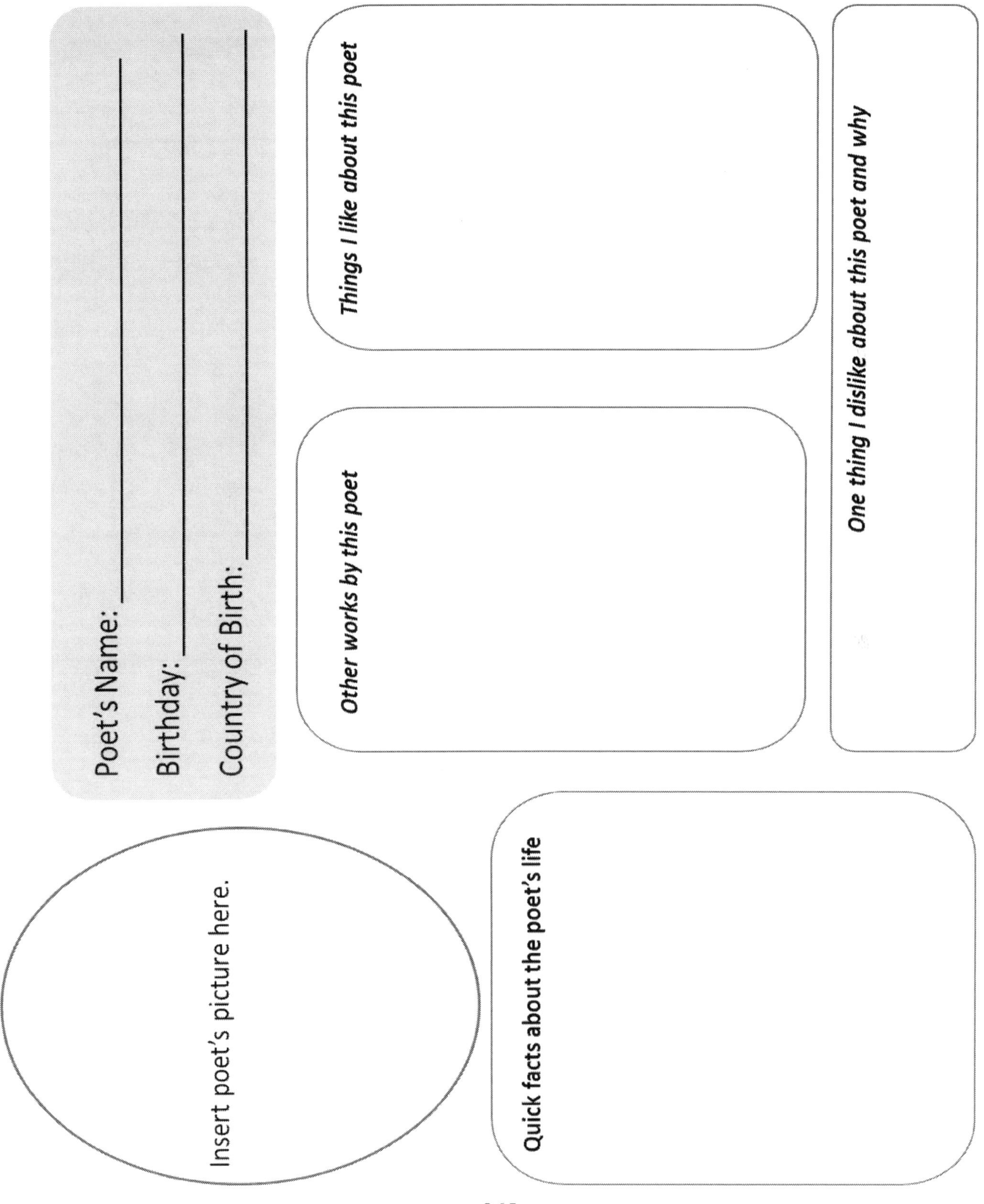

Literary Elements in "Dreaming Black Boy"

Directions. Write the literary elements identified by the presenter(s). After the presentation, you will be allowed time to identify these elements for yourself and compare your answers to the presenters' answers. Revise your notes on each element if you are unsure. Complete the table as follows:

1. Write the presenters' identifications.
2. Tick whether you agree or disagree with each identification.
3. Whether you agree or disagree, write one piece of evidence from the poem to support your decision.

Characters		
Persona:	**Agree**	**Disagree**
Evidence:		
Tone:	**Agree**	**Disagree**
Evidence:		
Other characters:	**Agree**	**Disagree**
Evidence:		
Type of Narration:	**Agree**	**Disagree**
Evidence:		

Setting		
Time and Place:	**Agree**	**Disagree**
Evidence:		
Mood:	**Agree**	**Disagree**
Evidence:		

Theme		
1st Theme Category: **Message *(one sentence):***	**Agree**	**Disagree**
Evidence		
2nd Theme Category: **Message *(one sentence):***	**Agree**	**Disagree**
Evidence		

Plot in "Dreaming Black Boy"

Directions. Make a list of the persona's dreams/wishes as presented in each stanza of the poem. Use suitable transition words and phrases to make the paragraph more coherent. Remember to use your own words.

Stanza 1:

Stanza 2:

Stanza 3:

Stanza 4:

Stanza 5:

Stylistics in "Dreaming Black Boy"

We will look at the form of the poem and the literary devices used.

Form of "Dreaming Black Boy"

Directions. Fill in the blanks with information from "Dreaming Black Boy"

"Dreaming Black Boy" is a __________________ (*Type of poem*). The poem consists of __________ (*Number of lines*) lines which are divided into _______________ (*Number of stanzas*) stanzas. The first three stanzas are ________________ (*Type of stanza*) and the last two stanzas are _____________ (*Type of stanza*). The poem has ______________ (*Type of rhyme scheme*) and is written in ________________ (*Type of rhythm*)

Why do you think there is a change in the types of stanza?

____

____

____

____

Literary Devices in "Dreaming Black Boy"

Activity 1: Identifying the Devices

Directions. Write the names of FOUR literary devices used in the poem. Then, write an example of each of the listed devices from the poem. Ensure you write the line number(s) for each example given.

Literary Devices	Examples
1. ________________________:	______________________________________ ______________________________________
2. ________________________:	______________________________________ ______________________________________
3. ________________________:	______________________________________ ______________________________________
4. ________________________:	______________________________________ ______________________________________

If you have identified a simile or metaphor, explain it by using the formula.

Activity 2. Allusions in "Dreaming Black Boy"

Directions. Examine THREE allusions used in the poem. Be sure to go through all the steps listed on pages 210 – 211.

Activity 3: Effect and Effectiveness

Directions. Choose TWO other literary devices identified in "Dreaming Black Boy" and comment on their effect and effectiveness. If you need to remind yourself of what is required when you are asked to examine or comment on the use of a literary device, read the notes presented of **pages 52 – 53** of this Workbook.

Device	**Evidence**
Effect:	
Effectiveness:	

Device	**Evidence**
Effect:	
Effectiveness:	

Assessing Your Peers' Presentation

Directions. Compare the information your peers provided with your own analysis and rate your classmates' analysis of "Dreaming Black Boy" by shading the stars below. Five stars mean you believe the analysis was excellent. Then, justify your rating.

Your Rating	Your Justification
☆☆☆☆☆	

What is the most common rating received by the presenter from your classmates? ____________

What is your teacher's rating? ____________

If you have the same rating as your teacher, you earn a .

Choose ONE element of poetry that you think the presenters need to make improvement in analyzing and make TWO recommendations to the presenters on how they can improve in analyzing that element.

Selected area: ____________

Recommendation 1: ____________

Recommendation 2: ____________

Now that you have finished analyzing "Dreaming Black Boy", look back at the predictions you made before you analyzed the poem and answer the following questions.

1. To what extent were your predictions right?

   Not at all ☐ A small extent ☐ Somewhat ☐ To a large extent ☐ Spot on ☐

2. Explain your selection for question 1. ______________________________

   ____
   ____
   ____
   ____

3. Identify ONE similarity and ONE difference between the dreams of the persona and your dreams.

   ____
   ____
   ____
   ____
   ____

4. In what way did the historical background of the poem contribute to your understanding of the poem? ______________________________

   ____
   ____
   ____
   ____
   ____

5. "Dreaming Black Boy" and "Once Upon A Time" focus on an individual's dreams OR desires.

   Write an essay in which you outline EACH persona's dream OR desire. In this essay, you must discuss the role EACH persona plays in the accomplishment of his dream and examine ONE device that is used to explore dreams OR desires in EACH poem.

Use the rubric for poetry essays in the CXC English syllabus to assess your essay writing skills. Then, ask your classmate to use the same rubric to assess your essay while you do the same for him/her. Revise your essay before presenting it to your teacher.

Checking My Progress

You have just finished the activities on "Dreaming Black Boy". Before we move to the activities on the next poem, review what you have learnt or are still uncertain about. Do so by first checking the objectives you have accomplished so far.

Directions. Go back to the objectives at the beginning of the activities on "Dreaming Black Boy". If you think you have accomplished an objective, without looking back at your notes, put a tick in the box ☐ before the objective. If you are unsure you have accomplished the objective, put a question mark (?) and if you are sure you have not accomplished the objective, leave it unchecked (blank). Ensure you pay more attention to your unchecked boxes and the boxes with your question marks as you study. Also, ensure that you can perform the number indicated in each objective (e.g., list **three** genres). You have accomplished the objective when you can list the indicated number (three).

Now complete the 3-2-1 activity below. It works as follows:

Three – Write **three** things you learned from the activities on "Dreaming Black Boy".

Two – Write **two** things you found interesting or about which you would like to learn more.

One – Write **one** question you still have about the material.

Share your question with your classmates and listen to their responses. Did they clarify things? If not, maybe it is time you did some independent research.

Finally, record ONE question from one of your classmates and provide an answer to that classmate.

Checking What I Know!!!

3. ____

____

____

2. ____

____

1. ____

Helping My Peers!!!

Peer's question: ____

____

My answer: ____

____

____

"Test Match Sabina Park" by Stewart Brown

Objectives

After completing the activities on "Test Match Sabina Park", you should be able to accurately:

- ☐ make predictions based on the title of the poem;
- ☐ identify the elements of poetry in the poem;
- ☐ critically assess your peers' presentation and analysis of the poem;
- ☐ examine the effect and effectiveness of literary devices used in the poem;
- ☐ create an advertisement for a place.

Getting Started

Activity 1: Before you begin …

Before you begin to read any piece of writing, it is usually a good idea to think about what you already know about the topic. Write down what you know about the title of the poem by completing the table below. The table should be completed as follows:

It says … - Write the title of the poem.

I know … - Write what you know about the title. In this case, what is a test match? What and where is Sabina Park?

And so … - Make a prediction about what you think the poem will be about based on the stated title and what you know about the title.

It says …	
I know …	
And so …	

Activity 2: Team Challenge – Cricket Lovely Cricket

Directions. Sabina Park is a historical cricket ground in Jamaica. It is also listed on Trip Advisor as a tourist attraction. The Jamaica Tourist Board (JTB) wants to increase interest in cricket and visits to Sabina Park, so the Board has approached your advertising company to create a TV advertisement to be shown locally, regionally and internationally. In groups of four or five, create a TV advertisement to help the JTB achieve its objective. Present your advertisement as a video.

Use the checklist below to ensure your advertisement is well-crafted. Your peers and your teacher may use the same checklist to give you feedback. After you have finished putting a tick beside each statement, make recommendations to yourself about how you may improve your advertisement. Ask your peers and your teacher to give you recommendations as well.

Checklist for Sabina Park Advertisement

Directions. The checklist below consists of a list of statements highlighting important things to consider when creating your advertisement and three emojis. If your answer to the statement is yes, put a tick beside the statement and under the happy face. If your answer to the statement is no, put a tick beside the statement and under the sad face. If you are unsure, put a tick beside the statement and under the unsure face.

Checklist for Sabina Park Advertisement			
1. Advertisement is no more than 60 seconds long.			
2. Advertisement has a simple and creative headline or tagline.			
3. Advertisement includes at least one influencer.			
4. Advertisement provides relevant details of the place (including what it offers, what sets it apart, and how to get there).			
5. Advertisement includes at least THREE historical cricket moments at Sabina Park.			
6. Advertisement includes important places in Sabina Park.			
7. Advertisement includes appropriate sound effects, pictures and video clips.			
8. Advertisement is organized properly.			
9. Advertisement is free from grammatical errors.			

For guidelines on how to create a TV advertisement, visit:

https://www.wikihow.com/Make-a-Commercial

https://smallbiztrends.com/2017/10/creating-an-effective-tv-commercial.html

You can use Windows Movie Maker to make your video.

My Recommendations

Make recommendations to yourself about how you may improve your advertisement. Ask your peers and your teacher for their recommendations on how you may improve as well.

Self	Peer
Teacher	

Peer reviewed by: ______________________________ Date: __________________________

Teacher reviewed by: ______________________________ Date: ________________________

Based on the feedback from yourself, your peers and teacher, make the necessary changes.

Earn a 

for creating the best advertisement.

Activity 3: The Featured Presentation

Use the checklist below to assess your peers' recitation of "Test Match Sabina Park".

Checklist for the Poetry Recitation

Directions. The checklist below consists of a list of statements highlighting important things to consider when reciting a poem and three emojis. If your answer to the statement is yes, put a tick beside the statement and under the happy face. If your answer to the statement is no, put a tick beside the statement and under the sad face. If you are unsure, put a tick beside the statement and under the unsure face.

Checklist for Song Performance			
1. Performance is no longer than three minutes.			
2. The words of the poem are said exactly as presented in the text.			
3. The performer adapts the role of the persona in movement, posture and general demeanour.			
4. Performer conveys the appropriate emotion.			
5. Performer makes appropriate use of facial expression, gestures, tone etc. to convey the meaning of the poem.			
6. Performer makes appropriate use of stage.			
7. Performance is audible and confident.			
8. Performance is entertaining.			

Directions. Based on your ticks in the checklist, rate your classmates' recitation of "Test Match Sabina Park" by shading the stars below. Five stars mean you believe the recitation was excellent. Then justify your rating.

Your Rating	Your Justification
☆☆☆☆☆	

What is the most common rating received by the presenter from your classmates? ____________________

What is your teacher's rating? ____

If you have the same rating as your teacher, you earn a  .

Choose TWO areas from the checklist where you ticked 'no' or 'unsure' and make ONE recommendation to the presenters on how they could have improved in those areas.

Selected area 1: ____

Recommendation: ____

____

____

____

Selected area 2: ____

Recommendation: ____

____

____

____

Elements of Poetry in "Test Match Sabina Park"

Your classmates will present their analysis of "Test Match Sabina Park". In this analysis, they will identify, explain and discuss the historical background, literary elements, form and literary devices used in the poem. You will be expected to critically assess the analysis being presented. This will be done in a step-by-step process.

Step 1: Listen for Information – While you listen to the analysis, complete the different activities with information presented in the analysis.

Step 2: Consult Your Peers – Share with a peer to see if he/she heard anything you might have missed or if you heard anything, he/she missed.

Step 3: Rate the Analysis – Look at the number of answered and unanswered activities you have and rate the overall analysis.

Historical Background

Directions. In this section, the presenters are expected to provide relevant information for all the areas in the picture below. However, you are only expected to write the ***poet's name, birthday, country of birth, quick facts and other works by the poet*** from the presenters' analysis. Complete the other sections based on your own feelings about the poet.

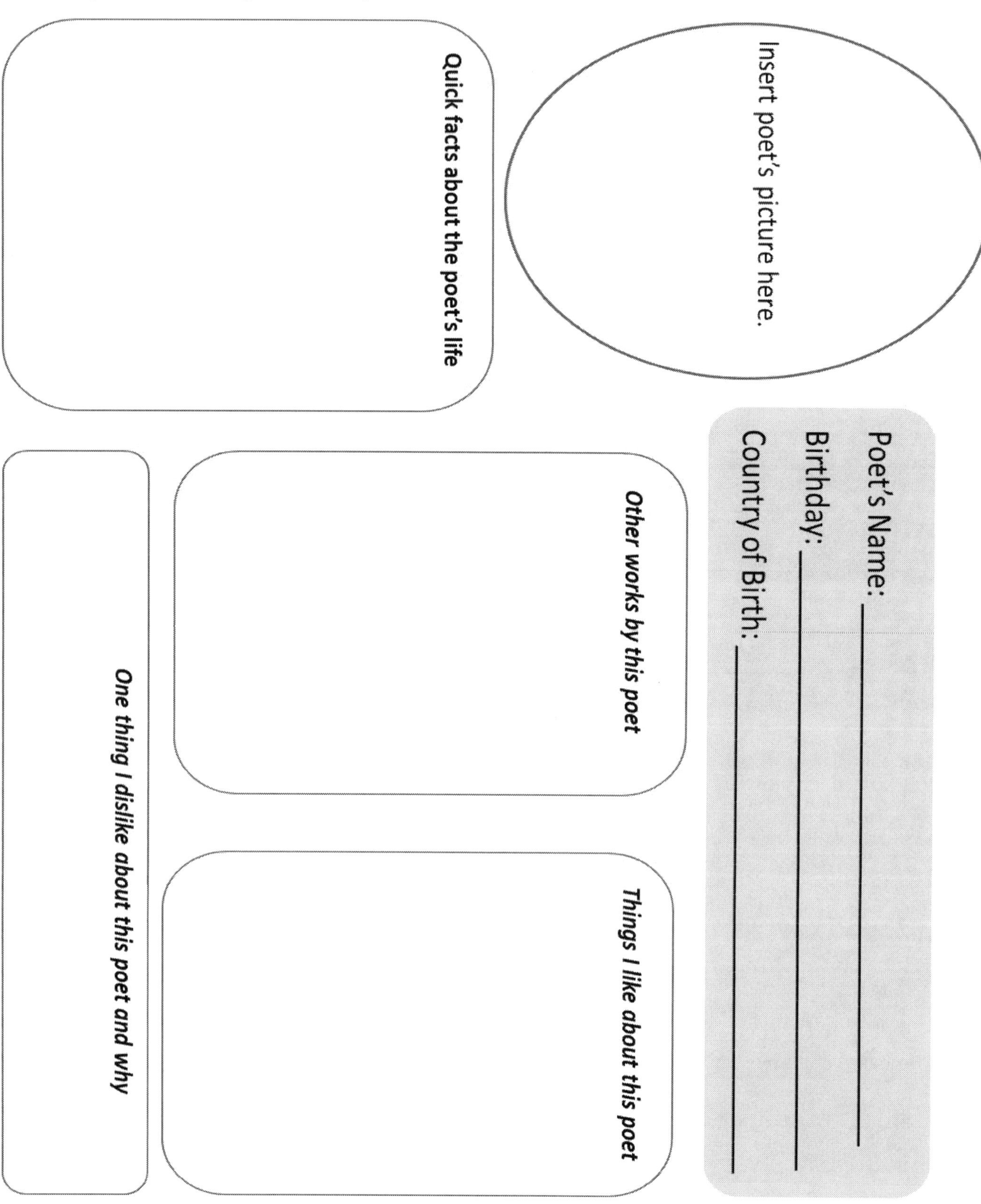

Literary Elements in "Test Match Sabina Park"

Directions. Write the literary elements identified by the presenter(s). After the presentation, you will be allowed time to identify these elements for yourself and compare your answers to the presenters' answers. Revise your notes on each element if you are unsure. Complete the table as follows:

1. Write the presenters' identifications.
2. Tick whether you agree or disagree with each identification.
3. Whether you agree or disagree, write one piece of evidence from the poem to support your decision.

<table>
<tr><th colspan="3">Characters</th></tr>
<tr><td>Persona:</td><td>Agree</td><td>Disagree</td></tr>
<tr><td colspan="3">Evidence:</td></tr>
<tr><td>Tone:</td><td>Agree</td><td>Disagree</td></tr>
<tr><td colspan="3">Evidence:</td></tr>
<tr><td>Other characters:</td><td>Agree</td><td>Disagree</td></tr>
<tr><td colspan="3">Evidence:</td></tr>
<tr><td>Type of Narration:</td><td>Agree</td><td>Disagree</td></tr>
<tr><td colspan="3">Evidence:</td></tr>
</table>

Setting		
Time and Place:	**Agree**	**Disagree**
Evidence:		
Mood:	**Agree**	**Disagree**
Evidence:		

Theme		
1st Theme Category: **Message *(one sentence):***	**Agree**	**Disagree**
Evidence		
2nd Theme Category: **Message *(one sentence):***	**Agree**	**Disagree**
Evidence		

Plot in "Test Match Sabina Park"

Directions. Summarize each stanza in a single sentence. Then, combine the sentences into a paragraph. Use suitable transition words and phrases to make the paragraph more coherent. Remember to use your own words.

Stanza 1:

Stanza 2:

Stanza 3:

Stanza 4:

Stanza 5:

Stylistics in "Test Match Sabina Park"

We will look at the form of the poem and the literary devices used.

Form of "Test Match Sabina Park"

Directions. Fill in the blanks with information from "Test Match Sabina Park".

"Test Match Sabina Park" is a ________________ (*Type of poem*). The poem consists of __________ (*Number of lines*) lines which are divided into ______________ (*Number of stanzas*) stanzas. The first three stanzas are ______________ (*Type of stanza*). The fourth and fifth are ____________ (*Type of stanza*), and the sixth is also a ____________ (*Type of stanza*). The poem has _________________ (*Type of rhythm*) and is written with ___________________________ (*Type of rhyme scheme*).

Activity 2A: A Poem with a Story Worth Performing

1. "Test Match Sabina Park" has features in common with a story. Identify these features below.

   Protagonist: ____________________________ **Antagonist:** ___________________________

   Conflict: ____

   ____

   Dialogue: ____

   ____

   Turning point: ____

   Resolution: ____

Activity 2B: Team Challenge – Test Match Sabina Park, The Play

Directions. In groups of five, dramatize the poem. Ensure you use sound, costume and lighting to enhance your performance.

Earn a 

for making the best performance.

Literary Devices in "Test Match Sabina Park"

Activity 1: Identifying the Devices

Directions. Write the names of FOUR literary devices used in the poem. Then, write an example of each of the listed devices from the poem. Ensure you write the line number(s) for each example given.

Literary Devices	Examples
1. ____________________:	______________________________
	______________________________
2. ____________________:	______________________________
	______________________________
3. ____________________:	______________________________
	______________________________
4. ____________________:	______________________________
	______________________________

If you have identified a simile or metaphor, explain it by using the formula.

____

____

____

____

____

____

____

____

Explain an allusion made in the poem.

____

____

____

____

____

____

____

Activity 2: That's So Punny

For this activity, we will focus on puns as a literary device used in poetry and literature in general. A pun is a play on words or phrases that have two meanings. They are usually created using homophones, homographs and homonyms. Puns are usually used to create humour and to highlight the wittiness of the speaker or poet. Like the other literary devices, puns are used in songs and everyday conversations as well.

Example. I'm on a see food diet. When I see food, I eat.

In the example, the pun is see food. When you hear the first see food, you might think the speaker only eats food from the sea (seafood). However, see food, as used in the second sentence in the example, shows that the speaker eats any food he/she sees. Can you think of any other example?

____

____

____

In examining or commenting on puns, you should:

- ✓ identify the pun;
- ✓ state the two meanings;
- ✓ assess the extent to which it was humourous or witty/clever.

Comment on TWO examples of puns used in "Test Match Sabina Park".

____

____

____

____

____

____

____

____

____

____

____

____

____

Activity 3: Effect and Effectiveness

Directions. Choose TWO devices identified in "Test Match Sabina Park" and comment on their effect and effectiveness. If you need to remind yourself of what is required when you are asked to examine or comment on the use of a literary device, read the notes presented of **pages 52 – 53** of this Workbook.

Device	Evidence
Effect:	
Effectiveness:	

Device	Evidence
Effect:	
Effectiveness:	

Assessing Your Peers' Presentation

Directions. Compare the information your peers provided with your own analysis and rate your classmates' analysis of "Test Match Sabina Park" by shading the stars below. Five stars mean you believe the analysis was excellent. Then, justify your rating.

Your Rating	Your Justification
☆☆☆☆☆	

What is the most common rating received by the presenter from your classmates? ______________

What is your teacher's rating? ______________________________

If you have the same rating as your teacher, you earn a ⚖.

Choose ONE element of poetry that you think the presenters need to make improvement in analyzing and make TWO recommendations to the presenters on how they can improve in analyzing that element.

Selected area: ______________________________

Recommendation 1: ______________________________

Recommendation 2: ______________________________

Now that you have finished analyzing "Test Match Sabina Park", look back at the predictions you made before you analyzed the poem and answer the following questions.

1. To what extent were your predictions right?

   Not at all ☐ A small extent ☐ Somewhat ☐ To a large extent ☐ Spot on ☐

2. Explain your selection for question 1. ______________________________

   ____

   ____

   ____

3. Identify FOUR contrasts made in the poem.

   ____

   ____

   ____

   ____

   ____

   ____

   ____

   ____

4. Would you attend a test match at Sabina Park? Why or Why not?

   ____

   ____

   ____

5. Choose TWO poems that you have studied from the prescribed list which present contrasting perspectives on racism.

   Write an essay in which you describe the speaker in EACH poem. In this essay, you must compare the attitude of EACH speaker to his own and the other race and examine ONE device that is used to explore racism as a theme in EACH poem.

Use the rubric for poetry essays in the CXC English syllabus to assess your essay writing skills. Then, ask your classmate to use the same rubric to assess your essay while you do the same for him/her. Revise your essay before presenting it to your teacher.

Checking My Progress

You have just finished the activities on "Test Match Sabina Park". Before we move to the activities on the next poem, review what you have learnt or are still uncertain about. Do so by first checking the objectives you have accomplished so far.

Directions. Go back to the objectives at the beginning of the activities on "Test Match Sabina Park". If you think you have accomplished an objective, without looking back at your notes, put a tick in the box ☐ before the objective. If you are unsure you have accomplished the objective, put a question mark (?) and if you are sure you have not accomplished the objective, leave it unchecked (blank). Ensure you pay more attention to your unchecked boxes and the boxes with your question marks as you study. Also, ensure that you can perform the number indicated in each objective (e.g., list **three** genres). You have accomplished the objective when you can list the indicated number (three).

Now complete the 3-2-1 activity below. It works as follows:

Three – Write **three** things you learned from the activities on "Test Match Sabina Park".

Two – Write **two** things you found interesting or about which you would like to learn more.

One – Write **one** question you still have about the material.

Share your question with your classmates and listen to their responses. Did they clarify things? If not, maybe it is time you did some independent research.

Finally, record ONE question from one of your classmates and provide an answer to that classmate.

Checking What I Know!!!

3. ______________________________

____

____

2. ______________________________

____

1. ______________________________

Helping My Peers!!!

Peer's question: ______________________________

____

My answer: ______________________________

____

____

"A Stone's Throw" by Elma Mitchell

Objectives

After completing the activities on "A Stone's Throw", you should be able to accurately:

- ☐ make predictions based on the title of the poem;
- ☐ identify the elements of poetry in the poem;
- ☐ critically assess your peers' presentation and analysis of the poem;
- ☐ examine the effect and effectiveness of literary devices used in the poem;
- ☐ examine devices with contradictions.

Getting Started

Activity 1: Before you begin …

Before you begin to read any piece of writing, it is usually a good idea to think of what you already know about the topic. Write down what you know about the title of the poem by completing the table below. The table should be completed as follows:

It says … - Write the title of the poem.

I know … - Write what you know about the title. In this case, what does a stone's throw mean in distance? Why do people throw stones?

And so … - Make a prediction about what you think the poem will be about based on the stated title and what you know about the title.

It says …	
I know …	
And so …	

Activity 2: Throwing Stones

Directions. Answer the following questions.

1. The park is just a stone's throw from my house? What does 'a stone's throw' mean in that sentence? ____

2. What does the proverb, 'if you live in a glass house, you should not throw stones' mean?

____

____

____

Activity 3A: Stone Throwing Stories

Directions. Interview a person of authority in a church near you and ask him/ her to share a story in the Bible that includes stone throwing.

Name of Interviewee: ______________________ Position: ______________________

Name of Church: ____

Story: ____

____

____

____

____

____

____

____

____

____

____

____

____

____

____

____

Signature of Interviewee: ______________________ Date: ______________

Activity 3: The Featured Presentation

Use the checklist below to assess your peers' recitation of "A Stone's Throw".

Checklist for the Poetry Recitation

Directions. The checklist below consists of a list of statements highlighting important things to consider when reciting a poem and three emojis. If your answer to the statement is yes, put a tick beside the statement and under the happy face. If your answer to the statement is no, put a tick beside the statement and under the sad face. If you are unsure, put a tick beside the statement and under the unsure face.

Checklist for Song Performance			
1. Performance is no longer than three minutes.			
2. The words of the poem are said exactly as presented in the text.			
3. The performer adapts the role of the persona in movement, posture and general demeanour.			
4. Performer conveys the appropriate emotion.			
5. Performer makes appropriate use of facial expression, gestures, tone etc. to convey the meaning of the poem.			
6. Performer makes appropriate use of stage.			
7. Performance is audible and confident.			
8. Performance is entertaining.			

Directions. Based on your ticks in the checklist, rate your classmates' recitation of "A Stone's Throw" by shading the stars below. Five stars mean you believe the recitation was excellent. Then, justify your rating.

Your Rating	Your Justification
☆☆☆☆☆	

What is the most common rating received by the presenter from your classmates? ____________________

What is your teacher's rating? ____

If you have the same rating as your teacher, you earn a  .

Choose TWO areas from the checklist where you ticked 'no' or 'unsure' and make ONE recommendation to the presenters on how they could have improved in those areas.

Selected area 1: ____

Recommendation: ____

____

____

____

Selected area 2: ____

Recommendation: ____

____

____

____

Elements of Poetry in "A Stone's Throw"

Your classmates will present their analysis of "A Stone's Throw". In this analysis, they will identify, explain and discuss the historical background, literary elements, form and literary devices used in the poem. You will be expected to critically assess the analysis being presented. This will be done in a step-by-step process.

Step 1: Listen for Information – While you listen to the analysis, complete the different activities with information presented in the analysis.

Step 2: Consult Your Peers – Share with a peer to see if he/she heard anything you might have missed or if you heard anything, he/she missed.

Step 3: Rate the Analysis – Look at the number of answered and unanswered activities you have and rate the overall analysis.

Historical Background

Directions. In this section, the presenters are expected to provide relevant information for all the areas in the picture below. However, you are only expected to write the ***poet's name, birthday, country of birth, quick facts and other works by the poet*** from the presenters' analysis. Complete the other sections based on your own feelings about the poet.

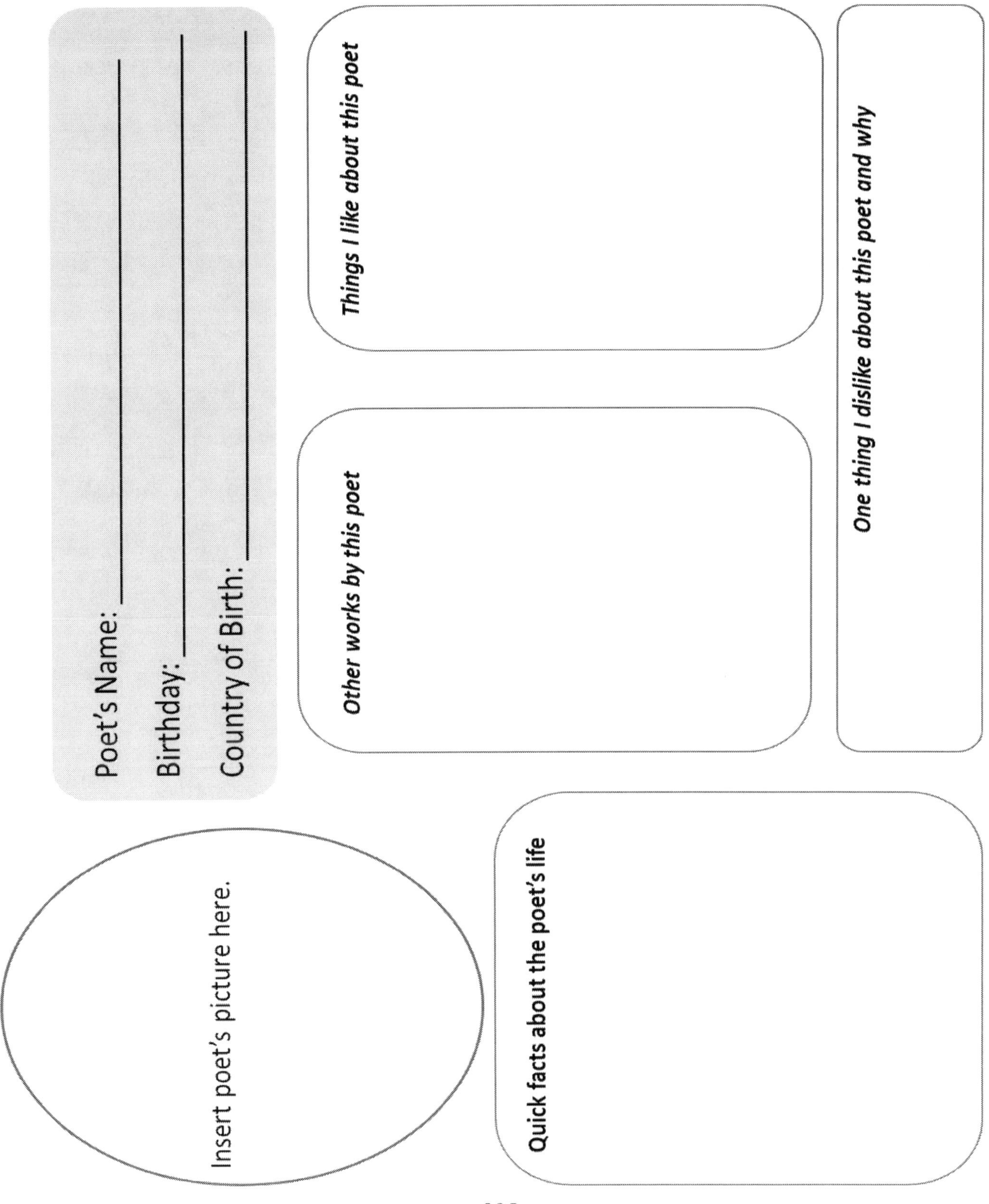

Literary Elements in "A Stone's Throw"

Directions. Write the literary elements identified by the presenter(s). After the presentation, you will be allowed time to identify these elements for yourself and compare your answers to the presenters' answers. Revise your notes on each element if you are unsure. Complete the table as follows:

1. Write the presenters' identifications.
2. Tick whether you agree or disagree with each identification.
3. Whether you agree or disagree, write one piece of evidence from the poem to support your decision.

<table>
<tr><th colspan="3">Characters</th></tr>
<tr><td>Persona:</td><td>Agree</td><td>Disagree</td></tr>
<tr><td colspan="3">Evidence:</td></tr>
<tr><td>Tone:</td><td>Agree</td><td>Disagree</td></tr>
<tr><td colspan="3">Evidence:</td></tr>
<tr><td>Other characters:</td><td>Agree</td><td>Disagree</td></tr>
<tr><td colspan="3">Evidence:</td></tr>
<tr><td>Type of Narration:</td><td>Agree</td><td>Disagree</td></tr>
<tr><td colspan="3">Evidence:</td></tr>
</table>

<table>
<tr><th colspan="3">Setting</th></tr>
<tr><td>Time and Place:</td><td>Agree</td><td>Disagree</td></tr>
<tr><td colspan="3">Evidence:</td></tr>
<tr><td>Mood:</td><td>Agree</td><td>Disagree</td></tr>
<tr><td colspan="3">Evidence:</td></tr>
<tr><th colspan="3">Theme</th></tr>
<tr><td>1st Theme Category:
Message (one sentence):</td><td>Agree</td><td>Disagree</td></tr>
<tr><td colspan="3">Evidence</td></tr>
<tr><td>2nd Theme Category:
Message (one sentence):</td><td>Agree</td><td>Disagree</td></tr>
<tr><td colspan="3">Evidence</td></tr>
</table>

Plot in "A Stone's Throw"

Directions. Summarize each stanza in a single sentence. Then, combine the sentences into a paragraph. Use suitable transition words and phrases to make the paragraph more coherent. Remember to use your own words.

Stanza 1:

Stanza 2:

Stanza 3:

Stanza 4:

Stanza 5:

Stanza 6:

Stylistics in "A Stone's Throw"

We will look at the form of the poem and the literary devices used.

Form of "A Stone's Throw"

Directions. Fill in the blanks with information from "A Stone's Throw".

"A Stone's Throw" is a ____________________ (*Type of poem*). The poem consists of ___________ (*Number of lines*) lines which are divided into _____________ (*Number of stanzas*) stanzas. Each stanza is a different type of stanza. The first two stanzas are ______________ (*Type of stanza*), the third is a ________________ (*Type of stanza*) the fourth is a ________________ (*Type of stanza*) and the fifth is a _________________ (*Type of stanza*) and the sixth is a _________________ (*Type of stanza*). The poem has __________________ (*Type of rhyme scheme*) and is written in ____________________________ (*Type of rhythm*).

Answer the following questions.

2. Why are some of the words in brackets? ____

   ____

   ____

3. "A Stone's Throw" has features in common with a story. Identify these features below.

   Protagonist: ____________________________ **Antagonist:** ___________________________

   Conflict: ____

   ____

   Dialogue: ____

   ____

   Turning point: ____

   Resolution: ____

   What is the sin of the woman? What is the accompanying punishment?

   ____

   ____

   ____

Literary Devices in "A Stone's Throw"

Activity 1: Identifying the Devices

Directions. Write the names of FOUR literary devices used in the poem. Then, write an example of each of the listed devices from the poem. Ensure you write the line number(s) for each example given.

Literary Devices	Examples
1. ____________________:	____
2. ____________________:	____
3. ____________________:	____
4. ____________________:	____

If you have identified a simile or metaphor, explain it by using the formula.

Devices with Contradiction

Devices with contradictions combine statements, ideas, or features that are the opposite of one another. They also mean the opposite of what is said. Examples of these devices are paradox, oxymoron, sarcasm and irony. In examining devices with contradictions, you should:

- ✓ identify the device;
- ✓ outline the contradiction;
- ✓ comment on the effect and/or effectiveness of the contradiction.

Activity 2. Explaining Contradictions

Directions. Answer the following questions.

"A Stone's Throw" makes use of devices with contradiction. Examine ONE of these devices.

____

List TWO other contradictions presented in the poem.

____

Activity 3: Effect and Effectiveness

Directions. Choose TWO devices identified in "A Stone's Throw" and comment on their effect and effectiveness. If you need to remind yourself of what is required when you are asked to examine or comment on the use of a literary device, read the notes presented of **pages 52 – 53** of this Workbook.

Device	**Evidence**
Effect:	
Effectiveness:	

Device	**Evidence**
Effect:	
Effectiveness:	

Assessing Your Peers' Presentation

Directions. Compare the information your peers provided with your own analysis and rate your classmates' analysis of "A Stone's Throw" by shading the stars below. Five stars mean you believe the analysis was excellent. Then justify your rating.

Your Rating	Your Justification
☆☆☆☆☆	

What is the most common rating received by the presenter from your classmates? ___________________

What is your teacher's rating? ___________________

If you have the same rating as your teacher, you earn a .

Choose ONE element of poetry that you think the presenters need to make improvement in analyzing and make TWO recommendations to the presenters on how they can improve in analyzing that element.

Selected area: ___________________

Recommendation 1: ___________________

Recommendation 2: ___________________

Now that you have finished analyzing "A Stone's Throw", look back at the predictions you made before you analyzed the poem and answer the following questions.

1. To what extent were your predictions right?

   Not at all ☐ A small extent ☐ Somewhat ☐ To a large extent ☐ Spot on ☐

2. Explain your selection for question 1.____

   ____

   ____

   ____

   ____

   ____

3. How is the meaning of a stone's throw (a short distance) reflected in the poem?

   ____

   ____

   ____

   ____

   ____

4. In what way did the biblical background of the poem contribute to your understanding of the poem?

   ____

   ____

   ____

   ____

   ____

5. "A Stone's Throw" and "Once Upon A Time" highlight contradictions in society."

   Write an essay in which you outline a societal contradiction presented in EACH poem. In this essay, you must also discuss how the persona in EACH poem feels about the contradiction and examine ONE device that is used to explore contradictions in EACH poem.

Checking My Progress

You have just finished the activities on "A Stone's Throw". Before we move to the activities on the next poem, review what you have learnt or are still uncertain about. Do so by first checking the objectives you have accomplished so far.

Directions. Go back to the objectives at the beginning of the activities on "A Stone's Throw". If you think you have accomplished an objective, without looking back at your notes, put a tick in the box ☐ before the objective. If you are unsure you have accomplished the objective, put a question mark (?) and if you are sure you have not accomplished the objective, leave it unchecked (blank). Ensure you pay more attention to your unchecked boxes and the boxes with your question marks as you study. Also, ensure that you can perform the number indicated in each objective (e.g., list **three** genres). You have accomplished the objective when you can list the indicated number (three).

Now complete the 3-2-1 activity below. It works as follows:

Three – Write **three** things you learned from the activities on "A Stone's Throw".

Two – Write **two** things you found interesting or about which you would like to learn more.

One – Write **one** question you still have about the material.

Share your question with your classmates and listen to their responses. Did they clarify things? If not, maybe it is time you did some independent research.

Finally, record ONE question from one of your classmates and provide an answer to that classmate.

Checking What I Know!!!

3. ______________________________

____

____

2. ______________________________

____

1. ______________________________

Helping My Peers!!!

Peer's question: ______________________________

____

My answer: ______________________________

____

____

"A Lesson for this Sunday" by Derek Walcott

Objectives

After completing the activities on "A Lesson for this Sunday", you should be able to accurately:

- ☐ make predictions based on the title of the poem;
- ☐ identify the elements of poetry in the poem;
- ☐ critically assess your peers' presentation and analysis of the poem;
- ☐ examine the effect and effectiveness of literary devices used in the poem;
- ☐ examine sound devices.

Getting Started

Activity 1: Before you begin …

Before you begin to read any piece of writing, it is usually a good idea to think of what you already know about the topic. Write down what you know about the title of the poem by completing the table below. The table should be completed as follows:

It says … - Write the title of the poem.

I know … - Write what you know about the title. In this case, what is a lesson? What are lessons taught on Sundays usually about?

And so … - Make a prediction about what you think the poem will be about based on the stated title and what you know about the title.

It says …	
I know …	
And so …	

Activity 2: Human Beings and Nature

Directions. This activity requires you to identify differences between human beings and nature and religion and science. In each square below, draw or paste a symbol or picture that represents human beings, nature science and religion. Then, on each symbol/picture write words or phrases that show differences between (1) human beings and nature (2) science and religion. Do NOT write sentences.

Humans	**Nature**
Science	**Religion**

Which of the differences identified do you consider to be the most significant one? Why?

____

____

Activity 2: My Sunday Lesson

Directions. Insert a picture of a church (or any other religious institution) you attend or is in your community.

Insert your picture here.

1. Write the name of your favourite or most memorable religious story. Be prepared to share this story with your classmates.

____

____

2. Write ONE lesson that you have learnt from this story.

____

____

____

3. Write THREE lessons you have been taught about human beings.

____

____

____

____

____

____

____

Activity 3: The Featured Presentation

Directions. Use the checklist below to assess your peers' recitation of "A Lesson for this Sunday".

Checklist for the Poetry Recitation

Directions. The checklist below consists of a list of statements highlighting important things to consider when reciting a poem and three emojis. If your answer to the statement is yes, put a tick beside the statement and under the happy face. If your answer to the statement is no, put a tick beside the statement and under the sad face. If you are unsure, put a tick beside the statement and under the unsure face.

Checklist for Poetry Recitation	(happy face)	(unsure face)	(sad face)
1. Performance is no longer than three minutes.			
2. The words of the poem are said exactly as presented in the text.			
3. The performer adapts the role of the persona in movement, posture and general demeanour.			
4. Performer conveys the appropriate emotion.			
5. Performer makes appropriate use of facial expression, gestures, tone etc. to convey the meaning of the poem.			
6. Performer makes appropriate use of stage.			
7. Performance is audible and confident.			
8. Performance is entertaining.			

Directions. Based on your ticks in the checklist, rate your classmates' recitation of "A Lesson for this Sunday" by shading the stars below. Five stars mean you believe the recitation was excellent. Then justify your rating.

Your Rating	**Your Justification**
☆☆☆☆☆	

What is the most common rating received by the presenter from your classmates? ____________________

What is your teacher's rating? ______________________________

If you have the same rating as your teacher, you earn a .

Choose TWO areas from the checklist where you ticked 'no' or 'unsure' and make ONE recommendation to the presenters on how they could have improved in those areas.

Selected area 1: ______________________________

Recommendation: ______________________________

____

____

____

Selected area 2: ______________________________

Recommendation: ______________________________

____

____

____

Elements of Poetry in "A Lesson for this Sunday"

Your classmates will present their analysis of "A Lesson for this Sunday". In this analysis, they will identify, explain and discuss the historical background, literary elements, form and literary devices used in the poem. You will be expected to critically assess the analysis being presented. This will be done in a step-by-step process.

Step 1: Listen for Information – While you listen to the analysis, complete the different activities with information presented in the analysis.

Step 2: Consult Your Peers – Share with a peer to see if he/she heard anything you might have missed or if you heard anything, he/she missed.

Step 3: Rate the Analysis – Look at the number of answered and unanswered activities you have and rate the overall analysis.

Historical Background

Directions. In this section, the presenters are expected to provide relevant information for all the areas in the picture below. However, you are only expected to write the ***poet's name, birthday, country of birth, quick facts and other works by the poet*** from the presenters' analysis. Complete the other sections based on your own feelings about the poet.

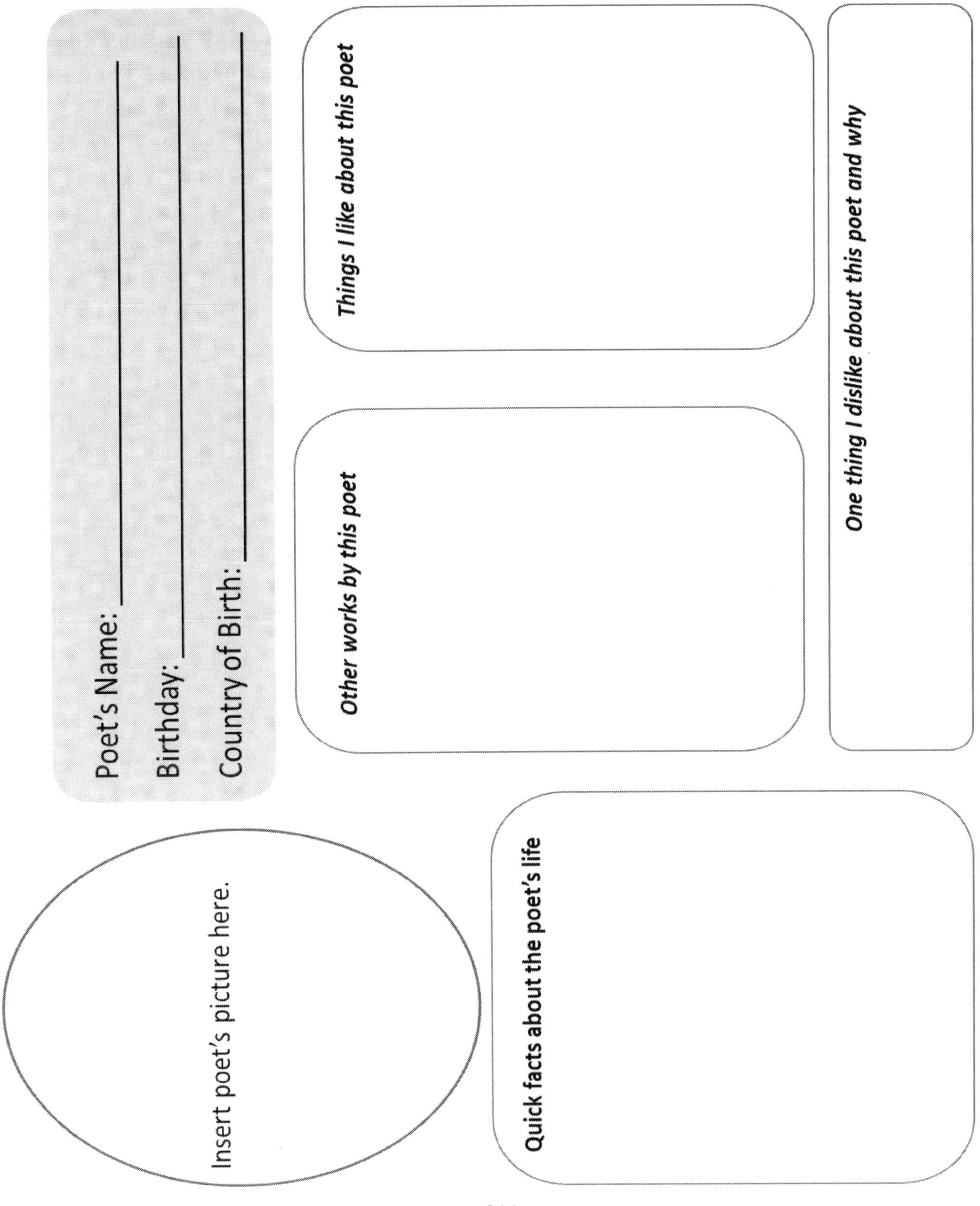

Literary Elements in "A Lesson for this Sunday"

Directions. Write the literary elements identified by the presenter(s). After the presentation, you will be allowed time to identify these elements for yourself and compare your answers to the presenters' answers. Revise your notes on each element if you are unsure. Complete the table as follows:

1. Write the presenters' identifications.
2. Tick whether you agree or disagree with each identification.
3. Whether you agree or disagree, write one piece of evidence from the poem to support your decision.

Characters		
Persona:	**Agree**	**Disagree**
Evidence:		
Tone:	**Agree**	**Disagree**
Evidence:		
Other characters:	**Agree**	**Disagree**
Evidence:		
Type of Narration:	**Agree**	**Disagree**
Evidence:		

<table>
<tr><th colspan="3">Setting</th></tr>
<tr><td>Time and Place:</td><td>Agree</td><td>Disagree</td></tr>
<tr><td colspan="3">Evidence:</td></tr>
<tr><td>Mood:</td><td>Agree</td><td>Disagree</td></tr>
<tr><td colspan="3">Evidence:</td></tr>
<tr><th colspan="3">Theme</th></tr>
<tr><td>1st Theme Category:
Message (one sentence):</td><td>Agree</td><td>Disagree</td></tr>
<tr><td colspan="3">Evidence</td></tr>
<tr><td>2nd Theme Category:
Message (one sentence):</td><td>Agree</td><td>Disagree</td></tr>
<tr><td colspan="3">Evidence</td></tr>
</table>

Plot in "A Lesson for this Sunday"

Directions. Summarize each stanza in a single sentence. Then, combine the sentences into a paragraph. Use suitable transitional words and phrases to make the paragraph more coherent. Remember to use your own words.

Stanza 1:

Stanza 2:

Stanza 3:

What are the main differences between human beings and nature highlighted in the poem? Write complete sentences.

____

____

Stylistics in "A Lesson for this Sunday"

We will look at the form of the poem and the literary devices used.

Form of "A Lesson for this Sunday"

Directions. Fill in the blanks with information from "A Lesson for this Sunday".

"A Lesson for this Sunday" is a ____________________ (*Type of poem*). The poem consists of ____________ (*Number of lines*) lines which are divided into ______________ (*Number of stanzas*) stanzas. Each stanza is a different type of stanza. The first stanza is ____________________ (*Type of stanza*), the second is a ____________________ (*Type of stanza*), and the third is a ____________________ (*Type of stanza*)

The poem has ________________________________ (*Type of rhyme scheme*) and is written in ____________________________ (*Type of rhythm*).

Answer the following questions.

1. List THREE words or phrases used in the poem to highlight each of the following:

   Science: ____

   Nature: ____

   Religion: ____

2. The persona uses the word 'frail' to describe the butterfly in line 2 and to describe the girl in line 22. What does the use of this word to describe both the butterfly and the girl tell you about the persona's attitude towards the girl?

   ____

   ____

   ____

   ____

   ____

3. What is the lesson presented in the poem?

   ____

   ____

   ____

Literary Devices in "A Lesson for this Sunday"

Activity 1: Identifying the Devices

Directions. Write the names of FOUR literary devices used in the poem. Then, write an example of each of the listed devices from the poem. Ensure you write the line number(s) for each example given.

Literary Devices	**Examples**
1. ______________________:	______________________________ ______________________________
2. ______________________:	______________________________ ______________________________
3. ______________________:	______________________________ ______________________________
4. ______________________:	______________________________ ______________________________

If you have identified a simile or metaphor, explain it by using the formula.

____

____

____

____

____

____

Explain an allusion made in the poem.

____

____

____

____

Explain a pun used in the poem.

____

____

____

____

Sound Devices

"A Lesson for this Sunday" makes use of sound devices to convey the sound and sense of the poem. Sound devices heighten the readers experience of the poem by appealing to the readers' sense of hearing. They also convey the tone of the persona and appeal to the readers' emotions. Examples of sound devices used in literature include alliteration, assonance, consonance, cacophony and onomatopoeia. Most of these devices are used in "A Lesson for this Sunday".

Activity 2. The Sound of Poetry

Directions. Complete the table below by putting in the missing information. The first one is done for you.

Sound Device	Evidence	What it allows you to hear
Alliteration	**The thought in things (L8)**	**Repetition of the 'th' sound causes me to hear the gentle wind that adds to the relaxing mood created in the first stanza. 'Th' is also a voiceless sound, so it heightens the contrast between the natural peace in the first stanza and the children's disruptive screams in the second stanza.**
	'cries', (L9), 'shrieks' (L16), 'scream' (L20)	Causes me to hear the disruption of the children.
	Teetering thing attempts its flight, (L20)	
Assonance		Repetition of the long 'o' sound causes me to hear the oooh people usually make while the weep
		Repetition of the 's' sound reminds me of the hiss (of a snake or a person) which usually signifies danger, disgust.

Activity 3: Effect and Effectiveness

Directions. Choose TWO devices identified in "A Lesson for this Sunday" and comment on their effect and effectiveness. If you need to remind yourself of what is required when you are asked to examine or comment on the use of a literary device, read the notes presented of **pages 52 – 53** of this Workbook.

<table>
<tr><td>Device</td><td>Evidence</td></tr>
<tr><td></td><td></td></tr>
<tr><td colspan="2">Effect:</td></tr>
<tr><td colspan="2">Effectiveness:</td></tr>
</table>

<table>
<tr><td>Device</td><td>Evidence</td></tr>
<tr><td></td><td></td></tr>
<tr><td colspan="2">Effect:</td></tr>
<tr><td colspan="2">Effectiveness:</td></tr>
</table>

Assessing Your Peers' Presentation

Directions. Compare the information your peers provided with your own analysis and rate your classmates' analysis of "A Lesson for this Sunday" by shading the stars below. Five stars mean you believe the analysis was excellent. Then, justify your rating.

Your Rating	Your Justification
☆☆☆☆☆	

What is the most common rating received by the presenter from your classmates? ________________

What is your teacher's rating? ________________

If you have the same rating as your teacher, you earn a .

Choose ONE element of poetry that you think the presenters need to make improvement in analyzing and make ONE recommendation to the presenters on how they can improve in analyzing that element.

Selected area: ________________

Recommendation 1: ________________

Recommendation 2: ________________

Now that you have finished analyzing "A Lesson for this Sunday", look back at the predictions you made before you analyzed the poem and answer the following questions.

1. To what extent were your predictions right?

   Not at all ☐ A small extent ☐ Somewhat ☐ To a large extent ☐ Spot on ☐

2. Explain your selection for question 1. ____

   ____

   ____

3. Circle the words that accurately describes the persona's attitude towards human beings and underline the words that accurately describes his attitude towards nature.

Annoyed	**Frustrated**	**Ambivalent**	**Compassionate**	**Hopeless**
Negative	**Appreciative**	**Disapproving**	**Celebratory**	**Positive**

4. "A Lesson for this Sunday" and "Birdshooting Season" focus on man's interaction with nature.

   Write an essay in which you describe how humans interact with nature in EACH poem. In this essay, you must also compare children's response to the interaction between man and nature and examine ONE device that is used to explore the theme of man and his environment in EACH poem.

5. Choose TWO poems that you have studied from the prescribed list which focus on religion.

   Write an essay in which you describe how God is presented in EACH poem. In this essay, you must also compare the speaker's attitude towards God and examine ONE device that is used to explore the theme of religion in EACH poem.

Use the rubric for poetry essays in the CXC English syllabus to assess your essay writing skills. Then, ask your classmate to use the same rubric to assess your essay while you do the same for him/her. Revise your essay before presenting it to your teacher.

Checking My Progress

You have just finished the activities on "A Lesson for this Sunday". Before we move to the activities on the next poem, review what you have learnt or are still uncertain about. Do so by first checking the objectives you have accomplished so far.

Directions. Go back to the objectives at the beginning of the activities on "A Lesson for this Sunday". If you think you have accomplished an objective, without looking back at your notes, put a tick in the ☐ box before the objective. If you are unsure you have accomplished the objective, put a question mark (?) and if you are sure you have not accomplished the objective, leave it unchecked (blank). Ensure you pay more attention to your unchecked boxes and the boxes with your question marks as you study. Also, ensure that you can perform the number indicated in each objective (e.g., list **three** genres). You have accomplished the objective when you can list the indicated number (three).

Now complete the 3-2-1 activity below. It works as follows:

Three – Write **three** things you learned from the activities on "A Lesson for this Sunday".

Two – Write **two** things you found interesting or about which you would like to learn more.

One – Write **one** question you still have about the material.

Share your question with your classmates and listen to their responses. Did they clarify things? If not, maybe it is time you did some independent research.

Finally, record ONE question from one of your classmates and provide an answer to that classmate.

Checking What I Know!!!

3. ____

____

____

2. ____

____

1. ____

Helping My Peers!!!

Peer's question: ____

____

My answer: ____

____

____

"The Woman Speaks to the Man Who Has Employed Her Son" by Lorna Goodison

Objectives

After completing the activities on "The Woman Speaks to the Man Who Has Employed Her Son", you should be able to accurately:

- ☐ make predictions based on the title of the poem;
- ☐ identify the elements of poetry in the poem;
- ☐ critically assess your peers' presentation and analysis of the poem;
- ☐ examine the effect and effectiveness of literary devices used in the poem;
- ☐ create black-out poems.

Getting Started

Activity 1: Before you begin …

Before you begin to read any piece of writing, it is usually a good idea to think of what you already know about the topic. Write down what you know about the title of the poem by completing the table below. The table should be completed as follows:

It says … - Write the title of the poem.

I know … - Write what you know about the title. In this case, based on the title, who is the speaker in the poem? What would a woman have to say to a man who has employed her son?

And so … - Make a prediction about what you think the poem will be about based on the stated title and what you know about the title.

It says …	
I know …	
And so …	

Activity 2A: A Mother's Love (Part 1)

Directions. Paste a picture of your mother or a person who has played a motherly role in your life in the heart below. Cut out words or phrases that describe this person as a mother from existing print documents (magazines, newspapers etc.) and paste them around the heart.

Activity 2B: This is How I Feel

Directions. Create a black out poem that expresses your response to your mother or the person who has played the role of a mother in your life. The source of your poem can be any printed document, but you get extra points for creating it from a poem, excerpt from a story or play on the CSEC English B prescribed list.

Earn a AWESOME JOB!! *for creating the best black out poem and a* DROPS MIC *for using a source document from the CSEC English B prescribed list.*

For information on how to create a black out poem, visit: https://www.scholastic.com/teachers/blog-posts/john-depasquale/blackout-poetry/

Activity 3: The Featured Presentation

Directions. Use the checklist below to assess your peers' recitation of "The Woman Speaks to the Man Who has Employed Her Son".

Checklist for the Poetry Recitation

Directions. The checklist below consists of a list of statements highlighting important things to consider when reciting a poem and three emojis. If your answer to the statement is yes, put a tick beside the statement and under the happy face. If your answer to the statement is no, put a tick beside the statement and under the sad face. If you are unsure, put a tick beside the statement and under the unsure face.

Checklist for Song Performance			
1. Performance is no longer than three minutes.			
2. The words of the poem are said exactly as presented in the text.			
3. The performer adapts the role of the persona in movement, posture and general demeanour.			
4. Performer conveys the appropriate emotion.			
5. Performer makes appropriate use of facial expression, gestures, tone etc. to convey the meaning of the poem.			
6. Performer makes appropriate use of stage.			
7. Performance is audible and confident.			
8. Performance is entertaining.			

Directions. Based on your ticks in the checklist, rate your classmates' recitation of "The Woman Speaks to the Man Who has Employed Her Son" by shading the stars below. Five stars mean you believe the recitation was excellent. Then, justify your rating.

Your Rating	Your Justification
☆☆☆☆☆	

What is the most common rating received by the presenter from your classmates? ____________

What is your teacher's rating? ___

If you have the same rating as your teacher, you earn a  .

Choose TWO areas from the checklist where you ticked 'no' or 'unsure' and make ONE recommendation to the presenters on how they could have improved in those areas.

Selected area 1: ___

Recommendation: ___

___

___

___

Selected area 2: ___

Recommendation: ___

___

___

___

Elements of Poetry in "The Woman Speaks to the Man Who has Employed Her Son

Your classmates will present their analysis of "The Woman Speaks to the Man Who has Employed Her Son". In this analysis, they will identify, explain and discuss the historical background, literary elements, form and literary devices used in the poem. You will be expected to critically assess the analysis being presented. This will be done in a step-by-step process.

Step 1: Listen for Information – While you listen to the analysis, complete the different activities with information presented in the analysis.

Step 2: Consult Your Peers – Share with a peer to see if he/she heard anything you might have missed or if you heard anything, he/she missed.

Step 3: Rate the Analysis – Look at the number of answered and unanswered activities you have and rate the overall analysis.

Historical Background

Directions. In this section, the presenters are expected to provide relevant information for all the areas in the picture below. However, you are only expected to write the ***poet's name, birthday, country of birth, quick facts and other works by the poet*** from the presenters' analysis. Complete the other sections based on your own feelings about the poet.

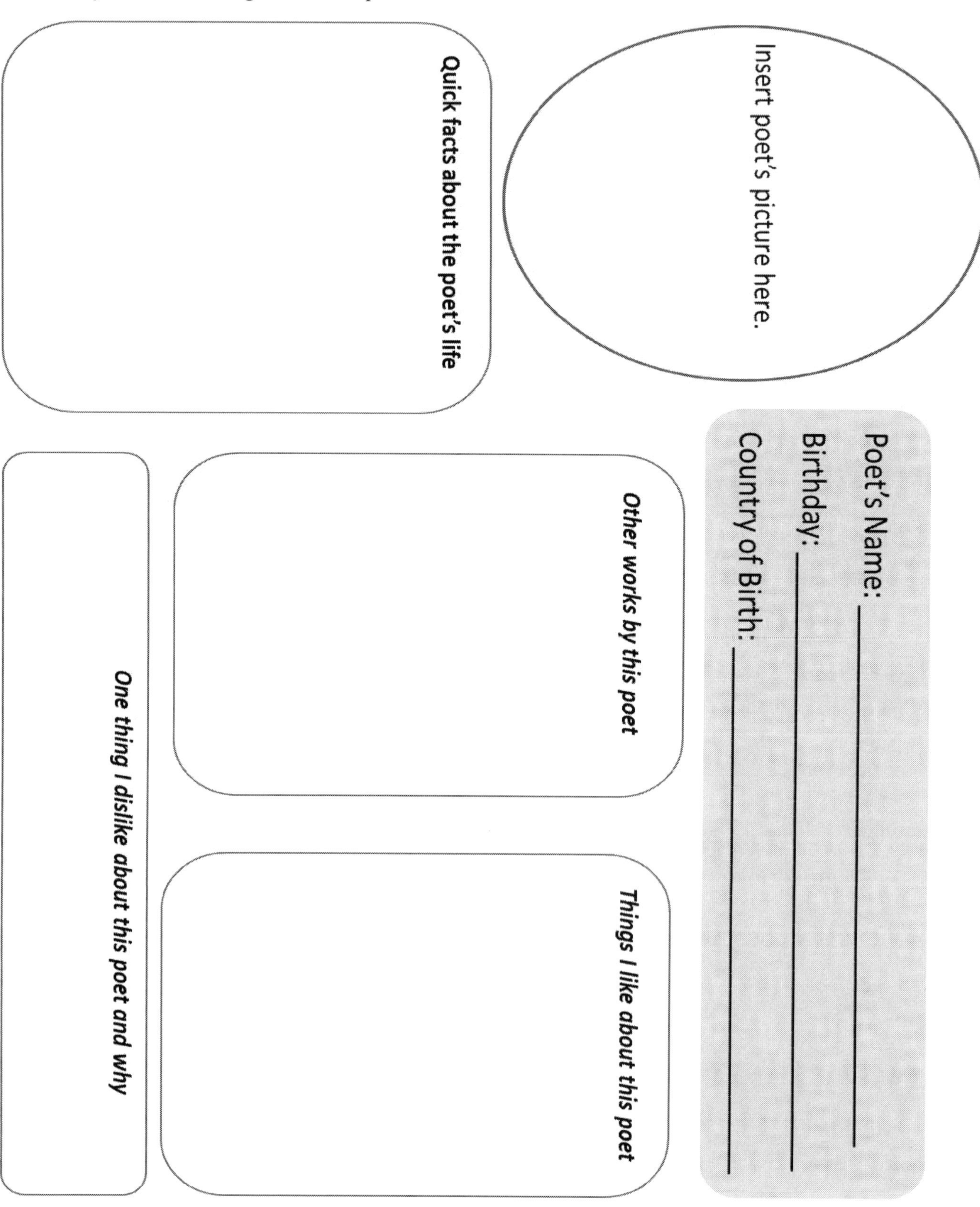

Literary Elements in "The Woman Speaks to the Man Who has Employed Her Son"

Directions. Write the literary elements identified by the presenter(s). After the presentation, you will be allowed time to identify these elements for yourself and compare your answers to the presenters' answers. Revise your notes on each element if you are unsure. Complete the table as follows:

1. Write the presenters' identifications.
2. Tick whether you agree or disagree with each identification.
3. Whether you agree or disagree, write one piece of evidence from the poem to support your decision.

Characters		
Persona:	**Agree**	**Disagree**
Evidence:		
Tone:	**Agree**	**Disagree**
Evidence:		
Other characters:	**Agree**	**Disagree**
Evidence:		
Type of Narration:	**Agree**	**Disagree**
Evidence:		

Setting		
Time and Place:	**Agree**	**Disagree**
Evidence:		
Mood:	**Agree**	**Disagree**
Evidence:		

Theme		
1st Theme Category: **Message *(one sentence):***	**Agree**	**Disagree**
Evidence		
2nd Theme Category: **Message *(one sentence):***	**Agree**	**Disagree**
Evidence		

Plot in "The Woman Speaks to the Man Who has Employed Her Son"

Directions. Summarize each stanza in a single sentence. Then, combine the sentences into a paragraph. Use suitable transition words and phrases to make the paragraph more coherent. Remember to use your own words.

Stanza 1:

Stanza 2:

Stanza 3:

Stanza 4:

Stanza 5:

Stanza 6:

Stylistics in "The Woman Speaks to the Man Who has Employed Her Son"

We will look at the form of the poem and the literary devices used.

Form of "The Woman Speaks to the Man Who has Employed Her Son"

Directions. Fill in the blanks with information from "The Woman Speaks to the Man Who has Employed Her Son".

"The Woman Speaks to the Man Who has Employed Her Son" is a ______________ (*Type of poem*). The poem consists of _________ (*Number of lines*) lines which are divided into __________________ (*Number and type of stanza*). The poem has __________________ (*Type of rhyme scheme*) and is written in ____________________________ (*Type of rhythm*).

Activity 2: A Poem that Tells a Story

Directions. "The Woman Speaks to the Man Who has Employed Her Son" includes features of a story. Use the diagram of the plot structure of a story to identify the components of the plot of the poem.

Climax

Rising Action

Falling Action

Exposition

Resolution

Describe the conflict in the story. ____

____

____

Literary Devices in "The Woman Speaks to the Man Who has Employed Her Son"

Activity 1: Identifying the Devices

Directions. Write the names of FOUR literary devices used in the poem. Then, write an example of each of the listed devices from the poem. Ensure you write the line number(s) for each example given.

Literary Devices	**Examples**
1. ______________________:	______________________________
	______________________________
2. ______________________:	______________________________
	______________________________
3. ______________________:	______________________________
	______________________________
4. ______________________:	______________________________
	______________________________

If you have identified a simile or metaphor, explain it by using the formula.

____

____

____

____

____

____

____

____

Explain an allusion made in the poem.

____

____

____

____

____

____

____

Activity 3: Effect and Effectiveness

Directions. Choose TWO devices identified in "The Woman Speaks to the Man Who has Employed Her Son" and comment on their effect and effectiveness. If you need to remind yourself of what is required when you are asked to examine or comment on the use of a literary device, read the notes presented of **pages 52 – 53** of this Workbook.

Device	**Evidence**
Effect:	
Effectiveness:	

Device	**Evidence**
Effect:	
Effectiveness:	

Assessing Your Peers' Presentation

Directions. Compare the information your peers provided with your own analysis and rate your classmates' analysis of "The Woman Speaks to the Man Who has Employed Her Son" by shading the stars below. Five stars mean you believe the analysis was excellent. Then, justify your rating.

Your Rating	Your Justification
☆☆☆☆☆	

What is the most common rating received by the presenters from your classmates? ________________

What is your teacher's rating? ________________________________

If you have the same rating as your teacher, you earn a ⚖ .

Choose ONE element of poetry that you think the presenters need to make improvement in analyzing and make TWO recommendations to the presenters on how they can improve in analyzing that element.

Selected area: ________________________________

Recommendation 1: ________________________________

____

____

____

____

Recommendation 2: ________________________________

____

____

____

____

Now that you have finished analyzing "The Woman Speaks to the Man Who has Employed Her Son", look back at the predictions you made before you analyzed the poem and answer the following questions.

1. To what extent were your predictions right?

   Not at all ☐ A small extent ☐ Somewhat ☐ To a large extent ☐ Spot on ☐

2. Explain your selection for question 1.

   ____

   ____

Activity 2: A Mother's Love (Part 2)

Directions. Paste a picture of the mother in the poem. Around the heart cut out words or phrases from existing print documents (magazines, newspapers etc.) that describe the persona as a mother.

1. Compare the mother in the poem to your own mother or the person who plays a motherly role in your life. ____

   ____

   ____

Checking My Progress

You have just finished the activities on "The Woman Speaks to the Man Who has Employed Her Son". Before we move to the activities on the next poem, review what you have learnt or are still uncertain about. Do so by first checking the objectives you have accomplished so far.

Directions. Go back to the objectives at the beginning of the activities on "The Woman Speaks to the Man Who has Employed Her Son". If you think you have accomplished an objective, without looking back at your notes, put a tick in the box ☐ before the objective. If you are unsure you have accomplished the objective, put a question mark (?) and if you are sure you have not accomplished the objective, leave it unchecked (blank). Ensure you pay more attention to your unchecked boxes and the boxes with your question marks as you study. Also, ensure that you can perform the number indicated in each objective (e.g., list **three** genres). You have accomplished the objective when you can list the indicated number (three).

Now complete the 3-2-1 activity below. It works as follows:

Three – Write three things you learned from the activities on "The Woman Speaks to the Man Who has Employed Her Son".

Two – Write two things you found interesting or about which you would like to learn more.

One – Write one question you still have about the material.

Share your question with your classmates and listen to their responses. Did they clarify things? If not, maybe it is time you did some independent research.

Finally, record ONE question from one of your classmates and provide an answer to that classmate.

Checking What I Know!!!

3. ____
____
____

2. ____
____

1. ____

Helping My Peers!!!

Peer's question: ____
____

My answer: ____
____
____

"Ol' Higue" by Mark McWatt

Objectives

After completing the activities on "Ol' Higue", you should be able to accurately:

- ☐ make predictions based on the title of the poem;
- ☐ identify the elements of poetry in the poem;
- ☐ critically assess your peers' presentation and analysis of the poem;
- ☐ examine the effect and effectiveness of literary devices used in the poem;
- ☐ examine different points of view used in literature.

Getting Started

Activity 1: Before you begin …

Before you begin to read any piece of writing, it is usually a good idea to think of what you already know about the topic. Write down what you know about the title of the poem by completing the table below. The table should be completed as follows:

It says … - Write the title of the poem.

I know … - Write what you know about the title. In this case, in which language is the title written? What is the English translation of the title?

And so … - Make a prediction about what you think the poem will be about based on the stated title and what you know about the title.

It says …	
I know …	
And so …	

Activity 2: The Strange and Supernatural

Directions. Draw a picture of a nice fairy OR scary monster of your creation. Be sure to give your fairy OR monster an original name and list its special powers.

Name: ______________________

Special Powers

____

____

____

____

____

____

____

____

____

____

____

____

Tell us about a mythical creature in your country (famous ghost, monster, talking animal)!

Name of the creature: ______________________

Special power of the creature: ______________________

Popular story about the creature: ______________________

____

____

____

____

____

____

____

____

____

Activity 3: The Featured Presentation

Use the checklist below to assess your peers' recitation of "Ol' Higue".

Checklist for the Poetry Recitation

Directions. The checklist below consists of a list of statements highlighting important things to consider when reciting a poem and three emojis. If your answer to the statement is yes, put a tick beside the statement and under the happy face. If your answer to the statement is no, put a tick beside the statement and under the sad face. If you are unsure, put a tick beside the statement and under the unsure face.

Checklist for Poetry Recitation			
1. Performance is no longer than three minutes.			
2. The words of the poem are said exactly as presented in the text.			
3. The performer adapts the role of the persona in movement, posture and general demeanour.			
4. Performer conveys the appropriate emotion.			
5. Performer makes appropriate use of facial expression, gestures, tone etc. to convey the meaning of the poem.			
6. Performer makes appropriate use of stage.			
7. Performance is audible and confident.			
8. Performance is entertaining.			

Directions. Based on your ticks in the checklist, rate your classmates' recitation of "Ol' Higue" by shading the stars below. Five stars mean you believe the recitation was excellent. Then, justify your rating.

Your Rating	Your Justification
☆☆☆☆☆	

What is the most common rating received by the presenters from your classmates? ____________________

What is your teacher's rating? ____

If you have the same rating as your teacher, you earn a  .

Choose TWO areas from the checklist where you ticked 'no' or 'unsure' and make ONE recommendation to the presenters on how they could have improved in those areas.

Selected area 1: ____

Recommendation: ____

____

____

____

Selected area 2: ____

Recommendation: ____

____

____

____

Elements of Poetry in "Ol' Higue"

Your classmates will present their analysis of "Ol' Higue". In this analysis, they will identify, explain and discuss the historical background, literary elements, form and literary devices used in the poem. You will be expected to critically assess the analysis being presented. This will be done in a step-by-step process.

Step 1: Listen for Information – While you listen to the analysis, complete the different activities with information presented in the analysis.

Step 2: Consult Your Peers – Share with a peer to see if he/she heard anything you might have missed or if you heard anything, he/she missed.

Step 3: Rate the Analysis – Look at the number of answered and unanswered activities you have and rate the overall analysis.

Historical Background

Directions. In this section, the presenters are expected to provide relevant information for all the areas in the picture below. However, you are only expected to write the ***poet's name, birthday, country of birth, quick facts and other works by the poet*** from the presenters' analysis. Complete the other sections based on your own feelings about the poet.

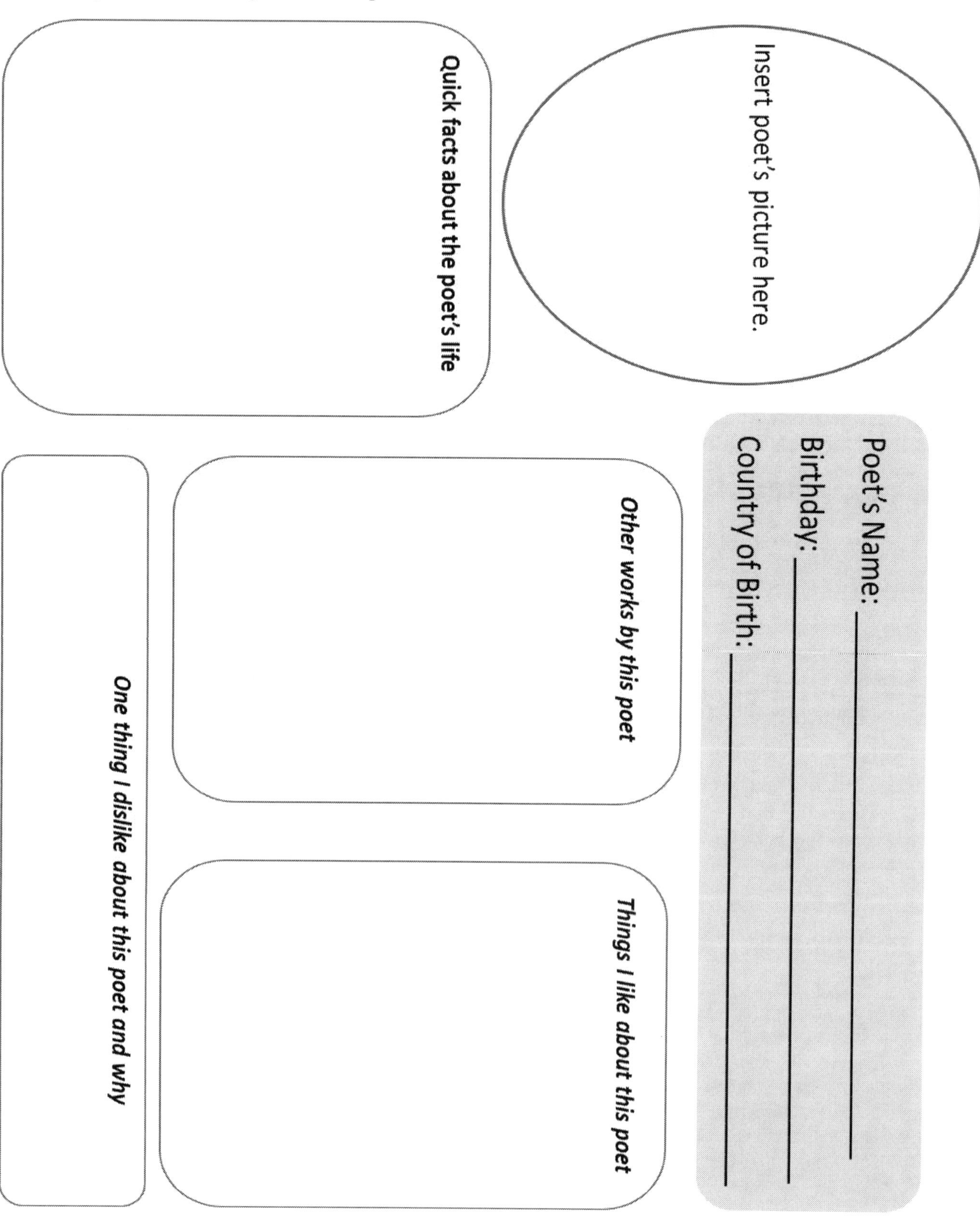

Literary Elements in "Ol' Higue"

Directions. Write the literary elements identified by the presenter(s). After the presentation, you will be allowed time to identify these elements for yourself and compare your answers to the presenters' answers. Revise your notes on each element if you are unsure. Complete the table as follows:

1. Write the presenters' identifications.
2. Tick whether you agree or disagree with each identification.
3. Whether you agree or disagree, write one piece of evidence from the poem to support your decision.

Characters		
Persona:	**Agree**	**Disagree**
Evidence:		
Tone:	**Agree**	**Disagree**
Evidence:		
Other characters:	**Agree**	**Disagree**
Evidence:		
Type of Narration:	**Agree**	**Disagree**
Evidence:		

Setting		
Time and Place:	**Agree**	**Disagree**
Evidence:		
Mood:	**Agree**	**Disagree**
Evidence:		

Theme		
1st Theme Category: **Message *(one sentence):***	**Agree**	**Disagree**
Evidence		
2nd Theme Category: **Message *(one sentence):***	**Agree**	**Disagree**
Evidence		

Plot in "Ol' Higue"

Directions. Summarize each stanza in a single sentence. Then, combine the sentences into a paragraph. Use suitable transition words and phrases to make the paragraph more coherent. Remember to use your own words.

Stanza 1:

Stanza 2:

Stanza 3:

Stylistics in "Ol' Higue"

We will look at the form of the poem, point of view and the literary devices used.

Form of "Ol' Higue"

Directions. Fill in the blanks with information from "Ol' Higue".

"Ol' Higue" is a ___________________ (*Type of poem*). The poem consists of ___________ (*Number of lines*) lines which are divided into ___________ (*Number of stanzas*) stanzas. Each stanza is a different type of stanza with first being a __________________ (*Type of stanza*), the second being a ____________________ (*Type of stanza*) and the third being a _________________ (*Type of stanza*). The poem has ____________________ (*Type of rhyme scheme*) and is written in ___________________________ (*Type of rhythm*).

Point of View

Point of view is the perspective from which a poet or author tells the story. It also refers to the position from which the story is told. There are three points of view used in literature:

1. First person – Where the story is told from the perspective of a character in the story. It is usually identified by the use of first-person pronouns *I, me, we, us*.

2. Second person – This type of narration is more commonly used in poetry than the other genres of literature. In second person point of view, the narrator or persona speaks directly to the audience. It is usually identified by the use of the personal pronouns *you* and *your* as the narrator/person is speaking directly to YOU.

3. Third person – Where the story is told from the perspective of a narrator who is outside the story. The narrator or person is not a participant in the action of the story. It is usually identified by the use of the third person pronouns *she, he, it, they, them*.

Activity 1: It Depends on Who Tells It

Directions. Read the description of the Ol' Higue below and answer the questions that follow.

On a bright Saturday morning, I shouldn't be chasing a cricket ball in the neighbor's yard. This happens when you have a little brother like Sammy. He's worse than a male mosquito.

"You do this on purpose." I want to clobber him. "Granny say Missis Withers is an Ole Higue. She suck her husband 'til he dead. She going suck you too."
"Daddy say is not true," says Sammy. "Ole Higue is only old people story. To frighten lil children."
"Is that so? Keep pestering Missis Withers. You going find out if is for true or not."

I march over to the Ole Higue's house at the street corner. Sammy lags behind.
"I got better things to do than go after your stupid cricket ball."
"Like kissing that smiley-face tall boy?
I turn around and glare at him. "You spying on me now?"

We pass the Ole Higue's dense five-foot high red hibiscus hedge. No one uses the padlocked gate to the sun-beaten, water-worn front staircase. We turn the corner to the side of the house. A thick metal chain secures the corroding wrought iron driveway gate. The Ole Higue's hearse waits under the house. The graying-white colonial-style wood house looms above us. It stands on eight robust ten-foot stilts like a giant black widow spider. Dark curtains trap the sunbeams piercing the glass windows.

I move towards the small service gate on the right. Sammy clutches my skirt; he hunches by my side. I shake the rusty bell. A young man, the Ole Higue's grandson, sticks his head out a window overhead. His oily black hair gleams in the sunlight.

"Is what you all want?"

Excerpt from The Ole Higue by Rosaliene Bacchus Guyana Journal, July 2008

1. Which point of view is used in the excerpt? Justify your identification.

____

____

2. Who is describing the Ole Higue? ______________________

3. Based on the events in the excerpt, use TWO adjectives to describe how you feel about the Ol' Higue. Justify EACH selection.

____

____

____

A popular superstition in Guyana is the Ol' Higue. She is always an old woman who lives a secluded life in the day, but removes her skin in the night, turns into a ball of fire and travels to her victims' home. She is believed to kill humans, especially babies, by sucking their blood. Ol' Higue can enter her victims' homes through small cracks and even key holes. However, one can prevent the Ol' Higue from entering the house by sprinkling rice grains around the house or turning the key in the keyhole while she is trying to enter. The Ol Higue can also be killed by putting salt or hot peppers in her skin before she returns for it.

Read the description of the Ol' Higue and answer the questions that follow.

1. Which point of view is used in the excerpt? Justify your identification.

 ____

 ____

2. Who is describing the Ole Higue? ______________________

3. Based on the events in the excerpt, use TWO adjectives to describe how you feel about the Ol' Higue. Justify EACH selection.

 ____

 ____

4. Who describes the experiences of the Ole Higue in the poem "Ol' Higue"? ____________

5. Based on the events in the poem, use TWO adjectives to describe how you feel about the Ol' Higue. Justify EACH selection.

 ____

 ____

 ____

 ____

6. Identify TWO details that the THREE pieces have in common.

 ____

 ____

 ____

 ____

7. Identify ONE difference between the poem and any of the other pieces.

 ____

 ____

Literary Devices in "Ol' Higue"

Activity 1: Identifying the Devices

Directions. Write the names of FOUR literary devices used in the poem. Then, write an example of each of the listed devices from the poem. Ensure you write the line number(s) for each example given.

Literary Devices	**Examples**
1. ____________________:	____
	____
2. ____________________:	____
	____
3. ____________________:	____
	____
4. ____________________:	____
	____

If you have identified a simile or metaphor, explain it by using the formula.

____

____

____

____

____

____

____

____

____

____

____

____

____

____

____

____

____

Activity 2: Effect and Effectiveness

Directions. Choose TWO devices identified in "Ol' Higue" and comment on their effect and effectiveness. If you need to remind yourself of what is required when you are asked to examine or comment on the use of a literary device, read the notes presented of **pages 52 – 53** of this Workbook.

Device	**Evidence**
Effect:	
Effectiveness:	

Device	**Evidence**
Effect:	
Effectiveness:	

Assessing Your Peers' Presentation

Directions. Compare the information your peers provided with your own analysis and rate your classmates' analysis of "Ol' Higue" by shading the stars below. Five stars mean you believe the analysis was excellent. Then, justify your rating.

Your Rating	Your Justification
☆☆☆☆☆	

What is the most common rating received by the presenters from your classmates? ___________

What is your teacher's rating? ___________

If you have the same rating as your teacher, you earn a ⚖ .

Choose ONE element of poetry that you think the presenters need to make improvement in analyzing and make TWO recommendations to the presenters on how they can improve in analyzing that element.

Selected area: ___________

Recommendation 1: ___________

Recommendation 2: ___________

Now that you have finished analyzing "Ol' Higue", look back at the predictions you made before you analyzed the poem and answer the following questions.

1. To what extent were your predictions right?

   Not at all ☐ A small extent ☐ Somewhat ☐ To a large extent ☐ Spot on ☐

2. Explain your selection for question 1. ______________________________

   ____

   ____

   ____

   ____

   ____

   ____

3. In what way did the historical background of the poem contribute to your understanding of the poem?

   ____

   ____

   ____

   ____

   ____

   ____

   ____

   ____

4. Choose TWO poems that you have studied from the prescribed list which focus on women in society.

   Write an essay in which you describe a woman that plays a major role in EACH poem. In this essay, you must discuss how women are presented in EACH poem and examine ONE device that contributes to the presentation of women in EACH poem.

Use the rubric for poetry essays in the CXC English syllabus to assess your essay writing skills. Then, ask your classmate to use the same rubric to assess your essay while you do the same for him/her. Revise your essay before presenting it to your teacher.

Checking My Progress

You have just finished the activities on "Ol' Higue". Before we move to the activities on the next poem, review what you have learnt or are still uncertain about. Do so by first checking the objectives you have accomplished so far.

Directions. Go back to the objectives at the beginning of the activities on "Ol' Higue". If you think you have accomplished an objective, without looking back at your notes, put a tick in the box ☐ before the objective. If you are unsure you have accomplished the objective, put a question mark (?) and if you are sure you have not accomplished the objective, leave it unchecked (blank). Ensure you pay more attention to your unchecked boxes and the boxes with your question marks as you study. Also, ensure that you can perform the number indicated in each objective (e.g., list **three** genres). You have accomplished the objective when you can list the indicated number (three).

Now complete the 3-2-1 activity below. It works as follows:

Three – Write **three** things you learned from the activities on "Ol' Higue".

Two – Write **two** things you found interesting or about which you would like to learn more.

One – Write **one** question you still have about the material.

Share your question with your classmates and listen to their responses. Did they clarify things? If not, maybe it is time you did some independent research.

Finally, record ONE question from one of your classmates and provide an answer to that classmate.

Checking What I Know!!!

3. ____

____

____

2. ____

____

1. ____

Helping My Peers!!!

Peer's question: ____

____

My answer: ____

____

____

"Mirror" by Sylvia Plath

Objectives

After completing the activities on "Mirror", you should be able to accurately:

- ☐ make predictions based on the title of the poem;
- ☐ identify the elements of poetry in the poem;
- ☐ critically assess your peers' presentation and analysis of the poem;
- ☐ examine the effect and effectiveness of literary devices used in the poem;
- ☐ examine the use of personification in poetry.

Getting Started

Activity 1: Before you begin …

Before you begin to read any piece of writing, it is usually a good idea to think of what you already know about the topic. Write down what you know about the title of the poem by completing the table below. The table should be completed as follows:

It says … - Write the title of the poem.

I know … - Write what you know about the title.

And so … - Make a prediction about what you think the poem will be about based on the stated title and what you know about the title.

It says …	
I know …	
And so …	

Activity 2: Mirror, Mirror, On the Wall

Directions. Insert a picture of a mirror below and write on it at least FOUR things you see when you look in the mirror. One of the things you see must be abstract.

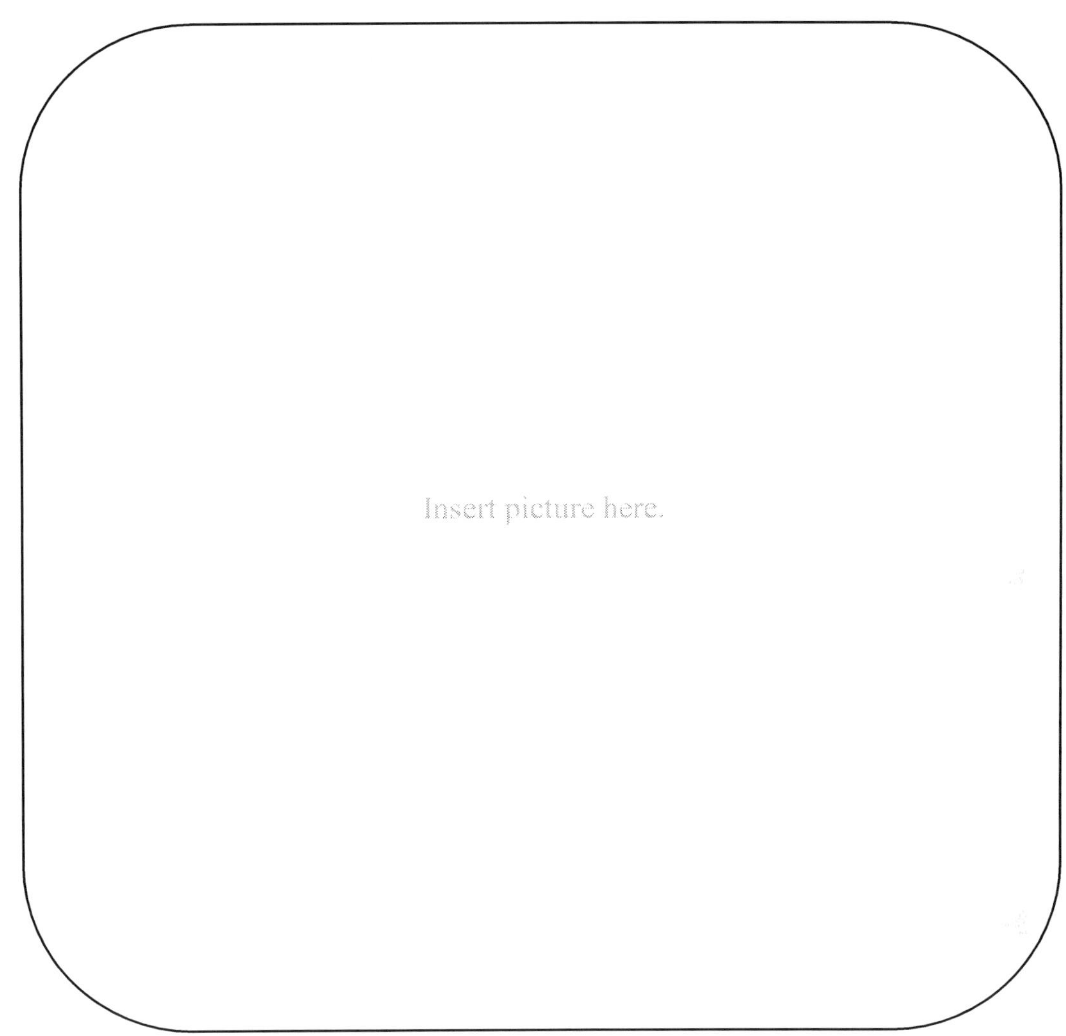

1. Imagine you are a mirror and list THREE things you see.

____

____

____

____

____

____

____

____

Activity 3: The Featured Presentation

Use the checklist below to assess your peers' recitation of "Mirror".

Checklist for the Poetry Recitation

Directions. The checklist below consists of a list of statements highlighting important things to consider when reciting a poem and three emojis. If your answer to the statement is yes, put a tick beside the statement and under the happy face. If your answer to the statement is no, put a tick beside the statement and under the sad face. If you are unsure, put a tick beside the statement and under the unsure face.

Checklist for Poetry Recitation			
1. Performance is no longer than three minutes.			
2. The words of the poem are said exactly as presented in the text.			
3. The performer adapts the role of the persona in movement, posture and general demeanour.			
4. Performer conveys the appropriate emotion.			
5. Performer makes appropriate use of facial expression, gestures, tone etc. to convey the meaning of the poem.			
6. Performer makes appropriate use of stage.			
7. Performance is audible and confident.			
8. Performance is entertaining.			

Directions. Based on your ticks in the checklist, rate your classmates' recitation of "Mirror" by shading the stars below. Five stars mean you believe the recitation was excellent. Then, justify your rating.

Your Rating	Your Justification
☆☆☆☆☆	

What is the most common rating received by the presenter from your classmates? ____________________

What is your teacher's rating? ____

If you have the same rating as your teacher, you earn a  .

Choose TWO areas from the checklist where you ticked 'no' or 'unsure' and make ONE recommendation to the presenters on how they could have improved in those areas.

Selected area 1: ____

Recommendation: ____

____

____

____

Selected area 2: ____

Recommendation: ____

____

____

____

Elements of Poetry in "Mirror"

Your classmates will present their analysis of "Mirror". In this analysis, they will identify, explain and discuss the historical background, literary elements, form and literary devices used in the poem. You will be expected to critically assess the analysis being presented. This will be done in a step-by-step process.

Step 1: Listen for Information – While you listen to the analysis, complete the different activities with information presented in the analysis.

Step 2: Consult Your Peers – Share with a peer to see if he/she heard anything you might have missed or if you heard anything, he/she missed.

Step 3: Rate the Analysis – Look at the number of answered and unanswered activities you have and rate the overall analysis.

Historical Background

Directions. In this section, the presenters are expected to provide relevant information for all the areas in the picture below. However, you are only expected to write the ***poet's name, birthday, country of birth, quick facts and other works by the poet*** from the presenters' analysis. Complete the other sections based on your own feelings about the poet.

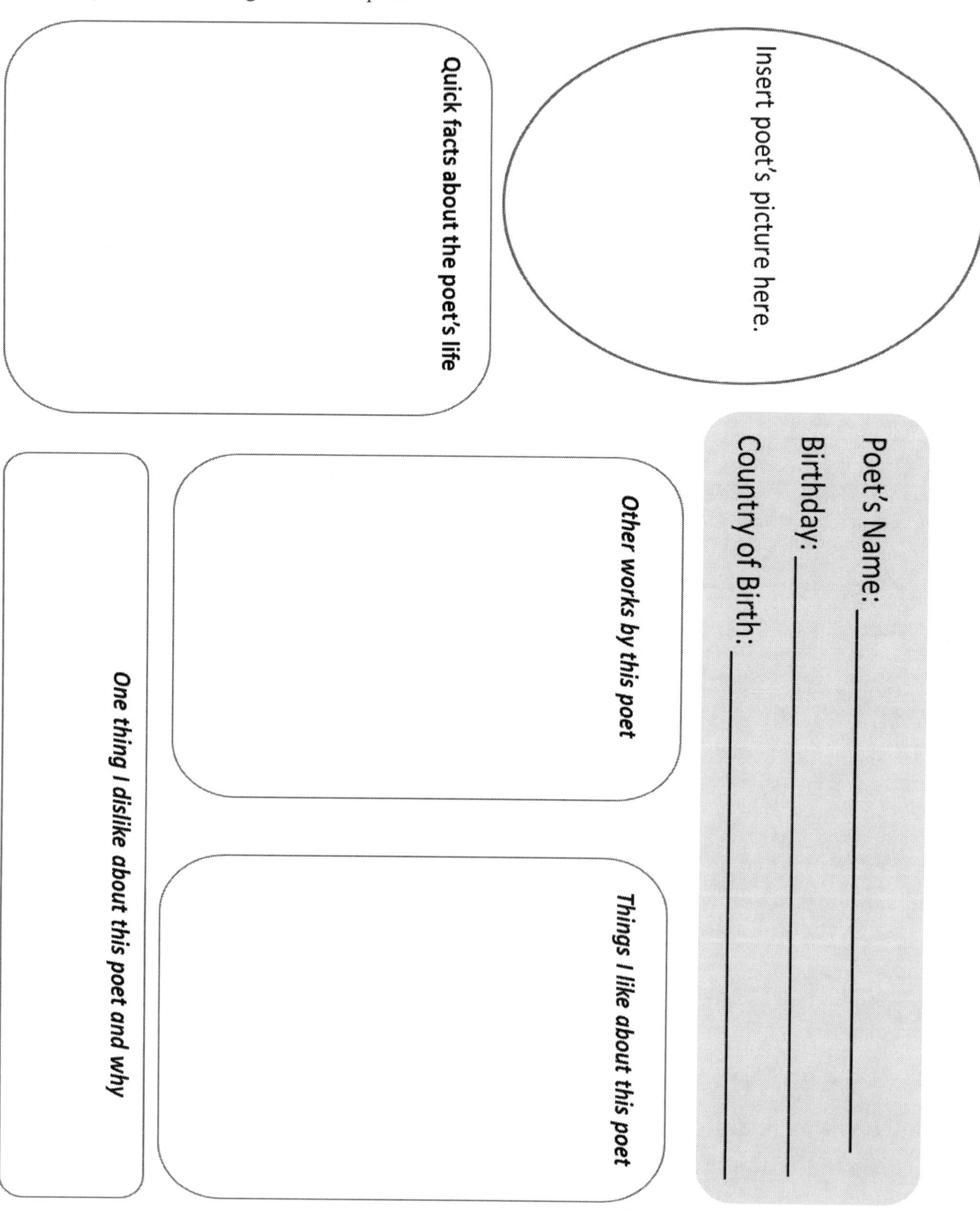

Literary Elements in "Mirror"

Directions. Write the literary elements identified by the presenter(s). After the presentation, you will be allowed time to identify these elements for yourself and compare your answers to the presenters' answers. Revise your notes on each element if you are unsure. Complete the table as follows:

1. Write the presenters' identifications.
2. Tick whether you agree or disagree with each identification.
3. Whether you agree or disagree, write one piece of evidence from the poem to support your decision.

Characters		
Persona:	**Agree**	**Disagree**
Evidence:		
Tone:	**Agree**	**Disagree**
Evidence:		
Other characters:	**Agree**	**Disagree**
Evidence:		
Type of Narration:	**Agree**	**Disagree**
Evidence:		

Setting		
Time and Place:	**Agree**	**Disagree**
Evidence:		
Mood:	**Agree**	**Disagree**
Evidence:		

Theme		
1st Theme Category: **Message *(one sentence):***	**Agree**	**Disagree**
Evidence		
2nd Theme Category: **Message *(one sentence):***	**Agree**	**Disagree**
Evidence		

Plot in "Mirror"

Directions. Summarize each stanza in a single sentence. Then, combine the sentences into a paragraph. Use suitable transition words and phrases to make the paragraph more coherent. Remember to use your own words.

Stanza 1:

Stanza 2:

____

____

____

____

____

____

____

____

____

____

Stylistics in "Mirror"

We will look at the form of the poem and the literary devices used.

Form of "Mirror"

Directions. Fill in the blanks with information from "Mirror".

"Mirror" is a __________________ (*Type of poem*). The poem consists of __________ (*Number of lines*) lines which are divided into __________________ (*Number and type of stanzas*). The poem has ________________ (*Type of rhyme scheme*) and is written in _____________________ (*Type of rhythm*).

Answer the following questions.

1. What does the consistent number of lines in the stanzas contribute to the poem?

____

____

____

____

____

____

____

2. What does the rhyme scheme or the absence of a rhyme scheme contribute to the poem?

____

____

____

____

____

____

____

Literary Devices in "Mirror"

Activity 1: Identifying the Devices

Directions. Write the names of FOUR literary devices used in the poem. Then, write an example of each of the listed devices from the poem. Ensure you write the line number(s) for each example given.

Literary Devices	Examples
1. ____________________:	______________________________
	______________________________
2. ____________________:	______________________________
	______________________________
3. ____________________:	______________________________
	______________________________
4. ____________________:	______________________________
	______________________________

If you have identified a simile or metaphor, explain it by using the formula.

____

____

____

____

____

____

____

____

____

____

____

____

____

____

____

Personification

Personification is a literary device in which human qualities (feelings, gestures, desires, speech etc.) are given to inanimate objects or abstract ideas. For example, the sun smiles down on us after the rain. In the example, the object 'sun' is given a human quality 'smiling'. In this example, the personification helps to highlight the persona's attitude towards the sun. Smiling usually show happiness and friendliness. Therefore, the persona has a positive attitude towards the sun. The persona views the sun with happiness. Personification helps to create vivid images and appeal to the emotions of the reader as well. We are more likely to share emotions with other human beings than with ideas and inanimate object. However, when these ideas and objects are personified, we get a better understanding of the object's feelings or movement. In examining personification, you should:

- ✓ identify the inanimate object or abstract idea;
- ✓ identify the human quality being given to the object or idea;
- ✓ describe at least one significant characteristic of the human quality;
- ✓ connect the described characteristic to the poem (theme, mood, setting, characterization etc.);
- ✓ comment on the effect and/or effectiveness of the personification.

Activity 2: The Personified Mirror

Directions. The poem, "Mirror" is described as a personification. Identify at least FOUR examples of the mirror in the poem being given human qualities.

____

____

____

____

____

____

____

____

____

____

____

____

Activity 3: Effect and Effectiveness

Directions. Choose THREE devices identified in "Mirror" and comment on their effect and effectiveness. If you need to remind yourself of what is required when you are asked to examine or comment on the use of a literary device, read the notes presented of **pages 52 – 53** of this Workbook.

Device	Evidence
Effect:	
Effectiveness:	

<table>
<tr><th>Device</th><th>Evidence</th></tr>
<tr><td></td><td></td></tr>
<tr><td colspan="2">Effect:</td></tr>
<tr><td colspan="2">Effectiveness:</td></tr>
</table>

<table>
<tr><th>Device</th><th>Evidence</th></tr>
<tr><td></td><td></td></tr>
<tr><td colspan="2">Effect:</td></tr>
<tr><td colspan="2">Effectiveness:</td></tr>
</table>

Assessing Your Peers' Presentation

Directions. Compare the information your peers provided with your own analysis and rate your classmates' analysis of "Mirror" by shading the stars below. Five stars mean you believe the analysis was excellent. Then, justify your rating.

Your Rating	Your Justification
☆☆☆☆☆	

What is the most common rating received by the presenters from your classmates? ______________

What is your teacher's rating? ______________________________

If you have the same rating as your teacher, you earn a ⚖.

Choose ONE element of poetry that you think the presenters need to make improvement in analyzing and make TWO recommendations to the presenters on how they can improve in analyzing that element.

Selected area: ______________________________

Recommendation 1: ______________________________

Recommendation 2: ______________________________

Now that you have finished analyzing "Mirror", look back at the predictions you made before you analyzed the poem and answer the following questions.

1. To what extent were your predictions right?

   Not at all ☐ A small extent ☐ Somewhat ☐ To a large extent ☐ Spot on ☐

2. Explain your selection for question 1. ______________________________

   ____

   ____

   ____

   ____

   ____

3. How important are mirrors to women? Explain your answer.

   ____

   ____

   ____

   ____

   ____

4. In what way did the historical background of the poem contribute to your understanding of the poem?

   ____

   ____

   ____

   ____

   ____

5. The events in "Ol' Higue" and "Mirror" are told from unconventional points of view.

   Write an essay in which you describe the unconventional point of view in EACH persona. In this essay, you must also discuss the contribution of point of view to the development of a NAMED theme in EACH poem and examine ONE device that is used to explore the NAMED theme as a whole in EACH poem.

Checking My Progress

You have just finished the activities on "Mirror". Before we move to the next set of activities, review what you have learnt or are still uncertain about. Do so by first checking the objectives you have accomplished so far.

Directions. Go back to the objectives at the beginning of the activities on "Mirror". If you think you have accomplished an objective, without looking back at your notes, put a tick in the box ☐ before the objective. If you are unsure you have accomplished the objective, put a question mark (?) and if you are sure you have not accomplished the objective, leave it unchecked (blank). Ensure you pay more attention to your unchecked boxes and the boxes with your question marks as you study. Also, ensure that you can perform the number indicated in each objective (e.g., list **three** genres). You have accomplished the objective when you can list the indicated number (three).

Now complete the 3-2-1 activity below. It works as follows:

Three – Write **three** things you learned from the activities on "Mirror".

Two – Write **two** things you found interesting or about which you would like to learn more.

One – Write **one** question you still have about the material.

Share your question with your classmates and listen to their responses. Did they clarify things? If not, maybe it is time you did some independent research.

Finally, record ONE question from one of your classmates and provide an answer to that classmate.

Checking What I Know!!!

3. ____

____

____

2. ____

____

1. ____

Helping My Peers!!!

Peer's question: ____

____

My answer: ____

____

____

Comparing Poems

In responding to essay questions on the poems, you will be required to compare two named poems. Therefore, it is useful to identify similarities and differences among the poems.

Activity 1: Themes in the Poems

The table below consists of the twenty poems and the categories of some of the popular themes in literature. Put a tick beside the poem and under the category if the theme is present in the poem.

Poems	Desire	Women	War	Nature	Racism	Childhood Exp.	Religion
South							
It is the Constant Image of Your Face							
Dreaming Black Boy							
Landscape Painter, Jamaica							
Sonnet Composed Upon Westminster Bridge							
West Indies, U.S.A.							
Test Match Sabina Park							
Mirror							
The Woman Speaks to the Man ...							
Death, be not proud ...							
Ol' Higue							
A Lesson for this Sunday							
An African Thunderstorm							
Birdshooting Season							
My Parents							
Once Upon A Time							
Little Boy Crying							
Dulce et Decorum Est							
This is the dark time, my love							
A Stone' s Throw							

Activity 2: Literary Devices in the Poems

The table below consists of the twenty poems and the categories of literary devices. Write the name of the specific device in the category that can be found in the poem.

	Sound	Double Meaning	Reference	Contradiction	Emphasis	Comparison
A Stone' s Throw						
This is the dark time, my love						
Dulce et Decorum Est						
Little Boy Crying						
Once Upon A Time						
My Parents						
Birdshooting Season						
An African Thunderstorm						
A Lesson for this Sunday						
Ol' Higue						
Death, be not proud ...						
The Woman Speaks to the Man …						
Mirror						
Test Match Sabina Park						
West Indies, U.S.A.						
Sonnet Composed Upon Westminster Bridge						
Landscape Painter, Jamaica						
Dreaming Black Boy						
It is the Constant Image of Your Face						
South						

References

Caribbean Examination Council. (2017). English Syllabus Effective for Examinations from May–June 2018. St. Michael, Barbados: Caribbean Examination Council.

Bacchus, B. (2008). The Ole Higue. *Guyana Journal*. Retrieved from: http://www.guyanajournal.com/Ole_Higue.html

Dictionary.com. (2019). Literature. Retrieved from: https://www.dictionary.com/browse/literature

McWatt, M. & Simmons-McDonald, H. (Eds.) (2005). *A World of Poetry for CSEC*. Essex: Pearson Education

MY STICKERS

BRILLIANT
SUPER STAR
AWESOME JOB!!
SUPERB!
DROPS MIC

BRILLIANT

BRILLIANT

BRILLIANT

BRILLIANT

BRILLIANT

BRILLIANT

SUPER STAR

SUPER STAR

SUPER STAR

SUPER STAR

SUPER STAR

AWESOME JOB!!

AWESOME JOB!!

AWESOME JOB!!

AWESOME JOB!!

AWESOME JOB!!

SUPERB!

SUPERB!

SUPERB!

SUPERB!

SUPERB!

SUPERB!

DROPS MIC

DROPS MIC

DROPS MIC

DROPS MIC

DROPS MIC

DROPS MIC

DROPS MIC

TEAM

TEAM

TEAM

TEAM

TEAM

TEAM

TEAM

TEAM

SUPER WRITING

SUPER WRITING

SUPER WRITING

SUPER WRITING

SUPER WRITING

SUPER WRITING

KEEP CALM
We Are
THE SUPER
TEAM!

KEEP CALM
We Are
THE SUPER
TEAM!

KEEP CALM
We Are
THE SUPER
TEAM!

KEEP CALM
We Are
THE SUPER
TEAM!

KEEP CALM
We Are
THE SUPER
TEAM!

KEEP CALM
We Are
THE SUPER
TEAM!

Made in the USA
Columbia, SC
10 June 2022

61548567R00209